JOHN WEBSTER

THE DUCHESS OF MALFI

OUR BOOKS ON LITERATURE

John Webster

THE DUCHESS OF MALFI

[Inclusive of Complete Text, Summary and Analysis of Text, Critical Analysis and Historical Context]

Aditya Nandwani
B.A. English (Hons) , Delhi University;
M.A. (English), IGNOU; Print Journalism (English) YMCA

ANMOL PUBLICATIONS PVT. LTD.
NEW DELHI - 110 002 (INDIA)

ANMOL PUBLICATIONS PVT. LTD.
H.O.: 4374/4B, Ansari Road, Daryaganj,
New Delhi-110 002 (India)
Ph.: 23278000, 23261597
B.O.: No. 1015, Ist Main Road, BSK IIIrd Stage
IIIrd Phase, IIIrd Block,
Bangalore - 560 085 (India)
Visit us at: www.anmolpublications.com

The Duchess of Malfi

First Published, 2009

PRINTED IN INDIA

Printed at Mehra Offset Press, Delhi.

Contents

Preface ix

1. **Introduction** 1
2. **A Note on Greek Tragedy** 5
3. **John Webster: Biography** 15
4. **Reception and Performance History** 18
5. **The Duchess of Malfi: As a Jacobean Drama** 23
6. **The Duchess of Malfi: As a Revenge Tragedy** 25
7. **The Duchess of Malfi: A Real Play** 34
8. **Act Wise Summary** 37
9. **Character Analysis** 41
10. **The Duchess of Malfi: Complete Text** 47
11. **Study Questions** 154

Q1. Give a brief introduction to Webster's 'The Duchess of Malfi'?
Or
Many Renaissance tragedies seem to have been influenced by Senecan tragedy. (Shakespeare's Hamlet, for example). Does the Duchess of Malfi have Senecan elements?
Or
State and discuss the various perceptions of "The Duchess of Malfi"
Or
Discuss 'The Duchess of Malfi' as Webster's masterpiece. 154

Q2. Briefly summarize the play,
"The Duchess of Malfi"
Write a short note on
"The Duchess of Malfi" 160

Q3. Draft a biographical sketch of John Webster.
Or
What do you know about the life of Webster. 161

Q4. Discuss the various themes in Webster's
'The Duchess of Malfi'
'The Duchess of Malfi' discusses sways
through themes of Horror,
Corruption and Reality. 164

Q5. Analyze and discuss Webster's play Act wise. 168

Q6. Present Webster's View of
"The Duchess of Malfi"
Or

Q7. Webster's play sways in the theme of
Unequal power relations. Discuss. 171

Q8. 16th Century play 'The Duchess of Malfi'
sends modern-day message. Discuss 172

Q9. Give a brief introduction to Webster's
'The Duchess of Malfi'?
Or
Many Renaissance tragedies seem to have
been influenced by Senecan tragedy.
(Shakespeare's Hamlet, for example).
Does the Duchess of Malfi have
Senecan elements?
Or
State and discuss the various perceptions
of "The Duchess of Malfi"
Or
Discuss 'The Duchess of Malfi' as
Webster's masterpiece. 175

Q10. Briefly summarize the play,
"The Duchess of Malfi"
Or
Write a short note on "The Duchess of Malfi" 181

Q11. What are the standards and values by which the court of Malfi lives? 182

Q12. Draft a biographical sketch of John Webster.
Or
What do you about the life of Webster. 187

Q13. Discuss the various themes in Webster's 'The Duchess of Malfi'
Or
'The Duchess of Malfi' discusses sways through themes of Horror, Corruption and Reality 189

Q14. Study the character of Bosola –Is he truly evil or just mislead? 193

Q15. What are the principal themes of the Duchess of Malfi? Does the play have a "moral"?
Or
Explore the theme of Victim v/s Villain in Webster's "The Duchess of Malfi" 196

Q16. The idea of entrapment and confinement is represented throughout the play. The soul is seen as a prisoner of the body, which will only be liberated in death. Discuss. 200

Q17. What implies when the lead character Duchess says. "I am Duchess of Malfi still"
Or
What is the effect and significance of the line "I am the Duchess of Malfi still" (Act 4, scene 2, line 128)? 203

Q18. Critically study the character of Bosola as presented by Webster.
Or
It is not a change of character from evil to good that we see in Bosola, but a battle of his conscience with his evil deeds. Do you agree?

Or
How does Bosola react to the growing conflict within him? What role does he attempt to play as the bellman? In what sense does the Duchess seem heroic? What is the source of her strength? How does her death contrast with that of Cariola? How does Webster keep Bosola a fairly sympathetic figure even though he has helped murder the Duchess? How might we explain Ferdinand's crazed reaction to the Duchess's death? What explains Bosola's sudden change from murderer to revenge of the Duchess's death? 206

Q19. Draft a character sketch of The Duchess.
Or
Does stoic philosophy cast light on the Duchess's story? Does she have the characteristics of a stoic?
Or
In the wooing and wedding scene that takes place in Act 1, scene 2, traditional gender roles are reversed. Is the Duchess's willingness to take the masculine role portrayed as heroic? Does she retain any traditional feminine qualities? 209

Q20. Reaffirm the Male Ambition in John Webster's The Duchess of Malfi 221

Q21. Critically study the play" The Duchess of Malfi".
Or
Drama arises from conflict of one sort or another. What is the principal conflict underlying the action of the play? 230

12. Critical Essays 233

13. Questions for Reading and Review 254

14. Quotations 259

Bibliography 261

Preface

With complete text of John Webster's The Duchess of Malfi the book incorporates the most recent editorial scholarship, including valuable information on Webster's biography, new critical methods, and textual theory and advanced criticism.

In his masterpiece, *The Duchess of Malfi,* Webster deals with a more innocent pair of lovers. The widowed Duchess of Malfi is forbidden to marry again by her brothers—Duke Ferdinand and the Cardinal—because they covet her estate. Unbeknownst to her brothers, however, the Duchess falls in love with her steward Antonio, and they marry secretly. The two lovers live happily for a time and the Duchess gives birth to three children, but when their marriage is discovered, the evil of the world stages a macabre dance around the little family from which there is no escape. A splendid nightmare, *The Duchess of Malfi* bears witness to a sensitive spirit, overwhelmed by the horror and despair of the world.

Webster's artistic development, defends him against charges of overindulgence in violence, and explores his sophisticated staging and scenic forms.

Author

Chapter 1

Introduction

Almost nothing is known about the private life of John Webster. Even the dates of his birth and death are a mystery; scholars speculate that he was born between 1570 and 1580, since he was writing plays in 1602, and he seems to have died before 1634, since in that year, he was referred to in the past tense by Thomas Heywood in *Hierarchy of Angels*. A John Webster was admitted to study law at the Middle Temple on August 1, 1598, but there is no evidence linking him to John Webster, the playwright. In addition, from a couple of obscure references, scholars speculate that Webster's brother (and Webster himself) may have been a Cartwright (i.e., a cart or coach builder), but this, too, is supported by no real evidence.

All we really know of Webster relates to his work. The first reference to him is in the diary of Philip Henslowe, manager of the Rose Theatre in London. In May 1602, Webster is listed with Thomas Dekker, Anthony Munday, Thomas Middleton, and Michael Drayton as the authors of a play called *Caesar's Fall*; this play has been lost. In October 1602, Webster was paid, along with several collaborators, for a play called *Lady Jane*, which was probably revised and printed in 1607 as *Sir Thomas Wyatt*, by Webster and Dekker. In November of 1602, Henslowe paid Webster in advance for *Christmas Comes But Once a Year*, another play which has been lost. In 1604, with Thomas Dekker, Webster wrote *Westward Ho*, a comedy, and in 1605, they wrote *Northward Ho*; both were printed in 1607. He wrote small pieces and collaborations for the next few years.

Webster's reputation as a major playwright rests mainly, however, on the four works he wrote alone between 1609 and 1619. The first of these was *The White Devil*; it was published in 1612, but was probably written around 1610. *The Duchess of Malfi* was not published until 1623, but we know that it was written before December 16, 1614, because William Ostler, one of the actors in the play, died on that day; scholars speculate that it was written in 1612 or 1613. Sometime before 1617, Webster probably wrote a play called *Guise*, which is lost. *The Devil's Law Case* was published in 1623, and was probably written between 1617 and 1621, but the dating of this play is debatable.

Webster collaborated on a number of plays with various authors after this, but the last record of his work is in 1625.

The Duchess of Malfi was performed sometime between 1612 and 1614 at both the Blackfriars and the Globe theatres, and Richard Burbage played a chief part. It probably took Webster a long time to write it; scholars believe that Webster wrote slowly and painstakingly; in fact, he himself admits as much, in the preface to *The White Devil*:

To those who report I was a long time in finishing this Tragedy, I confessed I do not write with a goose-quill, winged with two feathers, and if they will needs make it my fault, I must answered them with that of Euripides to Alcestides, a Tragic Writer: Alcestides objecting that Euripides had lonely in three daies composed three verses, whereas himself had written three hundreth: Thou telst truth (quoth he) but here's the difference, thine shall onely be read for three daies, whereas mine shall continue three ages.

The story in the play was based loosely on historical figures. King Federico of Naples had a half-brother, Enrico d'Aragona. Enrico had three children. The oldest, Lodovico, became a cardinal. The younger son, Carlo, inherited the father's title of Marquis of Gerace. Their sister, Giovanna, was married in 1490, at the age of 12 or less, to Alfonso Piccolomini, who became Duke of Amalfi in 1493 and died in 1498. Their son Alfonso was born in 1499, and she ruled Amalfi during his childhood. In 1510 she left Amalfi, ostensibly on a pilgrimage to Loretto, but really to meet Antonio Bologna, the former master of her household, whom she had secretly married. Antonio was killed in Milan in 1513, and it appears that the Duchess had been murdered along with her two younger children at Amalfi several months before. The historical record does not show whether Giovanna's brothers were responsible for her death.

A number of writers recorded the story, most in fictional form, and Webster almost certainly used at least two of these sources for his play. In addition, he culled speeches, themes, and lines from many other sources for his own use. If a writer did this now, he would be accused of plagiarism, but in Webster's time it was common practice to borrow from other writers, and was in fact a way for the writer to draw together various associations in a reader's or audience's mind.

Many critics have commented on the density of this play and its complexity of style and structure. The language is highly figurative, and there are numerous patterns of symbolism: fountains and springs, sight and blindness, knives and swords, among others. There is more than a hint of symbolic association between the Duchess and her children and the Holy Family: for example, her son is born just after December 18, in what is known as the "month of holy infancy." Later, when the Duchess, Antonio, and their children flee to escape their persecutors, their flight is reminiscent of that of the Holy Family from the persecution of the Innocents by Herod; and there are other connections and parallels, too numerous to be accidental, which lend a significance to the actions of the Duchess and the other characters beyond the events themselves.

Webster is exploring a number of themes in *The Duchess of Malfi*. Among them are

- The possibility of goodness and integrity in the face of evil;

- Corruption in the church and in the state;
- The falseness and inconstancy of security;
- The ease with which appearances deceive;
- The idea that suffering tests and defines a person's character.

Critics disagree about the significance of the Duchess's death. Because of the strength of her spirit, her integrity, and her faith, some see in her death an affirmation of life. Others believe that the fact that the Duchess dies is Webster's way of saying that her integrity was meaningless and without value, and likewise, life is random and meaningless. Whatever his ultimate intent, Webster certainly meant to contrast good and evil: he pits Ferdinand and the Cardinal against Antonio and the Duchess; he contrasts the relationship of Antonio and the Duchess with that of Julia and the Cardinal; he juxtaposes the Duchess's nobility and bravery in the face of death with the desperation and pleading of Cariola; he compares the Duchess's suffering with Ferdinand's; and in Bosola, he has a character who is the epitome of cynicism, an opportunist who discovers his conscience too late.

Chapter 2

A Note on Greek Tragedy

The word tragedy literally means "goat song," probably referring to the practice of giving a goat as a sacrifice or a prize at the religious festivals in honour of the god Dionysos. Whatever its origins, tragedy came to signify a dramatic presentation of high seriousness and noble character which examines the major questions of human existence: Why are we here? How can we know the will of the gods? What meaning does life have in the face of death? In tragedy people are tested by great suffering and must face decisions of ultimate consequence. Some meet the challenge with deeds of despicable cruelty, while others demonstrate their ability to confront and surpass adversity, winning our admiration and proving the greatness of human potential.

Background Information on Greek Theater

Ancient writers give us tantalizing glimpses of the possible origins of Greek theater. The fifth century historian Herodotus notes that in some cities the worship of Dionysos, god of wine and fertility, replaced earlier hero cults which had memorialized the hero's sufferings with tragic choruses. In his Poetics (1449a) Aristotle records that tragedy developed from improvisations on dithyrambs, a type of choral poetry celebrating mythological subjects. The Latin author Horace adds that Thespis invented tragedy, apparently being the first actor to portray the legendary characters of myth instead of narrating their exploits in song (Ars Poetica 275f). The earliest definite record we have of dramatic contests in Athens occurred in 501 BC (the typical date of 534 is based on an unreliable medieval text, see Scullion). The majority of evidence about Greek theater comes from the literature and performance records of the fifth century. This "Golden Age" witnessed major military encounters both with foreign invaders and fellow countrymen. A league of small city-states led by Athens defeated the Persian empire in two key battles at Marathon and Salamis. Our earliest extant tragedy, Persians by Aeschylus, records the humiliation of Xerxes and his mighty army only eight years after the event. The downfall of the Persian king demonstrates the folly of pride which provokes the wrath of the gods. During the following years Athens, under the leadership of Pericles, rose to prominence, celebrating its civic pride with a newly rebuilt Parthenon on the Acropolis. The annual festival held at the Theater of Dionysos, which lies on the hill beneath the Parthenon, brought visitors from miles around to see the dramatic contests and experience the glories of the city. In the final third of the century, civil war broke out between the Athenian league and the Spartan confederacy. Most of our extant plays come from this dark period: Euripides' Trojan Women depicts the horrors of war for the innocent victims left behind, while Aristophanes offers an unusual comic solution for ending the war: a sex-strike by the women of both sides, in Lysistrata [correctly pronounced Ly-SIS-tra-ta]. The themes of Greek tragedy and comedy reflect the political and social concerns of these exciting and troubled times.

Each spring Athens held a festival at which the contests for best tragedy (and comedy after 486) held a central part. Tragic playwrights submitted three serious dramas and a mythological spoof called a satyr play, often on a similar theme. Each playwright had a sponsor (choregos) who hired the three actors and the chorus of 12-15 performers. The playwright probably rehearsed his own cast much like a director would today. Actors wore masks which covered their entire heads like a helmet. These could be exchanged backstage to allow the same actor to play different characters; thus, only three actors were needed for all the parts in one play. The lead actor was called the protagonist, meaning first contestant. The chorus often portrayed the people of the city, responding to the protagonist as an ideal audience. During the choral odes their singing and dancing provided variety and spectacle, allowing time for the actors to change into other costumes for the next scene.

Plays were performed outdoors, often on a hillside which provided a natural seating area for the spectators. Benches of wood or stone surrounded an open circle of ground called the orchestra, or dancing space. The seating area, known as the theatron (literally "viewing space"), has given us our word for theater. Some ancient theaters could seat as many as 15,000 people. Excellent acoustics permitted such large audiences to hear the performance. At the back of the orchestra where most of the action took place stood the skené (pronounced "skay-NAY") or scene building, which provided a place to change costumes and store props. Actors could enter and exit from doors on the front of the skené or from large aisle ways on either side of the orchestra. There was little attempt at creating the illusion of a location other than using the scene building for a palace or temple. One popular special effect was the mechane or crane which lowered a god from the roof of the skené to the stage. In several plays gods or the spirits of dead heroes appear to proclaim a prophecy or resolve a crisis. We use the Latin phrase deus ex machina (god out of the machine) to describe a last-minute rescue which brings the play to a surprising, if improbable, conclusion. Another common device was a rolling platform (ekkyklema, literally "something rolled out") on which scenes of bloody carnage could be briefly revealed.

According to Aristotle, tragedies had certain recognizable sections which most of our surviving plays follow. A prologue, spoken by one or two characters, introduces the play's setting and major action. The parodos brings the chorus into the orchestra to become an audience and respondent to the characters. The body of the play alternates between episodes involving the principle actors and choral odes sung and danced by the chorus, to allow for the actors to change costumes and indicate the passage of time. The exodos concludes the play with all performers leaving the stage. Plays were written entirely in verse, although lyric passages and dramatic dialogue differed considerably in style. Choral odes exhibit a wide variety of meters, nearly impossible to convey in translation, which indicate changes in mood and subject, whether religious, solemn, excited, etc. Actors spoke verse sounding more like common speech but using heightened rhetoric for specific purposes: rhesis (persuasive speech), monody (musical solo), agon (formal debate), stychomythia (rapid exchange of dialogue) are the major forms. These make up the formal elements of tragedy.

Although hundreds of playwrights competed in the dramatic festivals in Athens and other cities, the works of only four have survived. Aeschylus was the early master of the trilogy, three plays written to be performed together which continue the same story. Most of the seven plays we have of his were once part of trilogies, but The Oresteia, containing the plays Agamemnon, Libation Bearers, and Eumenides, is the only complete example still in existence. According to Aristotle, Aeschylus introduced the practice of using two actors, thus receiving credit for the invention of dramatic dialogue. His other plays include Persians, Suppliants, and Seven Against Thebes (the authorship of Prometheus Bound is disputed). Ironically, Aeschylus wanted to be remembered on his epitaph not for his tragedies but for fighting at the battle of Marathon. Sophocles is best known for his masterpieces Oedipus the King and Antigone. Both plays demonstrate excellent plot construction and skillful use of dramatic irony. Aristotle claims Sophocles was first to use a third actor. Other tragedies by Sophocles include Aias, Women of Trachis, Philoctetes, and Oedipus at Colonus.

Euripides was known as an innovator, experimenting with both the form and content of the traditional myths. Several of his plays depict women driven to violence because of their intense suffering, such as Electra, Medea, and Hecabe. Euripides seems to reflect current skeptical trends in philosophy in plays such as Heracles in which the title character questions the existence of the gods, at least in their popular manifestations. Because of his daring approach, Euripides was not as successful in the contests as the other two tragedians during his lifetime, but during the fourth century his fame grew; hence we have more of his plays than the combined total of Aeschylus and Sophocles.

The only comic writer whose works survive from this period, Aristophanes addressed current events in his plays, blending political satire with bawdy farce, in some of the most elegant Greek poetry ever written. Many of his plays are named after his fanciful choruses: Knights, Clouds, Wasps, Birds, Frogs. One other comic writer from the next century deserves mention. Menander is credited with perfecting what ancient critics called New Comedy, which influenced most of the subsequent comedies written in Western Civilization including Shakespeare and Moliere. Two of his plays, The Grouch and The Girl from Samos, have survived almost intact. The apostle Paul quotes from a play by Menander in 1 Cor. 15:33: "Evil companions corrupt good morals."

Aristotle's Definition of Tragedy

Aristotle first defined tragedy in his Poetics around 330 BC, and all subsequent discussions of tragic form have been influenced by his concepts. According to Aristotle, "Tragedy, then, is an imitation of a noble and complete action, having the proper magnitude; it employs language that has been artistically enhanced; it is presented in dramatic, not narrative form, and achieves, through the representation of pitiable and fearful incidents, the catharsis of such incidents" (ch. 6; Golden 11).

Several of these terms require clarification. "Imitation" (mimesis) does not refer exclusively to acting out something on stage. Aristotle recognizes many forms of imitation including epic poetry (Homer), painting, song, and dance. "Noble" does not mean that the characters are necessarily of high moral standing or that they must always be kings, heroes, or gods: the title character of Euripides' Medea is a wicked sorceress who kills her own children. According to Hardison, the term could be translated as larger than life, majestic, or serious (Golden 84).

"Magnitude" refers not to the greatness of the subject matter, as some have suggested, but to the appropriate length of a production. Earlier in the Poetics (ch. 5), Aristotle contrasts the shorter action of a play with that of an epic poem such as the Iliad. A story with the proper magnitude for drama can be presented within two or three hours' performance time. "Enhanced language" refers to the fact that all plays at that time were written in poetic verse rather than the language of everyday speech. As Steiner explains, "There is nothing democratic in the vision of tragedy. The royal and heroic characters whom the gods honour with their vengeance are set higher than we are in the chain of being, and their style of utterance must reflect this elevation".

Endless debates have centered on the term "catharsis" which Aristotle unfortunately does not define. Some critics interpret catharsis as the purging or cleansing of pity and fear from the spectators as they observe the action on stage; in this way tragedy relieves them of harmful emotions, leaving them better people for their experience. According to this interpretation, Aristotle may have been offering an alternative to Plato's charge that the dramatic poets were dangerous to society because they incited the passions.

However, it is uncharacteristic of Aristotle to define tragedy in terms of audience psychology; throughout the Poetics he focuses on dramatic form, not its effects on viewers. Therefore, commentators such as Else and Hardison prefer to think of catharsis not as the effect of tragedy on the spectator but as the resolution of dramatic tension within the plot. The dramatist depicts incidents which arouse pity and fear for the protagonist, then during the course of the action, he resolves the major conflicts, bringing the plot to a logical and foreseeable conclusion.

This explanation of catharsis helps to explain how an audience experiences satisfaction even from an unhappy ending. Human nature may cause us to hope that things work out for Antigone, but, because of the insurmountable obstacles in the situation and the ironies of fate, we come to expect the worst and would feel cheated if Haemon arrived at the last minute to rescue her, providing a happy but contrived conclusion. In tragedy things may not turn out as we wish, but we recognize the probable or necessary relation between the hero's actions and the results of those actions, and appreciate the playwright's honest depiction of life's harsher realities. Notice that Aristotle's definition does not include an unfortunate or fatal conclusion as a necessary component of tragedy. Usually we think of tragedy resulting in the death of the protagonist along with several others. While this is true of most tragedies (especially Shakespeare), Aristotle acknowledges that several Greek tragedies end happily. In Aeschylus' trilogy the Oresteia, Orestes must avenge the death of his father by killing his murderer, who happens to be Orestes' mother. The conflict is successfully resolved when Athena appoints a court of law to uphold justice in such cases, and Orestes is acquitted of any guilt. In Oedipus the King the hero inflicts his own punishment by blinding himself, but he goes into exile instead of dying. Sophocles wrote a sequel to this play called Oedipus at Colonus in which the hero finds a peaceful death after years of suffering to atone for his misdeeds, but his demise is seen as a happy ending to an unhappy life. In tragedy people must make difficult choices and face serious consequences, but they do not always meet with death.

The Tragic Hero

Aristotle distinguishes between tragedy which depicts people of high or noble character, and comedy which imitates those of low or base character (ch. 2). Renaissance scholars understood this passage to mean that tragic characters must always be kings or princes, while comedy is peopled with the working or servant classes, but Aristotle was not talking about social or political distinctions. For him character is determined not by birth but by moral choice. A noble person is one who chooses to act nobly. Tragic characters are those who take life seriously and seek worthwhile goals, while comic characters are "good-for-nothings" who waste their lives in trivial pursuits (Else 77). While it may be true that, as Arthur Miller argued, the common man is a potential subject for tragedy (in the sense that one need not be a king or a demigod to act nobly), the one thing a tragic protagonist cannot be is common. Ordinary humanity belongs on the sidelines in tragedy, represented by the Greek chorus. The tragic protagonist is always larger than life, a person of action whose decisions determine the fate of others and seems to shake the world itself.

The hero of tragedy is not perfect, however. To witness a completely virtuous person fall from fortune to disaster would provoke moral outrage at such an injustice. Likewise, the downfall of a villainous person is seen as appropriate punishment and does not arouse pity or fear. The best type of tragic hero, according to Aristotle, exists "between these extremes... a person who is neither perfect in virtue and justice, nor one who falls into misfortune through vice and depravity, but rather, one who succumbs through some miscalculation" (ch. 13). The term hamartia, which Golden translates as "miscalculation," literally means "missing the mark," taken from the practice of archery.

Much confusion exists over this crucial term. Critics of previous centuries once understood hamartia to mean that the hero must have a "tragic flaw," a moral weakness in character which inevitably leads to disaster. This interpretation comes from a long tradition of dramatic criticism which seeks to place blame for disaster on someone or something: "Bad things don't just happen to good people, so it must be someone's fault." This was the "comforting" response Job's friends in the Old Testament story gave him to explain his suffering: "God is punishing you for your wrongdoing." For centuries tragedies were held up as moral illustrations of the consequences of sin.

Given the nature of most tragedies, however, we should not define hamartia as tragic flaw. While the concept of a moral character flaw may apply to certain tragic figures, it seems inappropriate for many others. There is a definite causal connection between Creon's pride which precipitates his destruction, but can Antigone's desire to see her brother decently buried be called a flaw in her character which leads to her death? Her stubborn insistence on following a moral law higher than that of the state is the very quality for which we admire her.

Searching for the tragic flaw in a character often oversimplifies the complex issues of tragedy. For example, the critic predisposed to looking for the flaw in Oedipus' character usually points to his stubborn pride, and concludes that this trait leads directly to his downfall. However, several crucial events in the plot are not motivated by pride at all: (1) Oedipus leaves Corinth to protect the two people he believes to be his parents; (2) his choice of Thebes as a destination is merely coincidental and/or fated, but certainly not his fault; (3) his defeat of the Sphinx demonstrates wisdom rather than blind stubbornness. True, he kills Laius on the road, refusing to give way on a narrow pass, but the fact that this happens to be his father cannot be attributed to a flaw in his character. (A modern reader might criticize him for killing anyone, but the play never indicts Oedipus simply for murder.) Furthermore, these actions occur prior to the action of the play itself. The central plot concerns Oedipus' desire as a responsible ruler to rid his city of the gods' curse and his unyielding search for the truth, actions which deserve our admiration rather than contempt as a moral flaw. Oedipus falls because of a complex set of factors, not from any single character trait.

This misunderstanding can be corrected if we realise that Aristotle discusses hamartia in the Poetics not as an aspect of character (ch. 15) but rather as an incident in the plot (ch. 13). What Aristotle means by hamartia might better be translated as "tragic error" (Golden's miscalculation). Caught in a crisis situation, the protagonist makes an error in judgment or action, "missing the mark," and disaster results.

Most of Aristotle's examples show that he thought of hamartia primarily as a failure to recognize someone, often a blood relative. In his commentary Gerald Else sees a close connection between the concepts of hamartia, recognition, and catharsis. For Aristotle the most tragic situation possible was the unwitting murder of one family member by another. Mistaken identity allows Oedipus to kill his father Laius on the road to Thebes and subsequently to marry Jocasta, his mother; only later does he recognize his tragic error. However, because he commits the crime in ignorance and pays for it with remorse, self-mutilation, and exile, the plot reaches resolution or catharsis, and we pity him as a victim of ironic fate instead of accusing him of blood guilt. While Aristotle's concept of tragic error fits the model example of Oedipus quite well, there are several tragedies in which the protagonists suffer due to circumstances totally beyond their control. In the Oresteia trilogy, Orestes must avenge his father's death by killing his mother. Aeschylus does not present Orestes as a man whose nature destines him to commit matricide, but as an unfortunate, innocent son thrown into a terrible dilemma not of his making. In The Trojan Women by Euripides, the title characters are helpless victims of the conquering Greeks; ironically, Helen, the only one who deserves blame for the war, escapes punishment by seducing her former husband Menelaus. Heracles, in Euripides' version of the story, goes insane and slaughters his wife and children, not for anything he has done but because Hera, queen of the gods, wishes to punish him for being the illegitimate son of Zeus and a mortal woman. Hamartia plays no part in these tragedies.

Given these examples, we should remember that Aristotle's theory of tragedy, while an important place to begin, should not be used to prescribe one definitive form which applies to all tragedies past and present.

Chapter 3

John Webster: Biography

John Webster (c. 1580 – c. 1634) was an English Jacobean dramatist, a late contemporary of William Shakespeare. His tragedies The White Devil and The Duchess of Malfi are often regarded as masterpieces of the early 17th-century English stage.

Life and Career

Webster's life is obscure, and the dates of his birth and death are not known. His father, a coach maker also named John Webster, married a blacksmith's daughter named Elizabeth Coates on November 4, 1577, and it is likely that Webster was born not long after in or near London. On August 1, 1598, "John Webster, lately of the New Inn" was admitted to the Middle Temple, one of the Inns of Court; in view of the legal interests evident in his dramatic work, this is probably him. Webster married a 17-year-old girl named Sara Peniall on March 18, 1606, and their first child, John, was baptized at the parish of St Dunstan-in-the-West on May 8, 1606. Bequests in the will of a neighbour who died in 1617 indicate that other children were born to him.

Most of what is otherwise known of him relates to his theatrical activities. Webster was still writing plays as late as the mid-1620s, but Thomas Heywood's Hierarchie of the Blessed Angels (licensed November 7, 1634) speaks of him in the past tense, implying he was then dead.

Early Collaborations

By 1602 he was working with teams of playwrights on history plays, most of which were never printed. These included a tragedy Caesar's Fall (written with Michael Drayton, Thomas Dekker, Thomas Middleton and Anthony Munday), and a collaboration with Thomas Dekker entitled Christmas Comes but Once a Year (1602). With Dekker he also wrote Sir Thomas Wyatt, which was printed in 1607. He worked with Thomas Dekker again on two city comedies, Westward Ho in 1604 and Northward Ho in 1605. Also in 1604, he adapted John Marston's The Malcontent for staging by the King's Men.

The Major Tragedies

Despite his ability to write comedy, Webster is best known for his two brooding English tragedies based on Italian sources. The White Devil, a retelling of the intrigues involving Vittoria Accoramboni, an Italian woman assassinated at the age of 28, was a failure when staged at the Red Bull Theatre in 1612 (published the same year), being too unusual and intellectual for its audience. The Duchess of Malfi first performed by the King's Men about 1614 and published nine years later, was more successful. He also wrote a play called Guise, based on French history, of which little else is known as no text has survived.

The White Devil was performed in the Red Bull Theatre, an open air theatre that is believed to have specialized in providing simple, escapist drama for a largely working class audience, a factor that might explain why Webster's highly intellectual and complex play was unpopular with its audience. In contrast, The Duchess of Malfi was probably performed by the King's Men in the smaller, indoor Blackfriars Theatre, where it would have played to a more highly educated audience that might have appreciated it better. The two plays would thus have been very different in their original performances. The White Devil would have been performed, probably in one continuous action, by adult actors, with elaborate stage effects a possibility. The Duchess of Malfi was performed in a controlled environment, with artificial lighting, and musical interludes between acts — which allowed time, perhaps, for the audience to accept the otherwise strange rapidity with which the Duchess is able to have babies.

Late Plays

Webster wrote one more play on his own: The Devil's Law Case (c. 1617–19?), a tragicomedy. His later plays were collaborative city comedies: Anything for a Quiet Life (c. 1621), co-written with Thomas Middleton, and A Cure for a Cuckold (c. 1624), co-written with William Rowley. In 1624, he also co-wrote a topical play about a recent scandal, Keep the Widow Waking (with John Ford, Rowley and Dekker); the play itself is lost, although its plot is known from a court case. He is believed to have contributed to the tragicomedy The Fair Maid of the Inn with John Fletcher, Ford, and Phillip Massinger. His Appius and Virginia, probably written with Thomas Heywood, is of uncertain date

Chapter 4

Reception and Performance History

The play was written for and performed by the King's Men in 1613 or 1614. The double cast lists included in the 1623 quarto suggest a revival around 1619. Contemporary reference also indicated that the play was performed in 1618, for in that year Orazio Busino, Venetian ambassador to England, complained of the play's treatment of Catholics in the character of the Cardinal.

The quarto's cast list allows more precision about casting than is usually available. Richard Burbage and Joseph Taylor successively played Ferdinand to Henry Condell's Cardinal. John Lowin played Bosola; William Ostler was Antonio. Boy player Richard Sharpe originated the title role. Nicholas Tooley played Forobosco, and Robert Pallant doubled numerous minor roles, including Cariola.The quarto title page announces that the play was performed at both the Globe Theater and at Blackfriars; however, in tone and in some details of staging (particularly the use of special lighting effects) the play is clearly meant primarily for the indoor stage.

The play is known to have been performed for Charles at the Cockpit-in-Court in 1630; there is little reason to doubt that it was performed intermittently throughout the period.

The play remained current through the first part of the Restoration. Samuel Pepys reports seeing the play several times; it was performed by the Duke of York's company under Thomas Betterton.

By the early eighteenth century, Webster's violence and sexual frankness had gone out of taste. In 1733, Lewis Theobald wrote and directed an adaptation, The Fatal Secret; the play imposed neoclassical unities on the play, for instance by eliminating the Duchess's child and preserving the Duchess at the end. By mid-century, the play had fallen with Webster out of the repertory, where it stayed until the Romantic revival of Charles Lamb and William Hazlitt.

In 1850, after a generation of critical interest and theatrical neglect, the play was staged by Samuel Phelps at Sadler's Wells, with Isabella Glyn in the title role. The text was adapted by Richard Henry Horne. The production was favourably reviewed by The Athenaeum; George Henry Lewes, however, registered disapproval of the play's violence and what he termed its shoddy construction: "Instead of 'holding the mirror up to nature,' this drama holds the mirror up to Madame Tussauds." These would become the cornerstones of criticisms of Webster for the next century. Still, the play was popular enough for Glyn to revive her performance periodically for the next two decades.

Shortly after, Duchess came to the United States. Working with Horne's text, director James Stark staged a production in San Francisco; this version is noteworthy for a sentimental apotheosis Stark added, in which the Duchess and Ferdinand are reunited in heaven. The most popular American productions, however, were produced by Wilmarth Waller and his wife Emma.William Poel staged the play at the Opera Comique in 1892, with Mary Rorke as the Duchess and Murray Carson as Bosola.

Poel's playscript followed Webster's text closely apart from scene rearrangements; however, reaction had set in, and the production received generally scathing reviews. William Archer, England's chief proponent of Ibsen's new drama, took advantage of the occasion to lambast what he saw as the overestimation of Elizabethan theater in general.

In 1919, the Phoenix Society revived the play in London for the first time in two decades. The production featured Cathleen Nesbitt as the Duchess; Robert Forquerson played Ferdinand. The production was widely disparaged. For many of the newspaper critics, the failure indicated that Webster had become a "curio"; T. S. Eliot, conversely, argued that the production had failed to uncover the elements that made Webster a great dramatist—specifically his poetry.

A 1935 production at the Embassy Theatre received similarly negative reviews; Ivor Brown noted that the audience left "rather with superior smiles than with emotional surrender." In 1938, a production was broadcast on BBC television; it was no better received than the previous two stage productions.

In the aftermath of World War II, George Rylands directed a production at the Haymarket Theatre that, at last caught the public mood. John Gielgud, as Ferdinand, accentuated the element of incestuous passion in that character's treatment of the Duchess (played by Peggy Ashcroft). Cecil Trouncer was Bosola. Edmund Wilson was perhaps the first to note that the play struck an audience differently in the wake of the revelation of the Holocaust; this note is, from 1945 on, continually struck in discussions of the appropriateness of Webster for the modern age.

A 1946 production on Broadway did not fare as well; Rylands attempted to duplicate his London staging with John Carradine as Ferdinand and Elisabeth Bergner as the Duchess. W. H. Auden adapted Webster's text for the modern audience. However, the production's most notable innovation was in the character of Bosola, which was played by Canada Lee in whiteface. The production received savage reviews from the popular press, and it fared little better in the literary reviews.

The first successful postwar performance in America was staged at the off-Broadway Phoenix Theatre in 1957. Directed by Jack Landau, who had earlier staged a brief but well-reviewed White Devil, the production emphasized (and succeeded as) Grand Guignol. As Walter Kerr put it, "Blood runs right over the footlights, spreads slowly up the aisle and spills well out into Second Avenue."

Ashcroft returned as the Duchess in a 1960 production at the Aldwych Theatre. The play was directed by Donald McWhinnie; Eric Porter played Ferdinand and Max Adrian the Cardinal. Patrick Wymark played Bosola. The production received generally favourable but lukewarm reviews. In 1971, Clifford Williams directed the play for the Royal Shakespeare Company.

Judi Dench took the title role, with Geoffrey Hutchings as Bosola and Emrys James as the Cardinal. Dench's husband Michael Williams played Ferdinand, casting which highlighted the sexual element of the play's siblings.

In 1980, Adrian Noble directed the play at the Royal Exchange Theatre, Manchester. This production received excellent notices; it was transferred to London, where it won the London Drama Critic's Award for best play. Helen Mirren played the title role; Mike Gwilym played Ferdinand, and Bob Hoskins played Bosola. Pete Postlethwaite was Antonio. Mirren's performance received special acclaim.

The actor-centered troupe led by Ian McKellan and Edward Petherbridge chose Webster's play as one of their first productions. The production premiered in January 1986 in the Lyttelton Theatre of the Royal National Theatre. Philip Prowse's direction was highly stylized, the scenic backdrop segmented, and the actors' movements tightly controlled.

The result, as Jarka Burian noted, was "a unified, consistent mise-en-scene...without enough inner turbulence to create a completely satisfying theatre experience." Eleanor Bron played the Duchess; Mckellan played Bosola, Jonathan Hyde Ferdinand, and Petheridge the Cardinal.

The Swan staged a new production in 1989; Harriet Walter took the part of the Duchess; Nigel Terry and Stephen Boxer alternated as Bosola; Bruce Alexander was Ferdinand and Russell Dixon the Cardinal.

Gale Edwards directed the 2000 production at The Barbican. Aisling O'Sullivan played the Duchess; Tom Mannion played Bosola, and Colin Tierney was FerdinandPhillip Franks directed the 2006 production at the West Yorkshire Playhouse. Imogen Stubbs played the Duchess

Chapter 5

The Duchess of Malfi: As a Jacobean Drama

The Duchess of Malfi is a typical Jacobean Tragedy in that it is characterized by a melodramatic sense of impending doom, fatalistic spiritual despair and instability. In most tragedies, the protagonist - always an outstanding figure - begins with an act of defiance against established laws and conventions. The protagonists are usually to blame for their actions through some fatal flaw and, after coming to a state of greater understanding through mass-suffering, the plays usually ended with their death. More specifically, The Duchess Of Malfi is a revenge tragedy in which the villain's wrongdoing is eventually avenged. The dramas' recurrent pattern is a moral ending in which evil is its own undoing and, after defeating itself, is purged.

The malcontent is a frequent figure in Jacobean Tragedy - a disaffected servant who feels wronged and who is usually an instrument of treachery. There is often a Machiavellian villain and the plays often reflect on court life. The main qualities of Jacobean Tragedy are a powerfully oppressive sense of the passage of time and the transitory nature of things, high profile imagery of death and decay and reflections upon mortality, the overturning of traditional relationships, melancholy and the settling of love affairs by the sword. Among The Duchess Of Malfi's themes are darkness, deception and corruption and the wheel of fortune. Central characters include the Duchess, an intelligent but tragic heroine; the philosophising feral villain Bosola; the Duchess' wicked two brothers, Ferdinand and the immoral Cardinal; as well as Antonio, a well-meaning commoner who falls short of being a hero and hence, commands our sympathy.

In the play, the incestuous Ferdinand forbids his widowed sister to marry again but, when he discovers that she is not only married, but has children, he is driven insane with fury. An overwhelming desire for revenge takes over and the Duchess' secret love unleashes violence which, due to the dreadfully powerful characters and dark deeds, ends with the stage covered in blood.

Chapter 6

The Duchess of Malfi: As a Revenge Tragedy

The Jacobean age was one of questioning and uncertainty about many issues, such as religion, politics and law. At the same time it was rediscovering the potency of Classical texts of Rome and Greece, and reinterpreting tragic form to suit its own ends. *The Duchess of Malfi* is a revenge tragedy, but Webster has used the form for much more than just its entertainment value; he has used it as a vehicle for the exploration of some themes relevant to the society of his time.

Webster based his plot on a true story set in Italy, and kept the Italian setting because like Shakespeare and other playwrights of his day, he had to use politically-acceptable foreign settings in which to explore ideas such as those presented in *The Duchess of Malfi*, (which were really commentaries on the England of their own era), to do with inequality, injustice, and corruption, without causing outrage in response to his work.

Antonio and The Duchess

The fact that Antonio can never have an equal relationship with the Duchess has prompted some readers to feel that his importance as a character in the play is limited, while others suggest that his main role is as a mouthpiece for Webster's own judgements and opinions. To assess the importance of his role we need to consider it relation to the Duchess, and in the context of the play as a whole.

Inequalities of power associated with gender and social status are highlighted in the relationship between The Duchess and Antonio, and the reactions of others towards their relationship.

In Antonio's self-deprecating dying speech,

Antonio: We follow after bubbles, blown in th'air. [Act V, Scene iv]

We see that he admits to his life having been filled more with promise than performance. He is a good man, but has been no match for the situation in which Webster placed him.

Antonio is introduced into the play as an outsider to Amalfi, returning home along with his confidant Delio. Delio can be perceived as a more intelligent character than Antonio; almost the 'counsellors counsellor', and more down-to-earth than his friend. Their dialogue serves to introduce the audience to the theme of how a well-governed court could be run, which will contrast dramatically to the corrupt Antonio will find at Amalfi.

At the court they encounter Bosola, the malcontent, who later likens the virtuous Antonio to a 'cedar planted by a spring', an image which contrasts to Bolola's view of the Aragon brothers (The Duchess's brothers: The Cardinal and Ferdinand) as, plum trees, that grow crooked [Act 1, Scene i]

Being of lower social status, Antonio is perhaps an unlikely match for the scheming Duchess, and being an honest man he is uncomfortable with the plotting and deceit in which he becomes involved. Antonio is considered to be equal to the Duchess in that he has acquired the level of education necessary to be a counsellor; he has gained status, in terms of the Renaissance humanist tradition, by absorbing scholarship in order to improve himself, but as he well knows himself, he can never equal The Duchess in blood. His predicament shows that as well as creating him as a character in his own right, Webster is using him as a device with which to make points about the society of the time.

While it was quite common for a male figure of power to marry below his station, it was quite unacceptable for a noble female to conduct herself in that way.

Duchess: I am Duchess of Malfi still [Act !V, Scene ii]

Thus, even when married to her, Antonio can never be her equal in power. Powerful women, being considered by some to be unnatural and dangerous, provoked much controversy at the time, a pertinent example being Queen Elizabeth Tudor.

The Duchess is seen right from the start as a lusty character who is pursuing the affection of Antonio. Her dialogue is full of sexual innuendo, and she can be seen as being in the category of the renaissance stereotype the 'lusty widow'. She is presented as a powerful woman with a dominant will and right to the moment of her death is portrayed as strong and independent. Defying her brother's warnings not to remarry is further proof of her strength.

The Duchess's defiant insistence on marrying Antonio, her second husband, is an action which shows that she has her own desires, and a more dominant will than anybody around her. Webster has given her all the qualities that Antonio, her spouse, lacks, qualities which were not thought to be desirable in a woman of that era; she plots, schemes and has a bold and impetuous nature.

She is also a fundamentally good character, and her dislike of the darkness:

Duchess: They that enter there,

Must go upon their knees [Act 4, Scene ii]

shows how she is an opposite of Ferdinand who moves about her in a black disguise.

Thus *The Duchess of Malfi* hinges around a female protagonist, and, like Antonio's, her predicament shows how the play's themes are underpinned by Webster's thinking about social issues of his day. Ironically, he is making points about women's rights at a time when only men were allowed to act on the stage.

Like many playwrights of the time Webster had a legal background, and this served to make him more aware of the inequalities of the law involving women. He has a sensitive awareness of these inequalities and the play illustrates the ridiculous views taken by the community.

Duchess: We are forced to woo, because none dare woo us [Act 1, Scene ii]

In that line we can see that Webster has emphasised The Duchess's commanding character by his use of language. The play has been written mainly in unrhymed iambic pentameter of five stresses and ten syllables per line, which was the norm for the blank verse of renaissance dramas. Like all good playwrights of the time he has occasionally bent the rules of this set pattern to make the lines shorter or longer, for example to show a character's unbalanced nature. The Duchess's line breaks the metre by being slightly too long, showing that she refuses to be restrained, and adding power to the point she is making.

Antonio fears that his feelings for the Duchess are little more than 'mad ambition', and in this respect we can liken him to Banquet in Shakespeare's play Macbeth; a man who lacks drive because he believes that ambition brings about the downfall of good men. Antonio proves to be useless in any crisis and in Act 5 is even unaware that his wife and children have been needlessly murdered. The Duchess, in contrast, accepts death nobly and faces her fate with serenity.

Corruption is an Important Theme in The Play

Duchess: He [Ferdinand] left this with me

She shows the poignard.

Antonio: And it seems, did wish you would use it on yourself?

Duchess: His action seem'd to intend so much. [Act 3, Scene ii]

This interchange is just one small illustration of how moral corruption is rife throughout the court of Amalfi. The only characters seemingly not tainted are Antonio and the Duchess. The Duchess may have chosen Antonio for this very reason, as he is a good and honest man and not a sycophant of the court. Even the Cardinal, a representative of religion, is full of dishonesty and murders his mistress.

Paradoxically, the corruption rife in the religious orders is explained in humanist terms by Antonio's simile for politics and good government:

A prince's court

Is like a common fountain, whence should flow

Pure silver-drops in general. But if't chance

Some cursed example poison't near the head,

Death and diseases through the whole land spread [Act 1, Scene i]

The corrupt motives of those around them bring about the downfall of the couple, which is an inevitable outcome of a revenge tragedy. As we have seen, Webster has woven the play into this genre and also raised many points about beliefs of the Jacobean time. The Duchess has done nothing legally wrong and Webster's exposure of the Cardinal's hypocrisy reveals how unjust and tragic the fate of Antonio and his wife really is.

So we have seen that Antonio does have a substantial role in his own right. He is a good man who, due to his learning, had gained an intimacy with the Duchess, but he is the victim of a corrupt society. At the same time he has been shaped to show the inequalities of the period and highlight the corruption of nobility. The evidence shows that the presentation of Antonio serves to show both sides of an argument. His marriage could have been successful, but is deemed unorthodox, inappropriate and draws moral censure in at least three ways; it is unequal, it is in secret and it is the Duchess's second marriage.

As good man destroyed by an unjust and corrupt society, we can understand the despair in Antonio's dying words:

Antonio: Pleasure of life, what isn't? Only the good hours of an ague. [Act 5, Scene iv]

Ferdinand and Bosola

The character Ferdinand, the Duchess's brother, is notable for his exaggerated feelings and violent and abusive language. Some may feel that his characterization is so extreme that it makes it difficult to take *The Duchess of Malfi* seriously, but he plays a central role in the dynamics of the play, and represents a personality-type which could just as easily exist today as in Webster's time.

Ferdinand: And women like the part, which, like the lamprey,

Hath ne'er a bone isn't.

Duchess: Fie, sir!

Ferdinand: Nay,

I mean the tongue [Act 1, Scene ii]

This double-entendre shows Ferdinand's dark side. His persistent sexual innuendo aimed at his sister throughout the play shows that he has an abrasive temperament and unbalanced emotions. But discourteous and sickening as his behaviour is, he plays a pivotal role in the play.

Ferdinand is a younger repressed twin, and his wish for the death of The Duchess can be interpreted in many ways, his intentions towards his sister having been the source of much conjecture by critics. He obviously wants to dominate her and control her, but his wish appears somewhat futile, as she has been married before, and has thus gained her powerful status.

Ferdinand appears to lack the freedom of both of his siblings, as not only is his sister in a more powerful position than he is, but also his brother The Cardinal has the authority to practice politics on a much wider scale and can be present wherever he chooses. Ferdinand is torturously inhibited, and his brother's blasphemous affair and subsequent murder of his lover is painful to him, as is his brooding on his sister

In the shameful act of sin [Act 2, Scene v]

Incest was widely used as a theme in Elizabethan and Jacobean plays, Shakespeare's *Hamlet* (1600) and Beaumont and Fletcher's *A King And No King* (1611) being examples which Webster may have had in mind whilst writing *The Duchess of Malfi* (1614). The brother-sister incest theme was also take up later, spectacularly, by John Ford in *'Tis Pity She's a Whore* (1633).

Webster has given Ferdinand the capacity for extreme love and hate. He is not married and appears to be without a mistress, which adds to his sense of alienation and inability to relate to women. Therefore he turns upon his sister who with her new-found freedom is an obvious target. Powerful women were considered unnatural and dangerous at the time, and Ferdinand is used as a mouthpiece for the public's judgements.

Ferdinand: There is a kind of honey-dew that's deadly:
'Twill poison your fame. [Act 1, Scene ii]

A modern day parallel to the marriage of The Duchess and Antonio might be a couple marrying with a large age gap, or a homosexual relationship. As with the relationship between the Duchess and Antonio these relationships are perfectly legal, but in the eyes of a narrow-minded and inflexible society are seen as deplorable.

In Webster's time most widows did not remarry, usually because they found themselves in a state of freedom and those left wealthy had the means to enjoy it. Webster brings his background in the legal profession to bear on the issues, showing the loopholes in the law of verbal contracts as an acceptable form of marriage.

Ferdinand is completely legally wrong to label his sister's children as 'bastards':

Ferdinand: For though our national law distinguish bastards [Act 4, Scene i]

And he exasperates her further by his doubt about their christening. Ferdinand constantly torments his sister with his madness. He is the antithesis of the cruel and coldly-calculating Cardinal, whose behaviour is less sinister than Ferdinand's which is motivated by his wild and fiery spirit. Ferdinand revels in the dark and in the play it is mentioned that he suffers with lycanthropic, a disease that makes the host believe he is a werewolf. The Duchess in contrast shuns the dark that Ferdinand operates in around her.

Bosola, whose character puts him in the category of the Renaissance dramatists' 'type', 'the malcontent', is in the service of Ferdinand, acting as a spy on The Duchess. He provides a great comedy element to the play, even though he is actually disgustingly unpleasant.

Bosola: She resembled an abortive hedgehog. [Act 2, Scene i]

He is the character who appeals to the working class in the audience who go to plays to see a blood-bath as entertainment. Webster also enjoys a pun on his name as 'Boss' can mean a protuberance on the body, or be slang for masterfulness.

Bosola can be likened to Feste in Shakespeare's *Twelfth Night*, in that he has the independence to roam among all strata of society and support all sides at once. But The Duchess makes a big mistake by trusting him, as he is the one who kills her on the order of Ferdinand.

With his dying breath Ferdinand comments on fate with an intriguing metaphor:

Ferdinand: Like diamonds we are cut with our own dust [Act 5, Scene v]

The diamond is a recurring image, and here echoes a speech made by the Duchess just before she is strangled.

Duchess: What would it pleasure me to have my throat cut

With diamonds? [Act 4, Scene ii]

Ferdinand may be acknowledging the downfall of his family by the dust in relation to the blood tie. His demise is a slide into isolation where every last light is extinguished.

It has often been pointed out that *The Duchess of Malfi* is a flawed play. For example Ferdinand reveals to Bosola a possible motive for wanting his sister to be murdered:

Ferdinand: To have gained an infinite mass of treasure by her death. [Act 5, Scene ii]

But this sounds unconvincing, as Malfi is little more than a poor fishing village. Moments such as these in the play have led it to be criticized for its plot, and it has other flaws. For example is it plausible that the Duchess could marry Antonio and have children in secret? Webster tends to neglect the importance of The Duchess' sons, and in Act 5 we see Delio apparently with a false heir.

But in spite of these flaws *The Duchess of Malfi* has lasted and remained popular, not just for its potent entertainment value and Webster's masterful use of language, but also for the insights it gives us into Jacobean society.

Chapter 7

The Duchess of Malfi: A Real Play

The Duchess of Malfi was a historical character. Born in Giorvanna d'Aragon, she was married in 1490 at the age of 12 to Alfonso Piccolomini, son and heir of the first Duke of AMalfi. He succeeded to the dukedom in 1493 but died of gout in 1498. The Duchess then at the age of 19 already had a daughter named Caterina. Her son was born posthumously in 1499 and succeeded to the Dukedom, which she ruled for him as regent.

Despite French and Spanish invasions, the state flourished. The Duchess was able to pay off debts incurred by her husband and live prosperously. Antonio Bologna who came of a reputable family was brought up in the court of Naples. He became major-domo to Frederico, the state's last Aragonian king and followed his master into exile in France. Upon Frederico's death, Antonio returned to Naples where he was offered the post of major-domo in the household of the Duchess of Malfi, who herself was of the Royal House of Aragon. The young widow fell quickly and passionately in love with Antonio. Fearing the wrath of her brothers Lodovico who had resigned his title of Marquis of Gerace to become a Cardinal and Carlo (Webster's Ferdinand) who had succeeded it, she married Antonio in secret, with her waiting woman as the sole witness to the ceremony.

In real life, as in Webster's play, their marraige was successfully concealed for some years. The birth of their 1st child was undetected, but the birth of the 2nd caused rumours which, reaching the ears of the Aragonian brothers, led them to set spies to watch their sister. Antonio took his 2 children to Ancona, leaving the Duchess who was again pregnant, in her palace. Unbearably lonely, she found an excuse to set out with a great retinue on pilgrimage to Loretto, from whence she proceeded to join Antonio. Upon her arrival in Ancona, she revealed her marraige to her household and declared that she would renounce her rank and title to live privately wiht Antonio and their children. One of her astonished servants set out to inform the Cardinal what had happened. The rest deserted her and returned to Amalfi.

At Ancona where their third child was born, the Duchess and her husband were allowed only a few months' peace before the Cardinal of Aragon put pressure on Cardinal Gonzaga, Legate of Ancona to banish Antonio. Having foreseen this, Antonio had made preparations to take refuge with a friend in Siena. As soon as the decree of his banishment was issued in 1511, he set out with the Duchess and their children, thus evading any attempt that might have been made to capture or murder them.

The Cardinal continuing the exert his influence against them, the head of Signiory of Siena was persuaded to expel them. This time, Antonio and his family did not depart so quickly. One their way to Venice, they were overtaken by horsemen. By asserting that her brothers would not harm her in person, the Duchess was able to persuade Antonio to escape with their eldest child, a boy of 6 or 7 of age. They arrived safely in Milan, probably in the late summer of 1512. There is no evidence to connect the Aragonian brothers with the death of the Duchess, but after being taken back to her palace in Amalfi, neither she, her two youngest children nor her waiting woman were ever seen again.

Antonio did not know what had happened to them. But he was constantly warned that his life was in danger, one warning coming from a man named Delio who had heard Antonio's story from a neopolitan friend. On an October in 1513, Delio and a companion passed Antonio, who looked dismayed, with 2 servants on their way to mass at the church of S Francesco. A few minutes later, an uproar was heard. Looking back, Delio and friend realised that Antonio had been stabbed to death by a Lombard captain called Daniele de Bozolo and three accomplices. All 4 escaped.

Chapter 8

Act Wise Summary

Act I:

The Duchess of Malfi is divided into five acts, each comprising several scenes. In the three scenes of act 1, the major characters and conflicts are introduced. The setting is the Italian city of Malfi in the sixteenth century, in the audience chamber or "presence" of the widowed Duchess. Antonio, the Duchess's steward, talks with his friend Delio as they observe the others who pass through the chamber. The first to enter are the Cardinal and Bosola. Although Bosola has recently been released after serving seven years for a murder he committed at the behest of the Cardinal, the Cardinal is cold to him and will not acknowledge his debt.

Ferdinand, the Duke of Calabria, enters with his entourage. Ferdinand learns that Antonio has proven himself the best at a knightly competition, and he congratulates Antonio for his prowess and for his eloquent speech. When the Cardinal reenters with the Duchess, Antonio gives Delio his impression of the three siblings: the Cardinal is jealous and vengeful, Ferdinand is ""perverse and turbulent," and the Duchess is sweet and noble. Ferdinand asks the Duchess to accept Bosola as a servant, and she agrees; in fact, the brothers have hired Bosola to spy on the Duchess.

The two brothers warn the Duchess not to remarry, and she promises that she will not. However, as soon as they leave her chamber, she summons Antonio and the two perform a private marriage ceremony, with the Duchess's trusted servant Cariola as witness.

Act II:

The second act, which has five scenes, begins several months later, as the Duchess is about to give birth to a child. Her marriage to Antonio is still secret, and she has concealed her pregnancy by wearing loose clothing. Bosola, however, suspects that she is pregnant and tries to trap her by giving her a present of apricots. When she devours them hungrily and then vomits, he has confirmation of the pregnancy but does not reveal what he knows. The incident sends the Duchess into labour, and she is rushed to her chamber.

To avoid suspicion that the Duchess is giving birth, a ruse is invented: it is announced that jewels have been stolen, and everyone must stay in his or her room while a search is conducted. The Duchess delivers a healthy son, and when Cariola tells Antonio the good news, he prepares a set of calculations based on astrology to determine the baby's future. Meanwhile, Bosola sneaks out to the courtyard beneath the Duchess's window and hears her crying out. Antonio finds him there, and they argue about Bosola having left his room. As he leaves Bosola, Antonio accidentally drops the paper on which he has written his astrological notes, and Bosola retrieves it, discovering that a baby has been born to the Duchess—a baby who will have a short life. Bosola knows that Antonio is in on the secret but does not consider that a man of Antonio's social class could be the father.

In Rome, the Cardinal meets in his chamber with Julia, his mistress. Delio arrives and propositions Julia, but she refuses him. In another part of the Cardinal's palace, Ferdinand has received a letter from Bosola, telling him of the baby's birth. The Cardinal and Ferdinand discuss their sister's betrayal, and Ferdinand's rage takes him to the brink of insanity.

Act III:

Several years pass before the five scenes in act 3 take place. The Duchess has given birth to two more children, but her marriage is still a secret, and Bosola still has not discovered the identity of the father. Ferdinand, finally stirred to action, arrives at the Duchess's palace to confront her. To play an affectionate joke on her, Antonio and Cariola step out of the room while the Duchess is talking to herself in the mirror, and Ferdinand comes into the room at the same moment. He accuses her of shaming the family with her promiscuity, and although she tells him that she is married, he vows never to look at her again.

Afraid of Ferdinand's anger, the Duchess sends Antonio to safety by pretending that he has stolen money and been banished. Tenderly, the couple say goodbye to each other, planning to reunite in Ancona. In her grief, the Duchess confides in Bosola, telling him everything. Bosola plots to entrap the Duchess and Antonio. He speeds to Rome to tell what he knows and find his reward, and the brothers respond with expected fury. The Cardinal decides to contact the authorities at Ancona and have the Duchess and her family banished.

At the Shrine of Our Lady of Loretto, the Duchess and Antonio review their situation. Bosola brings a letter from Ferdinand calling for Antonio's death, and Antonio and the Duchess say goodbye again. They know that this will be their final parting. Antonio takes their oldest son and flees to Milan. The Duchess is arrested by Bosola, in disguise, and taken by guards to her palace.

Act IV:

Act 4: with its two scenes set in the Duchess's chambers, moves quickly. Trying to drive her to despair so that she will be damned as well as killed, Ferdinand arranges for a series of horrors. He visits the Duchess in a darkened room (because he has vowed never to see her again) and places in her hand a dead man's hand that she will assume to be Antonio's. He shows her wax figures that look like the bodies of Antonio and the three children. He arranges for eight madmen to scream outside her window. Through it all, the Duchess maintains her quiet nobility, saying “““”I am Duchess of Malfi still,”””” and Bosola begins to feel a grudging respect for her.

Finally, Bosola brings two executioners to the Duchess's chamber, and they strangle her. She faces her death with dignity. Cariola is also strangled, though she resists her death with all her energy. Off stage, the two younger children are strangled. When Ferdinand sees his dead sister, he has a dramatic change of heart, and rather than rewarding Bosola, he blames him for the murders.

Act V:

The action of the five scenes of act 5 is also rapid. Four days after the events in the Cardinal has had all of Antonio's property seized. Antonio decides to visit the Cardinal and attempt reconciliation. Ferdinand's madness has increased, and he has been seen digging up bodies in the cemetery and carrying a man's leg over his shoulder. Bosola arrives in Milan, and he and the Cardinal try to determine what the other knows. The Cardinal pretends that he does not know the Duchess is dead, so that he will not seem to have been involved in the murder, but Bosola persuades Julia to find out the truth. The Cardinal confesses to Julia that he has had his sister killed, but then he immediately kills Julia with a poisoned book.

Outside the Cardinal's home, Antonio and Delio speak with a ghostly echo that comes from the Duchess's grave. Bosola vows to protect Antonio from harm, but he accidentally kills Antonio with his sword, mistaking him for the Cardinal, who has promised to kill Bosola. In the final scene, an anguished Bosola kills the Cardinal's servant and stabs the Cardinal. Ferdinand rushes in and stabs Bosola and the Cardinal. Bosola stabs Ferdinand. As they all lie dead, Delio enters with Antonio's son and calls for a unified effort to support the young man as the new Duke.

Chapter 9

Character Analysis

Daniel de Bosola

Bosola is the Duchess's Provisor of Horse. As the play opens, he has just been released from imprisonment because of "a notorious murder" the Cardinal hired him to commit. Now, he is employed by Ferdinand, who arranges his position with the Duchess so he can spy on her and prevent her from marrying. In many ways, Bosola is the most complex character in the play, and the only one who's thinking and personality change from beginning to end. Antonio predicts this change at the beginning, when he comments that Bosola is "very valiant," but worries that his melancholy will "poison all his goodness." In fact, Bosola is capable of great evil.

He spies on the Duchess (though he is unable in three years to discover that Antonio is the Duchess's husband), supervises her murder and the murder of her children and of Cariola, accidentally kills Antonio, and deliberately kills the Cardinal, Ferdinand, and a servant. As he observes the nobility of the Duchess and Antonio in facing death and also sees that committing heinous acts for the Cardinal and Ferdinand does not win him gratitude or financial reward, he begins to question his belief that it is better "To appear a true servant, than an honest man." But, when the "stars" drive Bosola to kill Antonio, whom he has resolved to protect, he concludes that all human endeavor and human goodness are meaningless.

Antonio Bologna

Antonio is the steward, or the manager, of the Duchess of Malfi's palace. He is good with a horse and a lance, and he is widely known to be honest — so honest that the Cardinal rejects a suggestion that Antonio be hired to spy on the Duchess. He is also a good judge of character, delivering to his friend, Delio, insightful descriptions of the others as they appear. He is in awe of the Duchess, because of her beauty and her disposition, and humbly accepts her proposal of marriage without regard for the wealth he will obtain by marrying her.

In fact, he agrees to keep the marriage secret, and so he gains no power or prestige from it. After he is married, Antonio is less sharply drawn, but the glimpses given of him do not fulfill the promise of act 1. He loses the paper on which he has calculated the baby's future. He follows the Duchess's plans for avoiding capture, making no suggestions himself. Finally, he is killed as he walks to the Cardinal's door to ask for reconciliation. Still, he is a good man, and the Duchess clearly loves and trusts him until the end.

The Cardinal

The Cardinal is the brother of the Duchess and Ferdinand, as cold and calculating as Ferdinand is excitable. He is a high-ranking official in the Roman Catholic Church, but he does not live the life of a Christian saint: he has a mistress; he hires spies and murderers; and, he does not seem to have any religious duties or religious thought. As Antonio explains to Delio, "where he is jealous of any man, he lays worse plots for them than ever was imposed on Hercules, for he strews in his way flatterers, panders, intelligencers, atheists, and a thousand such political monsters."

The Cardinal is the quiet force behind the plotting against the Duchess. It is his idea to hire Bosola to spy on her, but even Bosola does not know of the Cardinal's involvement. When Bosola has killed the Duchess, the Cardinal pretends to have no knowledge of the crime. He shares Ferdinand's desire that the Duchess not marry, and Ferdinand's anger when she bears a child, but he "can be angry / without this rupture" of "intemperate noise." He demonstrates no love or loyalty, treating with startling coldness Bosola, who killed and was punished in his employment, and Julia, who is his mistress, and the Duchess and Ferdinand, who are his siblings. His motives for tormenting his sister are not clear. He does not want her money or her love, and he is incapable of feeling humiliation or shame. He does not care for his reputation or legacy; his final words are "now, I pray, let me / be laid by, and never thought of."

Delio

Delio is a courtier and a friend of Antonio. His main role in the story is to provide a sounding board for Antonio. Delio's curiosity about the court gives Antonio the opportunity to speak aloud about the characters of the Duchess, her brothers, and Bosola in the way an omniscient narrator might in a novel. Delio is also the friend in whom Antonio confides the secrets of his marriage and the births of his children; like Cariola, Delio guards the secrets carefully. Delio has no direct connection with any of the siblings, and he does not directly participate in their plots and deaths.

He is the faithful friend, always standing by to help Antonio when he is needed. In a scene in act 2, Delio comes to Rome and makes advances to Julia, who rebuffs him. Their interaction affects nothing else in the play, and the two never meet again. Delio speaks the last words in the play, when he enters "too late" with Antonio's oldest son after his parents have been killed. He urges the survivors to help the young man gain his inheritance and proclaims, "Integrity of life is fame's best friend, / which nobly, beyond death, shall crown the end."

Cariola

Cariola is the trustworthy servant of the Duchess, privy to all of the Duchess's secrets. Cariola witnesses the marriage between the Duchess and Antonio, helps deliver the Duchess's children, and is with the Duchess when the Duchess dies. In her own death, she is not as noble as the Duchess, but kicks and screams and tries to escape. Throughout the play, she is more cautious than the Duchess, thinking that marrying Antonio is "madness," and fearing that the trick of a false pilgrimage will prove unlucky.

The Duchess of Malfi

The Duchess of Malfi is the sister of the Cardinal and the twin sister of Ferdinand. She is never referred to by name throughout the play, but only by the labels that describe her roles as sister, duchess, and wife. As the play opens, she is a widow, but still in the bloom of youth. (According to Webster's source materials, the real duchess was a girl of twelve years old when she was married to a much older man; she became a widow when she was twenty.) Although her brothers forbid her to marry again, and she promises to obey them, she longs for a husband.

Secretly, she asks her steward Antonio to marry her, and they perform a private marriage ceremony. Afraid of her brothers' anger, the Duchess manages to keep her marriage a secret for years, even through the birth of three children. When the brothers do learn of the children, she flees with Antonio but is captured and murdered.

Early in the play, Antonio describes her as a woman, whose speech is "full of rapture," who has a "sweet countenance," who lives a life of "noble virtue." Although duchess' sweet nobility casts no spell over her brothers, her every word and action support Antonio's judgment of her and her subjects love and respect her. She is clever, able to match her brothers' wit in her exchanges with them, and able to quickly craft intricate plots for escape. She is affectionate with all, showing a tenderness that is far beyond the capabilities of the Cardinal and Ferdinand. And she is dignified in the face of her brothers' torments, stating even at the worst of it, "I am Duchess of Malfi still."

Some critics have commented that the duchess deserves death because of her rashness in marrying beneath her station, but most reject that notion, agreeing that there is nothing in the play to indicate that Webster found fault with the marriage of Antonio and the Duchess. What happens to her is not her fault, but the result of living in a "gloomy world."

Julia

Julia is the wife of an old nobleman and is the Cardinal's mistress. While she is staying with the Cardinal, she is propositioned by Delio, whom she refuses; she also tries to seduce Bosola. Ironically, the Cardinal kills her by tricking her into kissing a poisoned book, while she is swearing to keep his secret.

Ferdinand

Ferdinand, the Duke of Calbria, is the twin brother of the Duchess, younger than her by a few minutes. He is as emotional as his brother the Cardinal is icy, and his response to the idea of his sister marrying is beyond all bounds. Ferdinand's motivation has always been a central question for critics of this play, and many critics have seen incestuous feelings in his rage. Whatever the cause, when he learns that his sister has given birth to a child, he declares her a whore and "a sister damn'd," creates a mental picture of her "in the shameful act of sin," and imagines burning her and her lover in a coal pit with no vent, so that "their curs'd smoke might not ascend to heaven," or boiling her child into a soup and serving it to the father.

As with other characters, Antonio's early description of Ferdinand proves insightful. Antonio tells Delio that Ferdinand has "a most perverse, and turbulent nature." Even the Cardinal wonders whether Ferdinand is "stark mad," and after brooding over his sister's betrayal for a time, Ferdinand does approach insanity. After he has had the Duchess killed and sees her lying dead, he regrets that he ordered Bosola, "When I was distracted of my wits, / Go kill my dearest friend," but there has been no hint previously that he and the Duchess shared any closeness.

The realization of what he has done pushes Ferdinand over the edge into insanity; perhaps even to the point of imagining that he is a werewolf. He is found in the graveyard digging up dead bodies and is seen "with the leg of a man / upon his shoulder; and he howled fearful, / said he was a wolf." Ferdinand is not seen again until the last scene, when he charges in on the Cardinal and Bosola, and stabs them both. Bosola stabs him in return, and just before Ferdinand dies, he "seems to come to himself," saying, "Whether we fall by ambition, blood, or lust, / like diamonds, we are cut with our own dust."

Chapter 10

The Duchess of Malfi: Complete Text

Act I, scene i

The Court at Malfi

Enter Antonio and Delio

DELIO: You are welcome to your country, dear Antonio;
You have been long in France, and you return
A very formal Frenchman in your habit.

How do you like the French court?

ANTONIO: I admire it:

In seeking to reduce both state and people
To a fix'd order, their judicious king
Begins at home; quits first his royal palace
Of flattering sycophants, of dissolute
And infamous persons, which he sweetly terms
His master's masterpiece, the work of heaven;
Considering duly, that a prince's court
Is like a common fountain, whence should flow
Pure silver drops in general, but if't chance
Some curs'd example poison't near the head,
Death and diseases through the whole land spread.

And what is't makes this blessed government,
But a most provident council, who dare freely
Inform him the corruption of the times?

Though some o'th' court hold it presumption
To instruct princes what they ought to do,
It is a noble duty to inform them
What they ought to foresee. Here comes Bosola,
The only court-gall; yet I observe his railing
Is not for simple love of piety:
Indeed he rails at those things which he wants;
Would be as lecherous, covetous, or proud,
Bloody, or envious, as any man,
If he had means to be so. Here's the Cardinal.

Enter BOSOLA and CARDINAL

BOSOLA: I do haunt you still.

CARDINAL: So.

BOSOLA: I have done you better service
Than to be slighted thus.
Miserable age, where only the reward
Of doing well, is the doing of it!

CARDINAL: You enforce your merit too much.

BOSOLA: I fell into the galleys in your service,

Where, for two years together, I wore
Two towels instead of a shirt, with a knot on the shoulder,
After the fashion of a Roman mantle.
Slighted thus! I will thrive some way:
Black-birds fatten best in hard weather;
Why not I in these dog-days?

CARDINAL: Would you could become honest!

BOSOLA: With all your divinity do but direct me
The way to it. I have known many travel far for it,
And yet return as arrant knaves as they went forth,
Because they carried themselves always along with them.

Exit Cardinal

Are you gone?
Some fellows, they say, are possessed with the devil,

But this great fellow were able to possess the greatest Devil, and make him worse.

ANTONIO: He hath denied thee some suit?

BOSOLA: He and his brother are like plum-trees that grow crooked over standing-pools; they are rich, and o'erladen with Fruit, but none but crows, pies, and caterpillars feed on them.

Could I be one of their flattering panders, I Would hang on their ears like a horseleech, till I were full, and Then drop off. I pray leave me.

Who would rely upon these miserable dependencies; in expectation to be advanced to-morrow?

What creature ever fed worse, than hoping Tantalus? nor ever died any man more fearfully, than he that hoped For a pardon.

There are rewards for hawks and dogs, When they have done us service: but for a soldier that hazards his Limbs in a battle, nothing but a kind of geometry is his last Supportation.

DELIO: Geometry?

BOSOLA: Ay, to hang in a fair pair of slings, take his latter swing in the World upon an honourable pair of crutches, from hospital to hospital.

Fare ye well, sir: and yet do not you scorn us, for Places in the court are but like beds in the hospital, where this Man's head lies at that man's foot, and so lower and lower.

Exit BOSOLA

DELIO: I knew this fellow seven years in the galleys
For a notorious murder; and 'twas thought
The Cardinal suborn'd it: he was releas'd
By the French general, Gaston de Foix,
When he recover'd Naples.

ANTONIO: 'Tis great pity,
He should be thus neglected: I have heard
He's very valiant. This foul melancholy
Will poison all his goodness; for, I'll tell you,
If too immoderate sleep be truly said
To be an inward rust unto the soul,
It then doth follow want of action
Breeds all black malcontents, and their close rearing,
Like moths in cloth, do hurt for want of wearing.

Act I, Scene ii

Action continues from previous scene

ENTER ANTONIO. DELIO, FERDINAND, CASTRUCCIO, SILVIO

DELIO: The presence 'gins to fill: you promis'd me
To make me the partaker of the natures
Of some of your great courtiers.

ANTONIO: The lord cardinal's,
And other strangers, that are now in court?
I shall: here comes the great Calabrian Duke.

FERDINAND: Who took the ring oftenest?

SILVIO: Antonio Bologna, my lord.

FERDINAND: Our sister Duchess' great master of her household:
Give him the jewel. When shall we leave this sportive action,
And fall to action indeed?

CASTRUCHIO: Methinks, my lord,

You should not desire to go to war in person.

FERDINAND: Now, for some gravity; why, my lord?

CASTRUCHIO: It is fitting a soldier arise to be a prince, but not necessary
A prince descend to be a captain.

FERDINAND: No?

CASTRUCHIO: No, my lord;
He were far better do it by a deputy.

FERDINAND: Why should he not as well sleep, or eat by a deputy?
This might take idle, offensive, and base office from him,
Whereas the other deprives him of honour.

CASTRUCHIO: Believe my experience: that realm is never long in quiet,
Where the ruler is a soldier.

FERDINAND: Thou toldest me
Thy wife could not endure fighting.

CASTRUCHIO: True, my lord.

FERDINAND: And of a jest she broke of a captain
she met full of wounds: I have forgot it.

CASTRUCHIO: She told him, my lord, he was a pitiful fellow, to lie
Like the children of Ismael, all in tents.

FERDINAND: Why, there's a wit were able to undo
All the chirugeons o'th' city, for although
Gallants should quarrel, and had drawn their weapons,
And were ready to go to it, yet her persuasions would
Make them put up.

CASTRUCHIO: That she would, my lord.
How do you like my Spanish gennet?

RODERIGO: He is all fire.

FERDINAND: I am of Pliny's opinion, I think he was begot by the wind;
He runs as if he were ballassed with quicksilver.

SILVIO: True, my lord, he reels from the tilt often.

RODERIGO and GRISOLAN: Ha, ha, ha!

FERDINAND: Why do you laugh? methinks you that are courtiers

Should be my touchwood, take fire when I give fire;
That is, not laugh but when I laugh, were the subject never so witty.

CASTRUCHIO: True, my lord; I myself have heard a very good jest,
And have scorned to seem to have so silly a wit, as to understand it.

FERDINAND: But I can laugh at your fool, my lord.

CASTRUCHIO: He cannot speak, you know, but he makes faces:
My lady cannot abide him.

FERDINAND: No?

CASTRUCHIO: Nor endure to be in merry company; for she says
Too much laughing, and too much company, fills her
Too full of the wrinkle.

FERDINAND: I would then have a mathematical instrument
Made for her face,
That she might not laugh out of compass. I shall shortly
Visit you at Milan, Lord Silvio.

SILVIO: Your grace shall arrive most welcome.

FERDINAND: You are a good horseman, Antonio: you have excellent
Riders in France: what do you think of good horsemanship?

ANTONIO: Nobly, my lord: as out of the Grecian horse issued
Many famous princes, so out of brave horsemanship
Arise the first sparks of growing resolution, that raise
The mind to noble action.

FERDINAND: You have bespoke it worthily.

SILVIO: Your brother, the lord Cardinal, and sister Duchess.

Enter CARDINAL, DUCHESS, CARIOLA, and JULIA

CARDINAL: Are the galleys come about?

GRISOLAN: They are, my lord.

FERDINAND: Here's the Lord Silvio is come to take his leave.

DELIO: Now, sir, your promise: what's that Cardinal?
I mean his temper? They say he's a brave fellow,
Will play his five thousand crowns at tennis, dance,
Court ladies, and one that hath fought single combats.

ANTONIO: Some such flashes superficially hang on him, for form;
But observe his inward character: he is a melancholy
Churchman; the spring in his face is nothing but the
Engendering of toads; where he is jealous of any man,
He lays worse plots for him than ever was imposed on
Hercules, for he strews in his way flatterers, panders,
Intelligencers, atheists, and a thousand such political
Monsters. He should have been Pope, but instead of
Coming to it by the primitive decency of the church,
He did bestow bribes so largely, and so impudently, as if he would
Have carried it away without heaven's knowledge.
Some good he hath done-

DELIO: You have given too much of him: what's his brother?

ANTONIO: The duke there? a most perverse and turbulent nature:
What appears in him mirth is merely outside;
If he laugh heartily, it is to laugh
All honesty out of fashion.

DELIO: Twins?

ANTONIO: In quality.
He speaks with others' tongues, and hears men's suits
With others' ears; will seem to sleep o' th' bench

Only to entrap offenders in their answers;
Dooms men to death by information,
Rewards by hearsay.

DELIO: Then the law to him
Is like a foul black cobweb to a spider,
He makes it his dwelling and a prison
To entangle those shall feed him.

ANTONIO: Most true:
He never pays debts unless they be shrewd turns,
And those he will confess that he doth owe.
Last, for his brother there, the cardinal,
They that do flatter him most say oracles
Hang at his lips; and verily I believe them,
For the devil speaks in them.
But for their sister, the right noble duchess,
You never fix'd your eye on three fair medals
Cast in one figure, of so different temper.
For her discourse, it is so full of rapture,
You only will begin then to be sorry
When she doth end her speech, and wish, in wonder,
She held it less vain-glory, to talk much,
Than your penance to hear her: whilst she speaks,
She throws upon a man so sweet a look,
That it were able to raise one to a galliard
That lay in a dead palsy, and to dote
On that sweet countenance; but in that look
There speaketh so divine a continence,
As cuts off all lascivious and vain hope.
Her days are practic'd in such noble virtue,
That sure her nights, nay more, her very sleeps,
Are more in heaven, than other ladies' shrifts.
Let all sweet ladies break their flattering glasses,
And dress themselves in her.

DELIO: Fie, Antonio,
You play the wire-drawer with her commendation.

ANTONIO: I'll case the picture up: only thus much,
All her particular worth, grows to this sum;

She stains the time past, lights the time to come.
CARIOLA: You must attend my lady in the gallery,
Some half an hour hence.

ANTONIO: I shall.

Exit ANTONIO and DELIO

FERDINAND: Sister, I have a suit to you.

DUCHESS: To me, sir?

FERDINAND: A gentleman here, Daniel de Bosola,
One that was in the galleys—

DUCHESS: Yes, I know him.

FERDINAND: A worthy fellow h'is: pray let me entreat for
The provisorship of your horse.

DUCHESS: Your knowledge of him
Commends him and prefers him.

FERDINAND: Call him hither.

Exit Attendant

We are now upon parting. Good Lord Silvio,
Do us commend to all our noble friends
At the leaguer.

SILVIO: Sir, I shall.

FERDINAND: You are for Milan?

SILVIO: I am.

DUCHESS: Bring the carroches: we'll bring you down to the haven.

Exit all but the CARDINAL and FERDINAND

CARDINAL: Be sure you entertain that Bosola
For your intelligence: I would not be seen in't;
And therefore many times I have slighted him,
When he did court our furtherance, as this morning.

FERDINAND: Antonio, the great master of her household,
Had been far fitter.

CARDINAL: You are deceiv'd in him:
His nature is too honest for such business.
He comes: I'll leave you

Exit CARDINAL, enter BOSOLA

BOSOLA: I was lur'd to you.

FERDINAND: My brother here, the Cardinal could never
Abide you.

BOSOLA: Never since he was in my debt.

FERDINAND: May be some oblique character in your face
Made him suspect you.

BOSOLA: Doth he study physiognomy?
There's no more credit to be given to th' face,
Than to a sick man's urine, which some call
The physician's whore, because she cozens him.
He did suspect me wrongfully.

FERDINAND: For that
You must give great men leave to take their times.
Distrust doth cause us seldom be deceiv'd:
You see, the oft shaking of the cedar-tree
Fastens it more at root.

BOSOLA: Yet, take heed;
For to suspect a friend unworthily,
Instructs him the next way to suspect you,
And prompts him to deceive you.

FERDINAND: There's gold.

BOSOLA: So,
What follows? never rain'd such showers as these
Without thunderbolts i' th' tail of them: whose throat must I cut?

FERDINAND: Your inclination to shed blood rides post
Before my occasion to use you. I give you that
To live i'th' court here, and observe the duchess;
To note all the particulars of her 'haviour,
What suitors do solicit her for marriage,
And whom she best affects. She's a young widow:
I would not have her marry again.

BOSOLA: No, sir?
FERDINAND: Do not you ask the reason; but be satisfied
I say I would not.

BOSOLA: It seems you would create me
One of your familiars.

FERDINAND: Familiar! what's that?

BOSOLA: Why, a very quaint invisible devil in flesh;
As intelligencer.

FERDINAND: Such a kind of thriving thing
I would wish thee; and ere long, thou may'st arrive
At a higher place by't.

BOSOLA: Take your devils,
Which hell calls angels: these curs'd gifts would make
You a corrupter, me an impudent traitor;
And should I take these, they'd take me to hell.

FERDINAND: Sir, I'll take nothing from you, that I have given:
There is a place that I procur'd for you
This morning, the provisorship o'th'horse;
Have you heard on't?

BOSOLA: No.

FERDINAND: 'Tis yours: is't not worth thanks?

BOSOLA: I would have you curse yourself now, that your bounty
(Which makes men truly noble) e'er should make
Me a villain. O, that to avoid ingratitude
For the good deed you have done me, I must do

All the ill man can invent! Thus the devil
Candies all sins o'er; and what heaven terms vile
That names he complemental.

FERDINAND: Be yourself;
Keep your old garb of melancholy; 'twill express
You envy those that stand above your reach,
Yet strive not to come near 'em: this will gain
Access to private lodgings, where yourself
May, like a politic dormouse—

BOSOLA: As I have seen some,
Feed in a lord's dish, half asleep, not seeming
To listen to any talk; and yet these rogues
Have cut his throat in a dream. What's my place?
The provisorship o'th' horse? say, then, my corruption
Grew out of horse-dung: I am your creature.

FERDINAND: Away.

BOSOLA: Let good men, for good deeds, covet good fame,
Since place and riches, oft are bribes of shame:
Sometimes the devil doth preach.

Exit BOSOLA, enter DUCHESS, CARDINAL, and CARIOLA

CARDINAL: We are to part from you; and your own discretion
Must now be your director.

FERDINAND: You are a widow:
You know already what man is; and therefore
Let not youth, high promotion, eloquence—

CARDINAL: No,
Nor anything without the addition, honour,
Sway your high blood.

FERDINAND: Marry! they are most luxurious,
Will wed twice.

CARDINAL: O, fie!

FERDINAND: Their livers are more spotted
Than Laban's sheep.

DUCHESS: Diamonds are of most value,
They say, that have past through most jewellers' hands.

FERDINAND: Whores, by that rule, are precious.

DUCHESS: Will you hear me?
I'll never marry.

CARDINAL: So most widows say;
But commonly that motion lasts no longer
Than the turning of an hour-glass: the funeral sermon
And it, end both together.

FERDINAND: Now hear me:
You live in a rank pasture here, i'th' court;
There is a kind of honey-dew that's deadly;
'Twill poison your fame; look to't: be not cunning;
For they whose faces do belie their hearts,
Are witches ere they arrive at twenty years,
Ay, and give the devil suck.

DUCHESS: This is terrible good counsel.

FERDINAND: Hypocrisy is woven of a fine small-thread,
Subtler than Vulcan's engine: yet, believ't,
Your darkest actions, nay, your privat'st thoughts,
Will come to light.

CARDINAL: You may flatter yourself,
And take your own choice; privately be married
Under the eaves of night—

FERDINAND: Think't the best voyage
That e'er you made; like the irregular crab,
Which, though't goes backward, thinks that it goes right,
Because it goes its own way: but observe,
Such weddings may more properly be said
To be executed, than celebrated.

CARDINAL: The marriage night
Is the entrance into some prison.

FERDINAND: And those joys,
Those lustful pleasures, are like heavy sleeps
Which do forerun man's mischief.

CARDINAL: Fare you well.
Wisdom begins at the end: remember it.

Exit CARDINAL

DUCHESS: I think this speech between you both was studied,
It came so roundly off.

FERDINAND: You are my sister;
This was my father's poniard, do you see?
I'd be loath to see't look rusty, 'cause 'twas his.
I would have you to give o'er these chargeable revels,
A visor and a mask are whispering rooms
That were never built for goodness;— fare ye well,
And beware that part, which like the lamprey,
Hath never a bone in't.

DUCHESS: Fie, sir!

FERDINAND: Nay,
I mean the tongue; variety of courtship;
What cannot a neat knave with a smooth tale
Make a woman believe: Farewell, lusty widow.

Exit FERDINAND

DUCHESS: Shall this move me? If all my royal kindred
Lay in my way unto this marriage,
I'd make them my low footsteps; and even now,
Even in this hate, as men in some great battles,
By apprehending danger, have achiev'd
Almost impossible actions,— I have heard soldiers say so,—
So I through frights and threatenings will assay
This dangerous venture. Let old wives report
I wink'd, and chose a husband. Cariola,
To thy known secrecy I have given up
More than my life- my fame.

CARIOLA: Both shall be safe:
For I'll conceal this secret from the world,
As warily as those that trade in poison
Keep poison from their children.

DUCHESS: Thy protestation
Is ingenious and hearty: I believe it.
Is Antonio come?

CARIOLA: He attends you.

DUCHESS: Good dear soul,
Leave me; but place thyself behind the arras,
Where thou may'st overhear us. Wish me good speed,
For I am going into a wilderness
Where I shall find no path, nor friendly clew,
To be my guide.

Exit CARIOLA, enter ANTONIO

I sent for you: sit down;

Take pen and ink, and write: are you ready?

ANTONIO: Yes.

DUCHESS: What did I say?

ANTONIO: That I should write somewhat.

DUCHESS: O, I remember.
After these triumphs and this large expense,
It's fit, like thrifty husbands, we inquire
What's laid up for tomorrow.

ANTONIO: So please your beauteous excellence.

DUCHESS: Beauteous! Indeed I thank you:
I look young for your sake;
You have ta'en my cares upon you.

ANTONIO: I'll fetch your grace
The particulars of your revenue and expense.

DUCHESS: O, you are
An upright treasurer; but you mistook:
For when I said I meant to make inquiry
What's laid up for tomorrow, I did mean
What's laid up yonder for me.

ANTONIO: Where?

DUCHESS: In heaven.

I am making my will, (as 'tis fit princes should,
In perfect memory, and, I pray, sir, tell me
Were not one better make it smiling, thus,
Than in deep groans, and terrible ghastly looks,
As if the gifts we parted with procur'd
That violent distraction?

ANTONIO: O, much better.

DUCHESS: If I had a husband now, this care were quit:
But I intend to make you overseer.
What good deed shall we first remember? say.

ANTONIO: Begin with that first good deed begun i'th'world
After man's creation, the sacrament of marriage:
I'd have you first provide for a good husband;
Give him all.

DUCHESS: All?

ANTONIO: Yes, your excellent self.

DUCHESS: St. Winifred, that were a strange will!

ANTONIO: 'Twere strange if there were no will in you
To marry again.

DUCHESS: What do you think of marriage?

ANTONIO: I take't, as those that deny purgatory,
It locally contains, or heaven, or hell,
There's no third place in't.

DUCHESS: How do you affect it?

ANTONIO: My banishment, feeding my melancholy,
Would often reason thus.

DUCHESS: Pray, let's hear it.

ANTONIO: Say a man never marry, nor have children,
What takes that from him? only the bare name
Of being a father, or the weak delight
To see the little wanton ride a cock-horse

Upon a painted stick, or hear him chatter
Like a taught starling.

DUCHESS: Fie, fie, what's all this?
One of your eyes is blood-shot; use my ring to't,
They say 'tis very sovereign: 'twas my wedding ring,
And I did vow never to part with it
But to my second husband.

ANTONIO: You have parted with it now.

DUCHESS: Yes, to help your eye-sight.

ANTONIO: You have made me stark blind.

DUCHESS: How?

ANTONIO: There is a saucy and ambitious devil,
Is dancing in this circle.

DUCHESS: Remove him.

ANTONIO: How?

DUCHESS: There needs small conjuration, when your finger
May do it; thus; is it fit?
He kneels

ANTONIO: What said you?

DUCHESS: Sir, this goodly roof of yours, is too low built;
I cannot stand upright in't nor discourse,
Without I raise it higher; raise yourself;
Or, if you please, my hand to help you: so.

ANTONIO: Ambition, madam, is a great man's madness,
That is not kept in chains, and close-pent rooms,
But in fair lightsome lodgings, and is girt
With the wild noise of prattling visitants,
Which makes it lunatic beyond all cure.
Conceive not I am so stupid but I aim
Whereto your favours tend: but he's a fool,
That being a-cold, would thrust his hands i'th' fire
To warm them.

DUCHESS: So now the ground's broke,
You may discover what a wealthy mine
I make you lord of.

ANTONIO: O, my unworthiness!
DUCHESS: You were ill to sell yourself:
This darkening of your worth is not like that
Which tradesmen use i'th' city; their false lights
Are to rid bad wares off; and I must tell you,
If you will know where breathes a complete man,
(I speak it without flattery,) turn your eyes,
And progress through yourself.

ANTONIO: Were there nor heaven nor hell,
I should be honest: I have long serv'd virtue,
And ne'er ta'en wages of her.

DUCHESS: Now she pays it.
The misery of us that are born great!
We are forc'd to woo, because none dare woo us;
And as a tyrant doubles with his words,
And fearfully equivocates, so we
Are forc'd to express our violent passions
In riddles, and in dreams, and leave the path
Of simple virtue, which was never made
To seem the thing it is not. Go, go brag
You have left me heartless; mine is in your bosom:
I hope 'twill multiply love there. You do tremble:
Make not your heart so dead a piece of flesh,
To fear, more than to love me. Sir, be confident:
What is't distracts you? This is flesh and blood sir;
'Tis not the figure cut in alabaster,
Kneels at my husbands tomb. Awake, awake, man!
I do here put off all vain ceremony,
And only do appear to you a young widow
That claims you for her husband, and like a widow,
I use but half a blush in't.

ANTONIO: Truth speak for me:
I will remain the constant sanctuary
Of your good name.

DUCHESS: I thank you, gentle love:
and 'cause you shall not come to me in debt,
Being now my steward, here upon your lips
I sign your Quietus est. This you should have begg'd now;
I have seen children oft eat sweetmeats thus,
As fearful to devour them too soon.

ANTONIO: But for your brothers?

DUCHESS: Do not think of them:
All discord without this circumference
Is only to be pitied, and not fear'd:
Yet, should they know it, time will easily
Scatter the tempest.

ANTONIO: These words should be mine,
And all the parts you have spoke, if some part of it
Would not have savour'd flattery.

DUCHESS: Kneel.

Enter CARIOLA

ANTONIO: Ha!

DUCHESS: Be not amaz'd, this woman's of my counsel:
I have heard lawyers say, a contract in a chamber
Per verba presenti is absolute marriage.
Bless, heaven, this sacred gordian, which let violence
Never untwine!

ANTONIO: And may our sweet affections, like the spheres,
Be still in motion.

DUCHESS: Quickening, and make
The like soft music.

ANTONIO: That we may imitate the loving palms,
Best emblem of a peaceful marriage
That never bore fruit divided.

DUCHESS: What can the church force more?

ANTONIO: That fortune may not know an accident
Either of joy, or sorrow, to divide
Our fixed wishes.

DUCHESS: How can the church build faster?
We now are man and wife, and 'tis the church
That must but echo this. Maid, stand apart:
I now am blind.

ANTONIO: What's your conceit in this?

DUCHESS: I would have you lead your fortune by the hand
Unto your marriage bed:
(You speak in me this, for we now are one:)
We'll only lie, and talk together, and plot
T'appease my humourous kindred; and if you please,
Like the old tale in Alexander and Lodowick,
Lay a naked sword between us, keep us chaste.
O, let me shroud my blushes in your bosom,
Since 'tis the treasury of all my secrets!

They exit

CARIOLA: Whether the spirit of greatness, or of woman
Reign most in her, I know not; but it shows
A fearful madness: I owe her much of pity.

Act II, scene *i*

The Court at Malfi, a few months later

Enter BOSOLA and CASTRUCHIO

BOSOLA: You say you would fain be taken for an eminent courtier?

CASTRUCHIO: 'Tis the very main of my ambition.

BOSOLA: Let me see: you have a reasonable good face for't already,
And your night-cap expresses your ears sufficient largely.
I would have you learn to twirl the strings of your band
With a good grace, and in a set speech, at th'end of every sentence,
To hum three or four times, or blow your nose till it smart again,
To recover your memory. When you come to be a president

In criminal causes, if you smile upon a prisoner, hang him, but if
You frown upon him, and threaten him, let him be sure to 'scape
The gallows.

CASTRUCHIO: I would be a very merry president.

BOSOLA: Do not sup a' nights; 'twill beget you
An admirable wit.

CASTRUCHIO: Rather it would make me have a good stomach to quarrel;
For they say, your roaring boys eat meat seldom,
And that makes them so valiant.
But how shall I know whether the people take me
For an eminent fellow?

BOSOLA: I will teach a trick to know it:
Give out you lie a-dying, and if you
Hear the common people curse you,
Be sure you are taken for one of the prime night-caps.

Enter an OLD LADY

You come from painting now.

OLD LADY: From what?

BOSOLA: Why, from your scurvy face-physic.
To behold thee not painted inclines somewhat near
A miracle. These in thy face here, were deep ruts,
And foul sloughs, the last progress.
There was a lady in France that, having the small-pox,
Flay'd the skin off her face to make it more level;
And whereas before she looked like a nutmeg grater,
After she resembled an abortive hedgehog.

OLD LADY: Do you call this painting?

BOSOLA: No, no, but you call't careening of an old
Morphewed lady, to make her disembogue again.
There's rough-cast phrase to your plastic.

OLD LADY: It seems you are well acquainted with my closet.

BOSOLA: One would suspect it for a shop of witchcraft,
To find in it the fat of serpents, spawn of snakes, Jews' spittle,
And their young childrens' ordure; and all these for the face.
I would sooner eat a dead pigeon, taken from the soles of the feet
Of one sick of the plague, than kiss one of you fasting.
Here are two of you, whose sin of your youth is the very
Patrimony of the physician; makes him renew
His foot-cloth with the spring, and change his
High-priced courtesan with the fall of the leaf.
I do wonder you do not loathe yourselves.
Observe my meditation now:
What thing is in this outward form of man
To be belov'd? We account it ominous,
If nature do produce a colt, or lamb,
A fawn, or goat, in any limb resembling
A man, and fly from't as a prodigy.
Man stands amaz'd to see his deformity
In any other creature but himself.
But in our own flesh, though we bear diseases
Which have their true names only ta'en from beasts,
As the most ulcerous wolf and swinish measle;
Though we are eaten up of lice and worms,
And though continually we bear about us
A rotten and dead body, we delight
To hide it in rich tissue; all our fear,
Nay all our terror, is, lest our physician
Should put us in the ground, to be made sweet.
Your wife's gone to Rome: you two couple, and get you
To the wells at Lucca, to recover your aches.

Exit CASTRUCHIO and OLD LADY

I have other work on foot: I observe our Duchess
Is sick a-days, she pukes, her stomach seethes,
The fins of her eyelids look most teeming blue,
She wanes i'th' cheek, and waxes fat i'th'flank,
And, contrary to our Italian fashion,

Wears a loose-bodied gown; there's somewhat in't.
I have a trick may chance discover it,
A pretty one: I have bought some apricocks,
The first our spring yields.

Enter ANTONIO and DELIO

DELIO: And so long since married?
You amaze me.

ANTONIO: Let me seal your lips for ever,
For did I think, that anything but th' air
Could carry these words from you, I should wish
You had no breath at all. [*to BOSOLA*] Now, sir, in your contemplation?
You are studying to become a great wise fellow?

BOSOLA: O, sir, the opinion of wisdom,
Is a foul tetter, that runs
All over a man's body: if simplicity
Direct us to have no evil,
It directs us to a happy being: for the subtlest folly
Proceeds from the subtlest wisdom.
Let me be simply honest.

ANTONIO: I do understand your inside.

BOSOLA: Do you so?

ANTONIO: Because you would not seem to appear to th' world
Puff'd up with your preferment, you continue
This out-of-fashion melancholy: leave it, leave it.

BOSOLA: Give me leave to be honest in any phrase, in any
Compliment whatsoever. Shall I confess myself to you?
I look no higher than I can reach:
They are the gods that must ride on winged horses.
A lawyer's mule, of a slow pace, will both suit
My disposition and business: for, mark me,
When a man's mind rides faster than his horse can gallop,
They quickly both tire.

ANTONIO: You would look up to heaven, but I think
The devil, that rules i'th'air stands in your light.

BOSOLA: O, sir, you are lord of the ascendant,
Chief man with the duchess; a duke was your
Cousin-german, removed. Say you were lineally
Descended from King Pepin, or he himself,
What of this? search the heads of the greatest rivers
In the world, you shall find them
But bubbles of water. Some would think
The souls of princes were brought forth

By some more weighty cause, than those of meaner persons:
They are deceived, there's the same hand to them;
The like passions sway them; the same reason
That makes a vicar to go to law for a tithe-pig,
And undo his neighbours, makes them spoil
A whole province, and batter down
Goodly cities with the cannon.

Enter DUCHESS and LADIES

DUCHESS: Your arm, Antonio: do I not grow fat?
I am exceeding short-winded. Bosola,
I would have you, sir, provide for me a litter,
Such a one as the Duchess of Florence rode in.

BOSOLA: The duchess us'd one when she was great with child.

DUCHESS: I think she did. Come hither, mend my ruff,
Here; when? thou art such a tedious lady; and
Thy breath smells of lemon pills: would thou hadst done!
Shall I sound under thy fingers? I am
So troubled with the mother.

BOSOLA: [*aside*] I fear too much.

DUCHESS: I have heard you say, that the French courtiers
Wear their hats on ' fore the king.

ANTONIO: I have seen it.

DUCHESS: In the presence?

ANTONIO: Yes.

DUCHESS: Why should not we bring up that fashion?
'Tis ceremony more than duty, that consists
In the removing of a piece of felt:
Be you the example to the rest o'th' court,
Put on your hat first.

ANTONIO: You must pardon me:
I have seen, in colder countries than in France,
Nobles stand bare to th' prince; and the distinction
Methought show'd reverently.

BOSOLA: I have a present for your grace.

DUCHESS: For me, sir?

BOSOLA: Apricocks, madam.

DUCHESS: O, sir, where are they?
I have heard of none to- year.

BOSOLA: [*aside*] Good, her colour rises.

DUCHESS: Indeed I thank you: they are wondrous fair ones.
What an unskillful fellow is our gardener!
We shall have none this month.

BOSOLA: Will not your grace pare them?

DUCHESS: No, they taste of musk, methinks; indeed they do.

BOSOLA: I know not: yet I wish your grace had par'd 'em.

DUCHESS: Why?

BOSOLA: I forgot to tell you, the knave gardener,
Only to raise his profit by them the sooner,
Did ripen them in horse-dung.

DUCHESS: O, you jest.
You shall judge: pray, taste one.

ANTONIO: Indeed, madam,
I do not love the fruit.

DUCHESS: Sir, you are loath
To rob us of our dainties: 'tis a delicate fruit;
They say they are restorative.

BOSOLA: 'Tis a pretty art,
This grafting.

DUCHESS: 'Tis so: a bettering of nature.

BOSOLA: To make a pippin grow upon a crab,
A damson on a black-thorn. [*aside*] How greedily she eats them!
A whirlwind strike off these bawd farthingales!
For, but for that, and the loose-bodied gown,
I should have discover'd apparently
The young springal cutting a caper in her belly.

DUCHESS: I thank you, Bosola: they were right good ones,
If they do not make me sick.

ANTONIO: How now, madam?

DUCHESS: This green fruit and my stomach are not friends:
How they swell me!

BOSOLA: [*aside*] Nay, you are too much swell'd already.

DUCHESS: O, I am in an extreme cold sweat!

BOSOLA: I am very sorry.

Exit BOSOLA

DUCHESS: Lights to my chamber. O, good Antonio,

I fear I am undone!

DELIO: Lights there, lights.

Exit DUCHESS

ANTONIO: O my most trusty Delio, we are lost!

I fear she's fallen in labour; and there's left
No time for her remove.

DELIO: Have you prepar'd
Those ladies to attend her? and procur'd
That politic safe conveyance for the midwife,
Your duchess plotted?

ANTONIO: I have.

DELIO: Make use then of this forc'd occasion:
Give out that Bosola hath poison'd her
With these apricocks; that will give some colour
For her keeping close.

ANTONIO: Fie, fie, the physicians
Will then flock to her.

DELIO: For that you may pretend
She'll use some prepar'd antidote of her own,
Lest the physicians should re-poison her.

ANTONIO: I am lost in amazement: I know not what to think on't.
They exit

Act II, Scene ii

Action is continuous

Enter BOSOLA

BOSOLA: So, so, there's no question but her tetchiness
And most vulturous eating of the apricocks, are
Apparent signs of breeding. Now?

Enter an OLD LADY

OLD LADY: I am in haste, sir.

BOSOLA: There was a young waiting-woman, had a monstrous desire

To see the glass-house—

OLD LADY: Nay, pray let me go.

BOSOLA: And it was only to know what strange instrument it was,
Should swell up a glass to the fashion of a woman's belly.

OLD LADY: I will hear no more of the glass house.
You are still abusing women.

BOSOLA: Who I? no, only, by the way, now and then,
Mention your frailties. The orange-tree
Bears ripe and green fruit and blossoms,
Altogether: and some of you
Give entertainment for pure love, but more,
For precious reward. The lusty
Spring smells well; but drooping autumn tastes well. If we
Have the same golden showers, that rained in the time of Jupiter
The thunderer, you have the same Danaes still, to hold up
Their laps to receive them. Didst thou never study
The mathematics?

OLD LADY: What's that, sir?

BOSOLA: Why, to know the trick how to make a many lines meet

In one centre. Go, go, give your foster-daughters good counsel:
Tell them, that the devil takes delight to hang at a woman's girdle,
Like a false rusty watch, that she cannot discern
How the time passes.

Exit OLD LADY

Enter ANTONIO, RODERIGO, and GRISOLAN

ANTONIO: Shut up the court-gates.

RODERIGO: Why, sir? what's the danger?

ANTONIO: Shut up the posterns presently, and call
All the officers o'th'court.

GRISOLAN: I shall instantly.

He exits

ANTONIO: Who keeps the key o'th' park gate?

RODERIGO: Forobosco.

ANTONIO: Let him bring't presently.

Enter GRISOLAN and SERVANTS

SERVANT 1: O, gentlemen o'th' court, the foulest treason!

BOSOLA: [*aside*] If that these apricocks should be poison'd now,
Without my knowledge!

SERVANT 1: There was taken even now a Switzer in the duchess' bed-chamber-

SERVANT 2: A Switzer!

SERVANT 1: With a pistol in his great cod-piece.

BOSOLA: Ha, ha, ha!

SERVANT 1: The cod-piece was the case for't.

SERVANT 2: There was a cunning traitor; who would have search'd his cod-piece?

SERVANT 1: True, if he had kept out of the ladies' chambers:
and all the moulds of his buttons were leaden bullets.

SERVANT 2: O, wicked cannibal! a firelock in's codpiece!

SERVANT 1: 'Twas a French plot, upon my life.

SERVANT 2: To see what the devil can do!

ANTONIO: Are all the officers here?

SERVANTS: We are.

ANTONIO: Gentlemen,
We have lost much plate you know; and but this evening
Jewels, to the value of four thousand ducats,
Are missing in the duchess' cabinet.

Are the gates shut?

SERVANT 1: Yes.

ANTONIO: 'Tis the duchess' pleasure
Each officer be lock'd into his chamber
Till the sun-rising; and to send the keys
Of all their chests, and of their outward doors
Into her bed-chamber. She is very sick.

RODERIGO: At her pleasure.

ANTONIO: She entreats you tak't not ill: the innocent
Shall be the more approv'd by it.

BOSOLA: Gentlemen o'th' wood-yard, where's your Switzer now?

SERVANT 1: By this hand 'twas credibly reported by one o'th' blackguard.

Exit Gentlemen

DELIO: How fares it with the duchess?

ANTONIO: She's expos'd
Unto the worst of torture, pain and fear.

DELIO: Speak to her all happy comfort.

ANTONIO: How I do play the fool with mine own danger!
You are this night, dear friend, to post to Rome:
My life lies in your service.

DELIO: Do not doubt me.

ANTONIO: O, 'tis far from me! and yet fear presents me
Somewhat that looks like danger.

DELIO: Believe it,
'Tis but the shadow of your fear, no more:
How superstitiously we mind our evils!
The throwing down salt, or crossing of a hare,
Bleeding at nose, the stumbling of a horse,
Or singing of a cricket, are of power

To daunt whole man in us. Sir, fare you well:
I wish you all the joys of a blest father;
And, for my faith, lay this unto your breast,
Old friends, like old swords, still are trusted best.

Enter CARIOLA

CARIOLA: Sir, you are the happy father of a son:
Your wife commends him to you.

ANTONIO: Blessed comfort!
For heaven' sake tend her well: I'll presently
Go set a figure for's nativity.

They exit

Act II, scene iii

Later that night

Enter BOSOLA with a dark lantern

BOSOLA: Sure I did hear a woman shriek: list, ha!
And the sound came, if I receiv'd it right,
From the duchess' lodgings. There's some stratagem
In the confining all our courtiers
To their several wards: I must have part of it;
My intelligence will freeze else. List, again!
It may be 'twas the melancholy bird,
Best friend of silence and of solitariness,
The owl, that scream'd so. Ha! Antonio!

Enter ANTONIO

ANTONIO: I heard some noise. Who's there? what art thou? speak.

BOSOLA: Antonio? put not your face nor body
To such a forc'd expression of fear:
I am Bosola, your friend.

ANTONIO: Bosola!

[*aside*] This mole does undermine me— Heard you not
A noise even now?

BOSOLA: From whence?

ANTONIO: From the duchess' lodging.

BOSOLA: Not I: did you?

ANTONIO: I did, or else I dream'd.

BOSOLA: Let's walk towards it.

ANTONIO: No, it may be 'twas
But the rising of the wind.

BOSOLA: Very likely.
Methinks 'tis very cold, and yet you sweat.
You look wildly.

ANTONIO: I have been setting a figure
For the duchess' jewels.

BOSOLA: Ah, and how falls your question?
Do you find it radical?

ANTONIO: What's that to you?
'Tis rather to be question'd what design,
When all men were commanded to their lodgings,
Makes you a night-walker.

BOSOLA: In sooth I'll tell you:
Now all the court's asleep, I thought the devil
Had least to do here; I came to say my prayers,
And if it do offend you I do so,
You are a fine courtier.

ANTONIO: This fellow will undo me.
You gave the duchess apricocks to-day:
Pray heaven they were not poison'd.

BOSOLA: Poison'd! a Spanish fig
For the imputation.

ANTONIO: Traitors are ever confident,
Till they are discover'd. There were jewels stol'n too:
In my conceit, none are to be suspected
More than yourself.

BOSOLA: You are a false steward.

ANTONIO: Saucy slave, I'll pull thee up by the roots.

BOSOLA: Maybe the ruin will crush you to pieces.

ANTONIO: You are an impudent snake indeed, sir.
Are you scarce warm, and do you show your sting?
You libel well, sir.

BOSOLA: No, sir: copy it out,
And I will set my hand to't.

ANTONIO: [*aside*] My nose bleeds.
One that were superstitious would count
This ominous, when it merely comes by chance:
Two letters, that are wrote here for my name,
Are drown'd in blood!
Mere accident. — For you, sir, I'll take order
I'th' morn you shall be safe— 'tis that must colour
Her lying in— sir, this door you pass not:
I do not hold it fit that you come near
The duchess' lodgings, till you have quit yourself.—
The great are like the base, nay, they are the same,
When they seek shameful ways to avoid shame.

Exits

BOSOLA: Antonio hereabout did drop a paper.

Some of your help, false friend. O, here it is:

What's here? a child's nativity calculated!

The Duchess was delivered of a son, ' tween the hours twelve and one in the night, Anno Dom. 1504, (that's this year) decimo nono Decembris, (that's this night,) taken according to the Meridian of Malfi (that's our Duchess: happy discovery!) The lord of the first house being combust in the ascendant, signifies short life; and Mars being in a human sign, joined to the tail of the Dragon, in the eighth house, doth threaten a violent death. Caetera non scrutantur.

Why, now 'tis most apparent: this precise fellow

Is the duchess' bawd. I have it to my wish!

This is a parcel of intelligency

Our courtiers were cas'd up for: it needs must follow,
That I must be comm'tted, on pretence
Of poisoning her; which I'll endure, and laugh at.
If one could find the father now! but that
Time will discover. Old Castruchio
I'th' morning posts to Rome: by him I'll send
A letter, that shall make her brothers' galls
O'erflow their livers. This was a thrifty way.
Though lust do mask in ne'er so strange disguise,
She's oft found witty, but is never wise.

Exits

Act II, scene iv

The Cardinal's apartment in Rome

Enter CARDINAL and JULIA

CARDINAL: Sit: thou art my best of wishes. Prithee tell me,
What trick didst thou invent to come to Rome
Without thy husband?

JULIA: Why, my lord, I told him
I came to visit an old anchorite
Here, for devotion.

CARDINAL: Thou art a witty false one;
I mean, to him.

JULIA: You have prevail'd with me
Beyond my strongest thoughts: I would not now
Find you inconstant.

CARDINAL: Do not put thyself
To such a voluntary torture, which proceeds
Out of your own guilt.

JULIA: How, my lord?

CARDINAL: You fear
My constancy, because you have approv'd
Those giddy and wild turnings in yourself.

JULIA: Did you e'er find them?

CARDINAL: Sooth, generally for women;
A man might strive to make glass malleable,
Ere he should make them fixed.

JULIA: So, my lord.

CARDINAL: We had need go borrow that fantastic glass,
Invented by Galileo the Florentine,
To view another spacious world i'th' moon,
And look to find a constant woman there.

JULIA: This is very well, my lord.

CARDINAL: Why do you weep?
Are tears your justification? the self-same tears
Will fall into your husband's bosom, lady,
With a loud protestation that you love him
Above the world. Come, I'll love you wisely,
That's jealously, since I am very certain
You cannot make me cuckold.

JULIA: I'll go home
To my husband.

CARDINAL: You may thank me, lady:
I have taken you off your melancholy perch,
Bore you upon my fist, and show'd you game,
And let you fly at it. I pray thee kiss me.
When thou was't with thy husband, thou wast watch'd
Like a tame elephant: (still you are to thank me.)
Thou hadst only kisses from him, and high feeding,
But what delight was that? 'Twas just like one
That hath a little fing'ring on the lute,
Yet cannot tune it: (still you are to thank me.)

JULIA: You told me of a piteous wound i'th' heart,
And a sick liver, when you woo'd me first,
And spake like one in physic.

CARDINAL: Who's that?

Enter SERVANT

Rest firm, for my affection to thee,
Lightning moves slow to't.

SERVANT: Madam, a gentleman,
That's come post from Malfi, desires to see you.

CARDINAL: Let him enter, I'll withdraw.

He exits

SERVANT: He says,
Your husband, old Castruchio, is come to Rome,
Most pitifully tired with riding post.

He exits

Enter DELIO

JULIA: Signior Delio! [*aside*] 'tis one of my old suitors.

DELIO: I was bold to come and see you.

JULIA: Sir, you are welcome.

DELIO: Do you lie here?

JULIA: Sure, your own experience
Will satisfy you, no: our Roman prelates
Do not keep lodging for ladies.

DELIO: Very well:
I have brought you no commendations from your husband,
For I know none by him.

JULIA: I hear he's come to Rome.

DELIO: I never knew man and beast, of a horse and a knight,
So weary of each other; if he had had a good back,
He would have undertook to have borne his horse,
His breech was so pitifully sore.

JULIA: Your laughter
Is my pity.

DELIO: Lady, I know not whether
You want money, but I have bought you some.

JULIA: From my husband?

DELIO: No, from mine own allowance.

JULIA: I must hear the condition, ere I be bound to take it.

DELIO: Look on't, 'tis gold; hath it not a fine colour?

JULIA: I have a bird more beautiful.

DELIO: Try the sound on't.

JULIA: A lute-string far exceeds it:
It hath no smell, like cassia, or civet;
Nor is it physical, though some fond doctors
Persuade us seeth't in cullises. I'll tell you,
This is a creature bred by—

Enter SERVANT

SERVANT: Your husband's come,
Hath deliver'd a letter to the Duke of Calabria,
That to my thinking, hath put him out of his wits.

He exits

JULIA: Sir, you hear:
Pray let me know your business and your suit,
As briefly as can be.

DELIO: With good speed, I would wish you,
At such time as you are non-resident
With your husband, my mistress.

JULIA: Sir, I'll go ask my husband if I shall,
And straight return your answer.

She exits

DELIO: Very fine.
Is this her wit, or honesty, that speaks thus?
I heard one say the Duke was highly mov'd
With a letter sent from Malfi. I do fear
Antonio is betray'd: how fearfully
Shows his ambition now; unfortunate fortune!
They pass through whirlpools, and deep woes do shun,
Who the event weigh, ere the action's done.

He exits

Act II, scene v

Rome

Enter CARDINAL and FERDINAND with a letter

FERDINAND: I have this night digg'd up a mandrake.

CARDINAL: Say you?

FERDINAND: And I am grown mad with't.

CARDINAL: What's the prodigy?

FERDINAND: Read there, a sister damn'd; she's loose i'th' hilts,
Grown a notorious strumpet.

CARDINAL: Speak lower.

FERDINAND: Lower!
Rogues do not whisper't now, but seek to publish't,
As servants do the bounty of their lords,
Aloud; and with a covetous searching eye,
To mark who note them. O, confusion seize her!
She hath had most cunning bawds to serve her turn,
And more secure conveyances for lust,
Than towns of garrison for service.

CARDINAL: Is't possible?
Can this be certain?

FERDINAND: Rhubarb, O, for rhubarb
To purge this choler! here's the cursed day
To prompt my memory; and here't shall stick
Till of her bleeding heart I make a sponge
To wipe it out.

CARDINAL: Why do you make yourself
So wild a tempest?

FERDINAND: Would I could be one,
That I might toss her palace 'bout her ears,
Root up her goodly forests, blast her meads,
And lay her general territory as waste,
As she hath done her honour's.

CARDINAL: Shall our blood,
The royal blood of Arragon and Castile,
Be thus attainted?

FERDINAND: Apply desperate physic:
We must not now use balsamum, but fire,
The smarting cupping-glass, for that's the mean
To purge infected blood, such blood as hers.
There is a kind of pity in mine eye,
I'll give it to my handkerchief; and now 'tis here
I'll bequeath this to her bastard.

CARDINAL: What to do?

FERDINAND: Why, to make soft lint for his mother's wounds,
When I have hewed her to pieces.

CARDINAL: Curs'd creature!
Unequal nature, to place women's hearts
So far upon the left side!

FERDINAND: Foolish men,
That e'er will trust their honour in a bark
Made of so slight weak bulrush as is woman,
Apt every minute to sink it!

CARDINAL: Thus ignorance, when it hath purchas'd honour,
It cannot wield it.

FERDINAND: Methinks I see her laughing:
Excellent hyena! Talk to me somewhat, quickly,
Or my imagination will carry me
To see her in the shameful act of sin.

CARDINAL: With whom?

FERDINAND: Happily with some strong-thigh'd bargeman,
Or one o'th' wood-yard, that can quoit the sledge,
Or toss the bar, or else some lovely squire
That carries coals up to her privy lodgings.

CARDINAL: You fly beyond your reason.

FERDINAND: Go to, mistress!
'Tis not your whore's milk that shall quench my wild-fire,
But your whore's blood.

CARDINAL: How idly shows this rage, which carries you,
As men convey'd by witches through the air,
On violent whirlwinds! this intemperate noise
Fitly resembles deaf men's shrill discourse,
Who talk aloud, thinking all other men
To have their imperfection.

FERDINAND: Have not you
My palsy?

CARDINAL: Yes; I can be angry
Without this rupture: there is not in nature
A thing that makes man so deform'd, so beastly,
As doth intemperate anger. Chide yourself.
You have divers men, who never yet express'd
Their strong desire of rest, but by unrest,
By vexing of themselves. Come, put yourself
In tune.

FERDINAND: So: I will only study to seem
The thing I am not. I could kill her now,
In you, or in myself; for I do think
It is some sin in us, heaven doth revenge
By her.

CARDINAL: Are you stark mad?

FERDINAND: I would have their bodies
Burnt in a coal-pit with the ventage stopp'd,
That their curs'd smoke might not ascend to heaven;
Or dip the sheets they lie in in pitch or sulphur,
Wrap them in't, and then light them like a match;
Or else to boil their bastard to a cullis
And give't his lecherous father, to renew
The sin of his back.

CARDINAL: I'll leave you.

FERDINAND: Nay, I have done.
I am confident, had I been damn'd in hell,
And should have heard of this, it would have put me
Into a cold sweat. In, in, I'll go sleep.
Till I know who leaps my sister, I'll not stir:
That known, I'll find scorpions to string my whips,
And fix her in a general eclipse.

They exit

Act III, scene i

The court at Malfi, several years later

Enter ANTONIO and DELIO

ANTONIO: Our noble friend, my most beloved Delio!
O, you have been a stranger long at court:
Came you along with the Lord Ferdinand?

DELIO: I did, sir: and how fares your noble duchess?

ANTONIO: Right fortunately well. She's an excellent
Feeder of pedigrees; since you last saw her,
She hath had two children more, a son and daughter.

DELIO: Methinks 'twas yesterday; let me but wink,
And not behold your face, which to mine eye
Is somewhat leaner: verily I should dream
It were within this half hour.

ANTONIO: You have not been in law, friend Delio,
Nor in prison, nor a suitor at the court,
Nor begg'd the reversion of some great man's place,
Nor troubled with an old wife, which doth make
Your time so insensibly hasten.

DELIO: Pray, sir, tell me,
Hath not this news arriv'd yet to the ear
Of the lord Cardinal?

ANTONIO: I fear it hath:
The Lord Ferdinand, that's newly come to court,
Doth bear himself right dangerously.

DELIO: Pray, why?

ANTONIO: He is so quiet, that he seems to sleep
The tempest out, as dormice do in winter:
These houses that are haunted, are most still
Till the devil be up.

DELIO: What say the common people?

ANTONIO: The common rabble do directly say
She is a strumpet.

DELIO: And your graver heads,
Which would be politic, what censure they?

ANTONIO: They do observe I grow to infinite purchase
The left hand way, and all suppose the duchess
Would amend it, if she could. For, say they,
Great princes, though they grudge their officers
Should have such large and unconfined means
To get wealth under them, will not complain
Lest thereby they should make them odious
Unto the people; for other obligation
Of love or marriage, between her and me,
They never dream of.

DELIO: The Lord Ferdinand
Is going to bed.

Enter DUCHESS, FERDINAND, BOSOLA

FERDINAND: I'll instantly to bed,
For I am weary. I am to bespeak
A husband for you.

DUCHESS: For me, sir? Pray who is't?

FERDINAND: The great Count Malateste.

DUCHESS: Fie upon him:
A count? He's a mere stick of sugar-candy;
You may look quite through him. When I choose
A husband, I will marry for your honour.

FERDINAND: You shall do well in't. How is't, worthy
Antonio?

DUCHESS: But, sir, I am to have private conference with you
About a scandalous report is spread
Touching mine honour.

FERDINAND: Let me be ever deaf to't:
One of Pasquil's paper-bullets, court calumny,
A pestilent air, which princes' palaces
Are seldom purg'd of. Yet, say that it were true,
I pour it in your bosom, my fix'd love
Would strongly excuse, extenuate, nay deny
Faults were they apparent in you. Go, be safe
In your own innocency.

DUCHESS: O bless'd comfort!
This deadly air is purg'd.

Exit all but Ferdinand and Bosola

FERDINAND: Her guilt treads on
Hot burning cultures. Now, Bosola,
How thrives our intelligence?

BOSOLA: Sir, uncertainly:
'Tis rumour'd she hath had three bastards, but
By whom, we may go read i'th' stars.

FERDINAND: Why some
Hold opinion, all things are written there.

BOSOLA: Yes, if we could find spectacles to read them.
I do suspect, there hath been some sorcery
Us'd on the duchess.

FERDINAND: Sorcery! to what purpose?

BOSOLA: To make her dote on some desertless fellow,
She shames to acknowledge.

FERDINAND: Can your faith give way
To think there's power in potions, or in charms,
To make us love whether we will or no?

BOSOLA: Most certainly.

FERDINAND: Away, these are mere gulleries, horrid things
Invented by some cheating mountebanks,
To abuse us. Do you think that herbs, or charms,
Can force the will? Some trials have been made
In this foolish practice, but the ingredients
Were lenative poisons, such as are of force
To make the patient mad; and straight the witch
Swears by equivocation they are in love.
The witchcraft lies in her rank blood. This night
I will force confession from her. You told me
You had got, within these two days, a false key
Into her bed-chamber.

BOSOLA: I have.

FERDINAND: As I would wish.

BOSOLA: What do you intend to do?

FERDINAND: Can you guess?

BOSOLA: No.

FERDINAND: Do not ask then:
He that can compass me, and know my drifts,
May say he hath put a girdle 'bout the world,
And sounded all her quicksands.

BOSOLA: I do not think so.

FERDINAND: What do you think, then, pray?

BOSOLA: That you are
Your own chronicle too much, and grossly
Flatter yourself.

FERDINAND: Give me thy hand; I thank thee.
I never gave pension but to flatterers,
Till I entertained thee. Farewell.
That friend a great man's ruin strongly checks,
Who rails into his belief all his defects.

They exit

Act III, scene ii

The Duchess' chambers, later that night

Enter DUCHESS, ANTONIO, and CARIOLA

DUCHESS: Bring me the casket hither, and the glass.
You get no lodging here tonight, my lord.

ANTONIO: Indeed, I must persuade one.

DUCHESS: Very good:
I hope in time 'twill grow into a custom,
That noblemen shall come with cap and knee,
To purchase a night's lodging of their wives.

ANTONIO: I must lie here.

DUCHESS: Must? You are a lord of misrule.

ANTONIO: Indeed, my rule is only in the night.

DUCHESS: To what use will you put me?

ANTONIO: We'll sleep together.

DUCHESS: Alas, what pleasure can two lovers find in sleep?

CARIOLA: My lord, I lie with her often; and I know
She'll much disquiet you.

ANTONIO: See, you are complain'd of.

CARIOLA: For she's the sprawlingest bedfellow.

ANTONIO: I shall like her the better for that.

CARIOLA: Sir, shall I ask you a question?

ANTONIO: Ay, pray thee, Cariola.

CARIOLA: Wherefore still, when you lie with my lady,
Do you rise so early?

ANTONIO: Labouring men
Count the clock oftenest, Cariola,
Are glad when their task's ended.

DUCHESS: I'll stop your mouth. [*kisses him*]

ANTONIO: Nay, that's but one; Venus had two soft doves
To draw her chariot; I must have another.
When wilt thou marry, Cariola?

CARIOLA: Never, my lord.

ANTONIO: O, fie upon this single life; forego it.
We read how Daphne, for her peevish flight,
Became a fruitless bay-tree; Syrinx turn'd
To the pale empty reed; Anaxarete
Was frozen into marble: whereas those
Which married, or prov'd kind unto their friends,
Were by a gracious influence, transhap'd
Into the olive, pomegranate, mulberry,
Became flowers, precious stones, or eminent stars.

CARIOLA: This is vain poetry; but I pray you tell me,
If there were propos'd me, wisdom, riches, and beauty,
In three several young men, which should I choose?

ANTONIO: 'Tis a hard question: this was Paris' case,
And he was blind in't, and there was great cause;
For how was't possible he could judge right,
Having three amorous goddesses in view,
And they stark naked? 'twas a motion
Were able to benight the apprehension
Of the severest counselor of Europe.
Now I look on both your faces so well form'd,
It puts me in mind of a question I would ask.

CARIOLA: What is't?

ANTONIO: I do wonder why hard-favour'd ladies,
For the most part, keep worse-favour'd waiting women,
To attend them, and cannot endure fair ones.

DUCHESS: O, that's soon answer'd.
Did you ever in your life know an ill painter
Desire to have his dwelling next door to the shop
Of an excellent picture-maker? 'twould disgrace
His face-making, and undo him. I prithee,
When were we so merry? My hair tangles.

ANTONIO: [*aside to Cariola*] Pray thee, Cariola, let's steal forth the room,
And let her talk to herself: I have divers times
Serv'd her the like, when she hath chaf'd extremely.
I love to see her angry. Softly. Cariola.

They exit

DUCHESS: Doth not the colour of my hair 'gin to change?
When I wax gray, I shall have all the court
Powder their hair with arras, to be like me.
You have cause to love me; I enter'd you into my heart
Before you would vouchsafe to call for the keys.

Enter FERDINAND unseen

We shall one day have my brothers take you napping:
Methinks his presence, being now in court,
Should make you keep your own bed; but you'll say
Love mix'd with fear is sweetest. I'll assure you,
You shall get no more children till my brothers
Consent to be your gossips. Have you lost your tongue?
She sees FERDINAND holding a dagger

'Tis welcome:

For know, whether I am doom'd to live or die,

I can do both like a prince.

FERDINAND: Die then quickly.
Virtue, where art thou hid? what hideous thing
Is it that doth eclipse thee?

DUCHESS: Pray, sir, hear me—

FERDINAND: Or is it true thou art but a bare name,
And no essential thing?

DUCHESS: Sir—

FERDINAND: Do not speak.

DUCHESS: No, sir:
I will plant my soul in mine ears, to hear you.

FERDINAND: O, most imperfect light of human reason,
That mak'st us so unhappy to foresee
What we can least prevent! Pursue thy wishes,
And glory in them: there's in shame no comfort,
But to be past all bounds and sense of shame.

DUCHESS: I pray, sir, hear me: I am married—

FERDINAND: So.

DUCHESS: Happily, not to your liking: but for that,
Alas, your shears do come untimely now
To clip the bird's wings, that's already flown!
Will you see my husband?

FERDINAND: Yes.
If I could change eyes with a basilisk.

DUCHESS: Sure, you came hither
By his confederacy.

FERDINAND: The howling of a wolf
Is music to thee, screech-owl: prithee, peace.
Whate'er thou art that hast enjoy'd my sister,
For I am sure thou hear'st me, for thine own sake
Let me not know thee. I came hither prepar'd
To work thy discovery; yet am now persuaded
It would beget such violent effects
As would damn us both. I would not for ten millions
I had beheld thee: therefore use all means
I never may have knowledge of thy name;
Enjoy thy lust still, and a wretched life,
On that condition. And for thee, vile woman,
If thou do wish thy lecher may grow old
In thy embracements, I would have thee build
Such a room for him as our anchorites
To holier use inhabit. Let not the sun
Shine on him, till he's dead; let dogs and monkeys
Only converse with him, and such dumb things
To whom nature denies use to sound his name;
Do not keep a paraquito, lest she learn it;
If thou do love him, cut out thine own tongue
Lest it bewray him.

DUCHESS: Why might not I marry?
I have not gone about in this to create
Any new world or custom.

FERDINAND: Thou art undone;
And thou hast ta'en that massy sheet of lead
That hid thy husband's bones, and folded it
About my heart.

DUCHESS: Mine bleeds for't.

FERDINAND: Thine? thy heart?
What should I name't, unless a hollow bullet
Fill'd with unquenchable wild-fire?

DUCHESS: You are in this
Too strict; and were you not my princely brother,
I would say, too willful. My reputation
Is safe.

FERDINAND: Dost thou know what reputation is?
I'll tell thee, to small purpose, since th' instruction
Comes now too late.
Upon a time Reputation, Love, and Death
Would travel o'er the world; and it was concluded
That they should part, and take three several ways.
Death told them, they should find him in great battles,
Or cities plagu'd with plagues: Love gives them counsel
To enquire for him 'mongst unambitious shepherds,
Where dowries were not talk'd of, and sometimes
'Mongst quiet kindred, that had nothing left
By their dead parents. 'Stay,' quoth Reputation,
'Do not forsake me; for it is my nature
If once I part from any man I meet,
I am never found again.' And so, for you;
You have shook hands with Reputation,
And made him invisible. So fare you well:
I will never see you more.

DUCHESS: Why should only I,
Of all the other princes of the world
Be cas'd up, like a holy relic? I have youth,
And a little beauty.

FERDINAND: So you have some virgins
That are witches. I will never see thee more.

He exits

Enter CARIOLA and ANTONIO with a pistol

DUCHESS: You saw this apparition?

ANTONIO: Yes: we are
Betray'd. How came he hither? I should turn
This to thee, for that. [*turns pistol on Cariola*]

CARIOLA: Pray, sir, do; and when
That you have cleft my heart, you shall read there
Mine innocence.

DUCHESS: That gallery gave him entrance.

ANTONIO: I would this terrible thing would come again,
That, standing on my guard, I might relate
My warrantable love. Ha! what means this? [*seeing the dagger*]

DUCHESS: He left this with me.

ANTONIO: And it seems, did wish
You would use it on yourself.

DUCHESS: His action seem'd to intend so much.

ANTONIO: This hath a handle to't,
As well as a point: turn it towards him,
And so fasten the keen edge in his rank gall.
How now? who knocks? more earthquakes?

DUCHESS: I stand
As if a mine beneath my feet were ready
To be blown up.

CARIOLA: 'Tis Bosola.

DUCHESS: Away!
O misery, methinks unjust actions
Should wear these masks and curtains, and not we.
You must instantly part hence: I have fashion'd it already.

Exit ANTONIO, enter BOSOLA

BOSOLA: The duke your brother is ta'en up in a whirlwind;
Hath took horse, and 's rid post to Rome.

DUCHESS: So late?

BOSOLA: He told me, as he mounted into th' saddle,
You were undone.

DUCHESS: Indeed, I am very near it.

BOSOLA: What's the matter?

DUCHESS: Antonio, the master of our household,
Hath dealt so falsely with me in's accounts:
My brother stood engag'd with me for money
Ta'en up of certain Neapolitan Jews,
And Antonio lets the bonds be forfeit.

BOSOLA: Strange: [*aside*] this is cunning.

DUCHESS: And hereupon
My brother's bills at Naples are protested
Against. Call up our officers.

BOSOLA: I shall.

Exit BOSOLA, enter ANTONIO

DUCHESS: The place that you must fly to is Ancona:
Hire a house there; I'll send after you
My treasure, and my jewels. Our weak safety
Runs upon enginous wheels: short syllables
Must stand for periods. I must now accuse you
Of such a feigned crime, as Tasso calls
Magnanima mensogna, a noble lie,
'Cause it must shield our honours: hark, they are coming.

Enter BOSOLA and Gentlemen

ANTONIO: Will your grace hear me?

DUCHESS: I have got well by you; you have yielded me
A million of loss: I am like to inherit

The people's curses for your stewardship.
You had the trick in audit-time to be sick,
Till I had sign'd your Quietus; and that cur'd you
Without help of a doctor. Gentlemen,
I would have this man be an example to you all,
So shall you hold my favour; I pray, let him;
For h'as done that, alas! you would not think of,
And, because I intend to be rid of him,
I mean not to publish. Use your fortune elsewhere.

ANTONIO: I am strongly arm'd to brook my overthrow,
As commonly men bear with a hard year;
I will not blame the cause on't, but do think
The necessity of my malevolent star
Procures this, not her humour. O, the inconstant
And rotten ground of service, you may see;
'Tis even like him, that in a winter night,
Takes a long slumber o'er a dying fire,
As loath to part from't; yet parts thence as cold,
As when he first sat down.

DUCHESS: We do confiscate
Towards the satisfying of your accounts,
All that you have.

ANTONIO: I am all yours; and 'tis very fit
All mine should be so.

DUCHESS: So, sir, you have your pass.

ANTONIO: You may see, gentlemen, what 't is to serve
A prince with body and soul.

Exit

BOSOLA: Here's an example for extortion: what moisture
Is drawn out of the sea, when foul weather comes,
Pours down, and runs into the sea again.

DUCHESS: I would know what are your opinions
Of this Antonio.

2 OFFICER: He could not abide to see a pig's head
gaping. I thought your grace would find him a Jew.

3 OFFICER: I would you had been his officer, for your own sake.

4 OFFICER: He stopped his ears with black wool, and to those came to him for money, said he was thick of hearing.

2 OFFICER: Some said he was an hermaphrodite, for he could not abide a woman.

4 OFFICER: How scurvy proud he would look, when the treasury was full! well, let him go.

1 OFFICER: Yes, and the chippings of the buttery fly after him, to scour his gold chain.

DUCHESS: Leave us. [*they exit*]
What do you think of these?

BOSOLA: That these are rogues, that in's prosperity,
But to have waited on his fortune, could have wish'd
His dirty stirrup riveted through their noses;
And follow'd after's mule, like a bear in a ring.
Would have prostituted their daughters to his lust;
Made their first-born intelligencers; thought none happy
But such as were born under his blest planet,
And wore his livery: and do these lice drop off now?
Well, never look to have the like again:
He hath left a sort of flattering rogues behind him;
Their doom must follow. Princes pay flatterers
In their own money: flatterers dissemble their vices,
And they dissemble their lies; that's justice.
Alas, poor gentleman!

DUCHESS: Poor! he hath amply fill'd his coffers.

BOSOLA: Sure he was too honest. Plutus, the god of riches,
When he's sent by Jupiter to any man,
He goes limping, to signify that wealth
That comes on God's name, comes slowly; but when he's sent
On the devil's errand, he rides post and comes in by scuttles.

Let me show you what a most unvalued jewel
You have in a wanton humour thrown away,
To bless the man shall find him. He was an excellent
Courtier, and most faithful; a soldier, that thought it
As beastly to know his own value too little,
As devilish to acknowledge it too much.
Both his virtue and form deserv'd a far better fortune.
His discourse rather delighted to judge itself, than show itself:
His breast was fill'd with all perfection,
And yet it seemed a private whispering-room,
It made so little noise of't.

DUCHESS: But he was basely descended.

BOSOLA: Will you make yourself a mercenary herald,
Rather to examine men's pedigrees, than virtues?
You shall want him:
For know an honest statesman to a prince,
Is like a cedar planted by a spring:
The spring bathes the tree's root, the grateful tree
Rewards it with his shadow: you have not done so.
I would sooner swim to the Bermoothes on
Two politicians' rotten bladders, tied
Together with an intelligencer's heart-string,
Than depend on so changeable a prince's favour.
Fare thee well, Antonio, since the malice of the world
Would needs down with thee, it cannot be said yet
That any ill happened unto thee,
Considering thy fall was accompanied with virtue.

DUCHESS: O, you render me excellent music!

BOSOLA: Say you?

DUCHESS: This good one that you speak of, is my husband.

BOSOLA: Do I not dream? Can this ambitious age
Have so much goodness in't, as to prefer
A man merely for worth, without these shadows
Of wealth and painted honours? possible?

DUCHESS: I have had three children by him.

BOSOLA: Fortunate lady!
For you have made your private nuptial bed
The humble and fair seminary of peace.
No question but many an unbenefic'd scholar
Shall pray for you for this deed, and rejoice
That some preferment in the world can yet
Arise from merit. The virgins of your land
That have no dowries shall hope your example
Will raise them to rich husbands. Should you want
Soldiers, 'twould make the very Turks and Moors
Turn Christians, and serve you for this act.
Last, the neglected poets of your time,
In honour of this trophy of a man,
Rais'd by that curious engine, your white hand,
Shall thank you, in your grave, for't; and make that
More reverend than all the cabinets
Of living princes. For Antonio,
His fame shall likewise flow from many a pen,
When heralds shall want coats to sell to men.

DUCHESS: As I taste comfort in this friendly speech,
So would I find concealment.

BOSOLA: O, the secret of my prince,
Which I will wear on th' inside of my heart.

DUCHESS: You shall take charge of all my coin and jewels,
And follow him; for he retires himself
To Ancona.

BOSOLA: So.

DUCHESS: Whither, within few days,
I mean to follow thee.

BOSOLA: Let me think:
I would wish your grace to feign a pilgrimage
To Our Lady of Loretto, scarce seven leagues

From fair Ancona; so may you depart
Your country with more honour, and your flight
Will seem a princely progress, retaining
Your usual train about you.

DUCHESS: Sir, your direction
Shall lead me by the hand.

CARIOLA: In my opinion,
She were better progress to the baths at Lucca,
Or go visit the Spa
In Germany: for, if you will believe me,
I do not like this jesting with religion,
This feigned pilgrimage.

DUCHESS: Thou art a superstitious fool.
Prepare us instantly for our departure.
Past sorrows, let us moderately lament them,
For those to come, seek wisely to prevent them.

Exit DUCHESS and CARIOLA

BOSOLA: A politician is the devil's quilted anvil;
He fashions all sins on him, and the blows
Are never heard: he may work in a lady's chamber,
As here for proof. What rests but I reveal
All to my lord? O, this base quality
Of intelligencer! Why, every quality i'th' world
Prefers but gain or commendation.
Now, for this act I am certain to be rais'd,
And men that paint weeds to the life, are prais'd.

Exit

Act III, scene iii

The CARDINAL'S palace in Rome

Enter CARDINAL, FERDINAND, MALATESTE, PESCARA, DELIO, and SILVIO

CARDINAL: Must we turn soldier then?

MALATESTE: The emperor,
Hearing your worth that way, ere you attain'd
This reverend garment, joins you in commission
With the right fortunate soldier, the Marquis of Pescara,
And the famous Lannoy.

CARDINAL: He that had the honour
Of taking the French king prisoner?

MALATESTE: The same.
Here's a plot drawn for a new fortification

At Naples.

FERDINAND: This great count Malateste, I perceive,
Hath got employment.

DELIO: No employment, my lord;
A marginal note in the muster-book, that he is
A voluntary lord.

FERDINAND: He's no soldier?

DELIO: He has worn gunpowder in's hollow tooth, for the tooth-ache.

SILVIO: He comes to the leaguer with a full intent
To eat fresh beef and garlic, means to stay
Till the scent be gone, and straight return to court.

DELIO: He hath read all the late service,
As the City Chronicle relates it,
And keeps two pewterers going, only to express
Battles in model.

SILVIO: Then he'll fight by the book.

DELIO: By the almanac, I think,
To choose good days, and shun the critical;
That's his mistress' scarf.

SILVIO: Yes, he protests
He would do much for that taffata.

DELIO: I think he would run away from a battle,
To save it from taking prisoner.

SILVIO: He is horribly afraid
Gunpowder will spoil the perfume on't.

DELIO: I saw a Dutchman break his pate once
For calling him pot-gun; he made his head
Have a bore in't like a musket.

SILVIO: I would he had made a touchhole to't.
He is indeed a guarded sumpter-cloth,
Only for the remove of the court.

Enter BOSOLA

PESCARA: Bosola arriv'd! what should be the business?
Some falling out amongst the cardinals.
These factions amongst great men, they are like
Foxes, when their heads are divided,
They carry fire in their tails, and all the country
About them goes to wrack for't.

SILVIO: What's that Bosola?

DELIO: I knew him in Padua,- a fantastical scholar,
Like such who study to know how many knots was in
Hercules' club, of what colour Achilles' beard was,
Or whether Hector were not troubled
With the tooth-ache.
He hath studied himself half blear-eyed to know
The true symmetry of Caesar's nose by a shoeing-horn; and this

He did to gain the name of a speculative man.

PESCARA: Mark prince Ferdinand:
A very salamander lives in's eye,
To mock the eager violence of fire.

SILVIO: That Cardinal hath made more bad faces with his

oppression than ever Michael Angelo made good ones: he

lifts up's nose, like a foul porpoise before a storm.

PESCARA: The Lord Ferdinand laughs.

DELIO: Like a deadly cannon,
That lightens ere it smokes.

PESCARA: These are your true pangs of death,
The pangs of life, that struggle with great statesmen.

DELIO: In such a deformed silence, witches whisper their charms.

CARDINAL: Doth she make religion her riding hood
To keep her from the sun and tempest?

FERDINAND: That:
That damns her. Methinks her fault and beauty,
Blended together, show like leprosy,
The whiter, the fouler. I make it a question
Whether her beggarly brats were ever christen'd.

CARDINAL: I will instantly solicit the state of Ancona
To have them banish'd.

FERDINAND: You are for Loretto?
I shall not be at your ceremony; fare you well.
Write to the Duke of Malfi, my young nephew
She had by her first husband, and acquaint him
With's mother's honesty.

BOSOLA: I will.

FERDINAND: Antonio!
A slave that only smell'd of ink and counters
And never in's life look'd like a gentleman,
But in the audit-time. Go, go presently,
Draw me out an hundred and fifty of our horse,
And meet me at the fort-bridge.

They exit

Act III, scene iv

Enter TWO PILGRIMS to the Shrine of Our Lady of Loretto

FIRST PILGRIM: I have not seen a goodlier shrine than this,
Yet I have visited many.

SECOND PILGRIM: The cardinal of Arragon
Is this day to resign his cardinal's hat:
His sister duchess likewise is arriv'd
To pay her vow of pilgrimage. I expect
A noble ceremony.

FIRST PILGRIM: No question. They come.

Here the ceremony of the Cardinal's installment, in the habit of a soldier, performed in delivering up his cross, hat, robes, and ring, at the shrine, and investing him with sword, helmet, shield, and spurs: then Antonio, the Duchess, and their children, having presented themselves at the shrine, are, by a form of banishment in dumb-show expressed towards them by the Cardinal and the state of Ancona, banished. During all which ceremony, this ditty is sung to very solemn music, by divers churchmen, and then exit:

Arms, and honours deck thy story,
To thy fame's eternal glory:
Adverse fortune ever fly thee;
No disastrous fate come nigh thee.
I alone will sing thy praises,
Whom to honour virtue raises;
And thy study, that divine is,
.lts and shrimps? and darest thou
Pass by our dog-ship without reverence?'
' O,' quoth the salmon, ' sister, be at peace:
Thank Jupiter, we both have past the net!
Our value never can be truly known,
Till in the fisher's basket we be shown:
I' th' market then my price may be the higher,
Even when I am nearest to the cook and fire.'
So, to great men the moral may be stretched;
Men oft are valu'd high, when th' are most wretched.
But come, whither you please. I am arm'd 'gainst misery;
Bent to all sways of the oppressor's will:
There's no deep valley but near some great hill.

They exit

Act IV, scene i

The court at Malfi, now serving as her prison

Enter FERDINAND and BOSOLA

FERDINAND: How doth our sister Duchess bear herself
In her imprisonment?

BOSOLA: Nobly: I'll describe her.
She's sad, as one long us'd to't, and she seems
Rather to welcome the end of misery,
Than shun it; a behaviour so noble,
As gives a majesty to adversity:
You may discern the shape of loveliness
More perfect in her tears than in her smiles:
She will muse for hours together; and her silence,
Methinks, expresseth more than if she spake.

FERDINAND: Her melancholy seems to be fortified
With a strange disdain.

BOSOLA: 'Tis so; and this restraint,
Like English mastiffs that grow fierce with tying,
Makes her too passionately apprehend
Those pleasure's she's kept from.

FERDINAND: Curse upon her!
I will no longer study in the book
Of another's heart. Inform her what I told you.

Exit

Enter DUCHESS

BOSOLA: All comfort to your grace.

DUCHESS: I will have none.
Pray thee, why dost thou wrap thy poison'd pills
In gold and sugar?

BOSOLA: Your elder brother, the Lord Ferdinand,
Is come to visit you, and sends you word,
'Cause once he rashly made a solemn vow
Never to see you more, he comes i'th' night;

And prays you gently neither torch nor taper
Shine in your chamber: he will kiss your hand,
And reconcile himself; but, for his vow,
He dares not see you.

DUCHESS: At his pleasure.
Take hence the lights; he's come.

Enter FERDINAND

FERDINAND: Where are you?

DUCHESS: Here, sir.

FERDINAND: This darkness suits you well.

DUCHESS: I would ask you pardon.

FERDINAND: You have it;
For I account it the honourable'st revenge,
Where I may kill, to pardon. Where are your cubs?

DUCHESS: Whom?

FERDINAND: Call them your children,
For though our national law distinguish bastards
From true legitimate issue, compassionate nature
Makes them all equal.

DUCHESS: Do you visit me for this?
You violate a sacrament o'th' church
Shall make you howl in hell for't.

FERDINAND: It had been well,
Could you have liv'd thus always; for indeed,
You were too much i'th' light. But no more;
I come to seal my peace with you. Here's a hand,
Gives her a dead man's hand
To which you have vow'd much love; the ring upon't
You gave.

DUCHESS: I affectionately kiss it.

FERDINAND: Pray do, and bury the print of it in your heart.
I will leave this ring with you, for a love-token;

And the hand, as sure as the ring; and do not doubt
But you shall have the heart too: when you need a friend,
Send it to him that ow'd it: you shall see
Whether he can aid you.

DUCHESS: You are very cold:
I fear you are not well after your travel.
Ha! lights! O, horrible!

FERDINAND: Let her have lights enough.

Exit

DUCHESS: What witchcraft doth he practice, that he hath left

A dead man's hand here?

Here is discovered, behind a traverse, the artificial figures of Antonio and his children, appearing as *if they were dead*

BOSOLA: Look you, here's the piece from which 'twas ta'en.
He doth present you this sad spectacle,
That, now you know directly they are dead,
Hereafter you may wisely cease to grieve
For that which cannot be recovered.

DUCHESS: There is not between heaven and earth one wish
I stay for after this: it wastes me more
Than were't my picture, fashion'd out of wax,
Stuck with a magical needle, and then buried
In some foul dunghill; and yond's an excellent property
For a tyrant, which I would account mercy.

BOSOLA: What's that?

DUCHESS: If they would bind me to that lifeless trunk,
And let me freeze to death.

BOSOLA: Come, you must live.

DUCHESS: That's the greatest torture souls feel in hell;
In hell that they must live, and cannot die.

Portia, I'll new kindle thy coals again,
And revive the rare and almost dead example
Of a loving wife.

BOSOLA: O fie! despair? remember
You are a Christian.

DUCHESS: The church enjoins fasting:
I'll starve myself to death.

BOSOLA: Leave this vain sorrow.
Things being at the worst, begin to mend: the bee
When he hath shot his sting into your hand,
May then play with your eyelid.

DUCHESS: Good comfortable fellow,
Persuade a wretch that's broke upon the wheel
To have all his bones new set; entreat him live
To be executed again. Who must dispatch me?
I account this world a tedious theatre,
For I do play a part in't 'gainst my will.

BOSOLA: Come, be of comfort; I will save your life.

DUCHESS: Indeed I have not leisure to tend so small a business.

BOSOLA: Now, by my life, I pity you.

DUCHESS: Thou art a fool then,
To waste thy pity on a thing so wretched
As cannot pity itself. I am full of daggers.
Puff, let me blow those vipers from me.

Enter SERVANT

What are you?

SERVANT: One that wishes you long life.

DUCHESS: I would thou wert hang'd for the horrible curse
Thou hast given me: I shall shortly grow one
Of the miracles of pity. I'll go pray, no,
I'll go curse.

BOSOLA: O, fie!

DUCHESS: I could curse the stars.

BOSOLA: O, fearful!

DUCHESS: And those three smiling seasons of the year
Into a Russian winter: nay the world
To its first chaos.

BOSOLA: Look you, the stars shine still.

DUCHESS: O, but you must remember,
My curse hath a great way to go:
Plagues, that make lanes through largest families,
Consume them.

BOSOLA: Fie, lady.

DUCHESS: Let them like tyrants
Never be remember'd, but for the ill they have done;
Let all the zealous prayers of mortified
Churchmen forget them.

BOSOLA: O, uncharitable!

DUCHESS: Let heaven, a little while, cease crowning martyrs,
To punish them! Go, howl them this, and say, I long to bleed:
It is some mercy when men kill with speed.

Exit

Enter FERDINAND

FERDINAND: Excellent, as I would wish; she's plagu'd in art:
These presentations are but fram'd in wax,
By the curious master in that quality,
Vincentio Lauriola, and she takes them
For true substantial bodies.

BOSOLA: Why do you do this?

FERDINAND: To bring her to despair.

BOSOLA: 'Faith, end here,
And go no farther in your cruelty;
Send her a penitential garment to put on
Next to her delicate skin, and furnish her
With beads, and prayer-books.

FERDINAND: Damn her! that body of hers,
While that my blood ran pure in't, was more worth
Than that which thou wouldst comfort, called a soul.
I will send her masks of common courtesans,
Have her meat serv'd up by bawds and ruffians,
And, 'cause she'll needs be mad, I am resolv'd
To remove forth the common hospital
All the mad-folk, and place them near her lodging;
There let them practice together, sing and dance,
And set their gambols to the full o'th' moon:
If she can sleep the better for it, let her.
Your work is almost ended.

BOSOLA: Must I see her again?

FERDINAND: Yes.

BOSOLA: Never.

FERDINAND: You must.

BOSOLA: Never in mine own shape;
That's forfeited by my intelligence,
And this last cruel lie: when you send me next,
The business shall be comfort.

FERDINAND: Very likely;
Thy pity is nothing of kin to thee. Antonio
Lurks about Milan: thou shalt shortly thither,
To feed a fire as great as my revenge,
Which never will slack till it have spent his fuel:
Intemperate agues make physicians cruel.

They exit

Act IV, scene ii

Scene: same as before

Enter DUCHESS and CARIOLA

DUCHESS: What hideous noise was that?

CARIOLA: 'Tis the wild consort
Of madmen, lady, which your tyrant brother
Hath plac'd about your lodging: this tyranny,
I think, was never practic'd till this hour.

DUCHESS: Indeed, I thank him: nothing but noise and folly
Can keep me in my right wits; whereas reason
And silence make me stark mad. Sit down;
Discourse to me some dismal tragedy.

CARIOLA: O, 'twill increase your melancholy.

DUCHESS: Thou art dcceiv'd:
To hear of greater grief would lessen mine.
This is a prison?

CARIOLA: Yes, but you shall live
To shake this durance off.

DUCHESS: Thou art a fool:
The robin red-breast and the nightingale
Never live long in cages.

CARIOLA: Pray, dry your eyes:
What think you of, madam?

DUCHESS: Of nothing;
When I muse thus, I sleep.

CARIOLA: Like a madman, with your eyes open?

DUCHESS: Dost thou think we shall know one another
In th'other world?

CARIOLA: Yes, out of question.

DUCHESS: O, that it were possible we might
But hold some two days' conference with the dead!
From them I should learn somewhat, I am sure,
I never shall know here. I'll tell thee a miracle;

I am not mad yet, to my cause of sorrow:
Th' heaven o'er my head seems made of molten brass,
The earth of flaming sulphur, yet I am not mad.
I am acquainted with sad misery,
As the tann'd galley-slave is with his oar;
Necessity makes me suffer constantly,
And custom makes it easy. Whom do I look like now?

CARIOLA: Like to your picture in the gallery,
A deal of life in show, but none in practice;
Or rather like some reverend monument
Whose ruins are even pitied.

DUCHESS: Very proper;
And Fortune seems only to have her eyesight,
To behold my tragedy.
How now! What noise is that?

Enter SERVANT

SERVANT: I am come to tell you,
Your brother hath intended you some sport.
A great physician, when the pope was sick
Of a deep melancholy, presented him
With several sorts of madmen, which wild object
Being full of change and sport, forc'd him to laugh,
And so th' imposthume broke: the selfsame cure
The Duke intends on you.

DUCHESS: Let them come in.

Enter MADMEN

SERVANT: There's a mad lawyer; and a secular priest;
A doctor, that hath forfeited his wits
By jealousy; an astrologian
That in his works said, such a day o'th' month
Should be the day of doom, and failing of't,
Ran mad; an English tailor, craz'd i'th' brain
With the study of new fashion; a gentleman usher,
Quite beside himself with care to keep in mind
The number of his lady's salutations,
Or "How do you," she employ'd him in each morning;

A farmer too, an excellent knave in grain,
Mad 'cause he was hinder'd transportation;
And let one broker that's mad loose to these,
You'd think the devil were among them.

DUCHESS: Sit, Cariola. Let them loose when you please,
For I am chain'd to endure all your tyranny.

Here by a madman this song is sung, to a dismal kind of music.

O, let us howl some heavy note,
Some deadly dogged howl,
Sounding, as from the threatening throat
Of beasts and fatal fowl!
As ravens, screech-owls, bulls, and bears,
We'll bell, and bawl our parts,
Till irksome noise have cloy'd your ears,
And corrosiv'd your hearts.
At last, when as our quire wants breath,
Our bodies being blest,
We'll sing, like swans, to welcome death,
And die in love and rest.

MAD ASTROLOGER: Doomsday not come yet? I'll draw it nearer by a perspective, or make a glass that shall set all the world on fire upon an instant. I cannot sleep; my pillow is stuffed with a litter of porcupines.

MAD LAWYER: Hell is a mere glass-house, where the devils are continually blowing up women's souls on hollow irons, and the fire never goes out.

MAD PRIEST: I will lie with every woman in my parish the tenth night; I will tithe them over like haycocks.

MAD DOCTOR: Shall my 'pothecary outgo me, because I am a cuckold? I have found out his roguery; he makes alum of his wife's urine, and sells it to Puritans that have sore throats with overstraining.

MAD ASTROLOGER: I have skill in heraldry.

MAD LAWYER: Hast?

MAD ASTROLOGER: You do give for your crest a woodcock's head, with the brains picked out on't; you are a very ancient gentleman.

MAD PRIEST: Greek is turn'd Turk: we are only to be saved by the Helvetian translation.

MAD ASTROLOGER: Come on, sir, I will lay the law to you.

MAD LAWYER: O, rather lay a corrosive; the law will eat to the bone.

MAD PRIEST: He that drinks but to satisfy nature, is damn'd.

MAD DOCTOR: If I had my glass here, I would show a sight should make all the women here call me mad doctor.

MAD ASTROLOGER: What's he, a rope-maker?

MAD LAWYER: No, no, no, a snuffling knave, that while he shows the tombs, will have his hand in a wench's placket.

MAD PRIEST: Woe to the caroche, that brought home my wife from the mask at three a'clock in the morning! it had a large featherbed in it.

MAD DOCTOR: I have pared the devil's nails forty time, roasted them in ravens' eggs, and cur'd agues with them.

MAD PRIEST: Get me three hundred milch bats, to make possets to procure sleep.

MAD DOCTOR: All the college may throw their caps at me; I have made a soapboiler costive: it was my masterpiece.

Here the dance, consisting of eight madmen, with music answerable thereunto; after which, Bosola, like an old *man, enters*

DUCHESS: Is he mad too?

SERVANT: Pray question him. I'll leave you.

Exit all but the DUCHESS and BOSOLA

BOSOLA: I am come to make thy tomb.

DUCHESS: Ha! my tomb?
Thou speak'st, as if I lay upon my death-bed,
Gasping for breath: dost thou perceive me sick?

BOSOLA: Yes, and the more dangerously, since thy sickness

Is insensible.

DUCHESS: Thou art not mad, sure: dost thou know me?

BOSOLA: Yes.

DUCHESS: Who am I?

BOSOLA: Thou art a box of worm-seed, at best but a salvatory
Of green mummy. What's this flesh? a little cruded milk
Fantastical puff-paste. Our bodies are weaker than those
Paper-prisons boys use to keep flies in; more contemptible,
Since ours is to preserve earth-worms. Didst thou ever see
A lark in a cage? Such is the soul in the body: this world
Is like her little turf of grass, and the heaven o'er our heads,
Like her looking-glass, only gives us a miserable knowledge
Of the small compass of our prison.

DUCHESS: Am not I thy Duchess?

BOSOLA: Thou art some great woman, sure, for riot
Begins to sit on thy forehead (clad in gray hairs)
Twenty years sooner than on a merry milkmaid's.
Thou sleepest worse than if a mouse
Should be forced to take up her lodging in a cat's ear:
A little infant that breeds its teeth, should it lie with thee,
Would cry out, as if thou wert
The more unquiet bedfellow.

DUCHESS: I am Duchess of Malfi still.

BOSOLA: That makes thy sleep so broken:
Glories, like glowworms afar off shine bright,
But look'd to near, have neither heat nor light.

DUCHESS: Thou art very plain.

BOSOLA: My trade is to flatter the dead, not the living;
I am a tomb-maker.

DUCHESS: And thou com'st to make my tomb?

BOSOLA: Yes.

DUCHESS: Let me be a little merry:
Of what stuff wilt thou make it?

BOSOLA: Nay, resolve me first, of what fashion?

DUCHESS: Why, do we grow fantastical in our death-bed?
Do we affect fashion in the grave?

BOSOLA: Most ambitiously. Princes' images on their tombs
Do not lie, as they were wont, seeming to pray
Up to heaven; but with their hands under their cheeks,
As if they died of the tooth-ache: they are not carved
With their eyes fix'd upon the stars; but
As their minds were wholly bent upon the world,
The selfsame way they seem to turn their faces.

DUCHESS: Let me know fully therefore the effect
Of this thy dismal preparation,
This talk, fit for a charnel.

BOSOLA: Now I shall:

Enter Executioners with a coffin, cords, and a bell

Here is a present from your princely brothers,
And may it arrive welcome, for it brings
Last benefit, last sorrow.

DUCHESS: Let me see it:

I have so much obedience in my blood,
I wish it in their veins to do them good.

BOSOLA: This is your last presence chamber.

CARIOLA: O, my sweet lady!

DUCHESS: Peace; it affrights not me.

BOSOLA: I am the common bellman,
That usually is sent to condemn'd persons
The night before they suffer.

DUCHESS: Even now thou said'st
Thou wast a tomb-maker.

BOSOLA: 'Twas to bring you
By degrees to mortification. Listen:
Rings the bell
Hark, now everything is still,
The screech-owl, and the whistler shrill,
Call upon our dame aloud,
And bid her quickly don her shroud!
Much you had of land and rent;
Your length in clay's now competent:
A long war disturb'd your mind;
Here your perfect peace is sign'd.
Of what is't fools make such vain keeping?
Sin their conception, their birth weeping;
Their life a general mist of error,
Their death a hideous storm of terror.
Strew your hair with powders sweet,
Don clean linen, bathe your feet,
And (the foul fiend more to check)
A crucifix let bless your neck:
'Tis now full tide 'tween night and day;
End your groan, and come away.

CARIOLA: Hence, villains, tyrants, murderers! alas!
What will you do with my lady? Call for help.

DUCHESS: To whom, to our next neighbours? they are mad-folks.

BOSOLA: Remove that noise.

DUCHESS: Farewell, Cariola.
In my last will, I have not much to give:
A many hungry guests have fed upon me;
Thine will be a poor reversion.

CARIOLA: I will die with her.

DUCHESS: I pray thee, look thou giv'st my little boy
Some syrup for his cold, and let the girl
Say her prayers ere she sleep.

CARIOLA is forced out
Now what you please: What death?

BOSOLA: Strangling; here are your executioners.

DUCHESS: I forgive them:
The apoplexy, catarrh, or cough o'th' lungs,
Would do as much as they do.

BOSOLA: Doth not death fright you?

DUCHESS: Who would be afraid on't,
Knowing to meet such excellent company
In th' other world?

BOSOLA: Yet, methinks,
The manner of your death should much afflict you;
This cord should terrify you?

DUCHESS: Not a whit:
What would it pleasure me to have my throat cut
With diamonds? or to be smothered
With cassia? or to be shot to death with pearls?
I know death hath ten thousand several doors
For men to take their exits; and 'tis found
They go on such strange geometrical hinges,
You may open them both ways: any way, for heaven sake,
So I were out of your whispering. Tell my brothers,
That I perceive death, now I am well awake,
Best gift is they can give, or I can take.
I would fain put off my last woman's fault,
I'd not be tedious to you.

EXECUTIONERS: We are ready.

DUCHESS: Dispose my breath how please you, but my body
Bestow upon my women, will you?

EXECUTIONERS: Yes.

DUCHESS: Pull, and pull strongly, for your able strength,
Must pull down heaven upon me:
Yet stay, heaven gates are not so highly arch'd
As princes' palaces; they that enter there,
Must go upon their knees. Come, violent death,
Serve for mandragora, to make me sleep:
Go, tell my brothers, when I am laid out,
They then may feed in quiet.

They strangle her

BOSOLA: Where's the waiting-woman?
Fetch her: some other strangle the children.

Enter CARIOLA

Look you, there sleeps your mistress.

CARIOLA: O, you are damn'd
Perpetually for this! My turn is next;
Is't not so order'd?

BOSOLA: Yes, and I am glad
You are so well prepar'd for't.

CARIOLA: You are deceiv'd, sir,
I am not prepared for't; I will not die:
I will first come to my answer, and know
How I have offended.

BOSOLA: Come, dispatch her.
You kept her counsel, now you shall keep ours.

CARIOLA: I will not die, I must not; I am contracted
To a young gentleman.

EXECUTIONERS: Here's your wedding-ring.

CARIOLA: Let me but speak with the duke; I'll discover
Treason to his person.

BOSOLA: Delays: throttle her.

EXECUTIONERS: She bites and scratches.

CARIOLA: If you kill me now,
I am damn'd; I have not been at confession
This two years.

BOSOLA: When?

CARIOLA: I am quick with child.

BOSOLA: Why then,
Your credit's sav'd.
They strangle her
Bear her into the next room;
Let this lie still.

Enter FERDINAND

FERDINAND: Is she dead?

BOSOLA: She is what
You'd have her. But here begin your pity:
Shows the children strangled
Alas! how have these offended?

FERDINAND: The death
Of young wolves is never to be pitied.

BOSOLA: Fix your eye here.

FERDINAND: Constantly.

BOSOLA: Do you not weep?
Other sins only speak; murder shrieks out:
The element of water moistens the earth,
But blood flies upwards and bedews the heavens.

FERDINAND: Cover her face; mine eyes dazzle: she died young.

BOSOLA: I think not so; her infelicity

Seem'd to have years too many.

FERDINAND: She and I were twins;
And should I die this instant, I had liv'd
Her time to a minute.

BOSOLA: It seems she was born first:
You have bloodily approv'd the ancient truth,
That kindred commonly do worse agree
Than remote strangers.

FERDINAND: Let me see her face again.
Why didst not thou pity her? what an excellent
Honest man might'st thou have been
If thou hadst born her to some sanctuary;
Or, bold in a good cause, oppos'd thyself,
With thy advanced sword above thy head,
Between her innocence and my revenge.
I had thee, when I was distracted of my wits,
Go kill my dearest friend, and thou hast done't.
For let me but examine well the cause:
What was the meanness of her match to me?
Only I must confess I had a hope,
Had she continu'd widow, to have gain'd
An infinite mass of treasure by her death;
And that was the main cause — her marriage!
That drew a stream of gall quite through my heart.
For thee, as we observe in tragedies
That a good actor many times is curs'd
For playing a villain's part, I hate thee for't,
And for my sake say thou hast done much ill, well.

BOSOLA: Let me quicken your memory, for I perceive
You are falling into ingratitude; I challenge
The reward due to my service.

FERDINAND: I'll tell thee
What I'll give thee.

BOSOLA: Do.

FERDINAND: I'll give thee a pardon
For this murder.

BOSOLA: Ha!

FERDINAND: Yes, and 'tis
The largest bounty I can study to do thee.
By what authority didst thou execute
This bloody sentence?

BOSOLA: By yours.

FERDINAND: Mine? Was I her judge?
Did any ceremonial form of law,
Doom her to not being? Did a complete jury
Deliver her conviction up i'th' court?
Where shalt thou find this judgment register'd,
Unless in hell? See, like a bloody fool,
Th' hast forfeited thy life, and thou shalt die for't.

BOSOLA: The office of justice is perverted quite,
When one thief hangs another. Who shall dare
To reveal this?

FERDINAND: O, I'll tell thee;
The wolf shall find her grave, and scrape it up,
Not to devour the corpse, but to discover
The horrid murder.

BOSOLA: You, not I, shall quake for't.

FERDINAND: Leave me.

BOSOLA: I will first receive my pension.

FERDINAND: You are a villain.

BOSOLA: When your ingratitude
Is judge, I am so.

FERDINAND: O horror!
That not the fear of him, which binds the devils,
Can prescribe man obedience.
Never look upon me more.

BOSOLA: Why, fare thee well:
Your brother and yourself are worthy men:
You have a pair of hearts are hollow graves,
Rotten, and rotting others; and your vengeance,
Like two chain'd bullets, still goes arm in arm.
You may be brothers; for treason, like the plague,
Doth take much in a blood. I stand like one
That long hath ta'en a sweet and golden dream:
I am angry with myself, now that I wake.

FERDINAND: Get thee into some unknown part o'th' world,
That I may never see thee.

BOSOLA: Let me know
Wherefore I should be thus neglected? Sir,
I serv'd your tyranny, and rather strove,
To satisfy yourself, than all the world:
And though I loath'd the evil, yet I lov'd
You that did counsel it; and rather sought
To appear a true servant, than an honest man.

FERDINAND: I'll go hunt the badger by owl-light:
'Tis a deed of darkness.

Exit

BOSOLA: He's much distracted. Off, my painted honour!
While with vain hopes our faculties we tire,
We seem to sweat in ice and freeze in fire.
What would I do, were this to do again?
I would not change my peace of conscience
For all the wealth of Europe. She stirs; here's life:
Return, fair soul, from darkness, and lead mine
Out of this sensible hell: She's warm, she breathes:
Upon thy pale lips I will melt my heart,
To store them with fresh colour. Who's there?
Some cordial drink! Alas! I dare not call:
So pity would destroy pity. Her eye opes,
And heaven in it seems to ope, that late was shut,
To take me up to mercy.

DUCHESS: Antonio!

BOSOLA: Yes, madam, he is living;
The dead bodies you saw, were but feign'd statues;
He's reconcil'd to your brothers; the Pope hath wrought
The atonement.

DUCHESS: Mercy!

She dies

BOSOLA: O, she's gone again! there the cords of life broke.

O, sacred innocence, that sweetly sleeps
On turtles' feathers, whilst a guilty conscience
Is a black register, wherein is writ

All our good deeds and bad, a perspective
That shows us hell! That we cannot be suffer'd
To do good when we have a mind to it!
This is manly sorrow;
These tears, I am very certain, never grew
In my mother's milk. My estate is sunk
Below the degree of fear: where were
These penitent fountains, while she was living?
O, they were frozen up! Here is a sight
As direful to my soul, as is the sword
Unto a wretch hath slain his father. Come,
I'll bear thee hence,
And execute thy last will; that's deliver
Thy body to the reverend dispose
Of some good women: that, the cruel tyrant
Shall not deny me. Then I'll post to Milan,
Where somewhat I will speedily enact
Worth my dejection.

Exit

Act V, scene i

Rome, a few months later

Enter ANTONIO and DELIO

ANTONIO: What think you of my hope of reconcilement
To the Aragonian brethren?

DELIO: I misdoubt it;
For though they have sent letter of safe conduct
For your repair to Milan, they appear
But nets to entrap you. The Marquis of Pescara,
Under whom you hold certain land in cheat,
Much 'gainst his noble nature hath been mov'd
To seize those lands, and some of his dependents
Are at this instant making it their suit

To be invested in your revenues.
I cannot think they mean well to your life,
That do deprive you of your means of life,
Your living.

ANTONIO: You are still an heretic
To any safety I can shape myself.

DELIO: Here comes the marquis: I will make myself
Petitioner for some part of your land,
To know whither it is flying.

ANTONIO: I pray do.

Enter PESCARA

DELIO: Sir, I have a suit to you.

PESCARA: To me?

DELIO: An easy one:
There is the citadel of St. Bennet,
With some demesnes, of late in the possession
Of Antonio Bologna; please you bestow them on me.

PESCARA: You are my friend; but this is such a suit,
Nor fit for me to give, nor you to take.

DELIO: No, sir?

PESCARA: I will give you ample reason for't,
Soon in private: here's the cardinal's mistress.

Enter JULIA

JULIA: My lord, I am grown your poor petitioner,
And should be an ill beggar, had I not
A great man's letter here, the cardinal's,
To court you in my favour.

PESCARA: He entreats for you
The citadel of St. Bennet, that belong'd
To the banish'd Bologna.

JULIA: Yes.

PESCARA: I could not have thought of a friend I could rather
Pleasure with it: 'tis yours.

JULIA: Sir, I thank you;
And he shall know how doubly I am engag'd
Both in your gift, and speediness of giving,
Which makes your grant the greater.

She exits

ANTONIO: [*aside*] How they fortify
Themselves with my ruin!

DELIO: Sir, I am
Little bound to you.

PESCARA: Why?

DELIO: Because you denied this suit to me, and gave't
To such a creature.

PESCARA: Do you know what it was?
It was Antonio's land; not forfeited
By course of law, but ravish'd from his throat
By the cardinal's entreaty: it were not fit
I should bestow so main a piece of wrong
Upon my friend; 'tis a gratification
Only due to a strumpet, for it is injustice.
Shall I sprinkle the pure blood of innocents
To make those followers I call my friends
Look ruddier upon me? I am glad
This land, ta'en from the owner by such a wrong,
Returns again unto so foul an use,
As salary for his lust. Learn, good Delio,
To ask noble things of me, and you shall find
I'll be a noble giver.

DELIO: You instruct me well.

ANTONIO: [*aside*] Why, here's a man now, would fright impudence
From sauciest beggars.

PESCARA: Prince Ferdinand's come to Milan,
Sick, as they give out, of an apoplexy;

But some say, 'tis a frenzy: I am going
To visit him.

He exits

ANTONIO: 'Tis a noble old fellow.

DELIO: What course do you mean to take, Antonio?

ANTONIO: This night I mean to venture all my fortune,
Which is no more than a poor lingering life,
To the cardinal's worst of malice. I have got
Private access to his chamber; and intend
To visit him about the mid of night,
As once his brother did our noble duchess.
It may be that the sudden apprehension
Of danger, for I'll go in mine own shape,
When he shall see it fright with love and duty,
May draw the poison out of him, and work
A friendly reconcilement: if it fail,
Yet is shall rid me of this infamous calling;
For better fall once, than be ever falling.

DELIO: I'll second you in all danger, and, howe'er;
My life keeps rank with yours.

ANTONIO: You are still my lov'd and best friend.

They exit

Act V, scene ii

The CARDINAL'S palace in Rome

Enter PESCARA and DOCTOR

PESCARA: Now, doctor, may I visit your patient?

DOCTOR: If't please your lordship: but he's instantly
To take the air here in the gallery
By my direction.

PESCARA: Pray thee, what's his disease?

DOCTOR: A very pestilent disease, my lord,
They call lycanthropia.

PESCARA: What's that?
I need a dictionary to't.

DOCTOR: I'll tell you.
In those that are possess'd with't there o'erflows
Such melancholy humour, they imagine
Themselves to be transformed into wolves;
Steal forth to churchyards in the dead of night,
And dig dead bodies up: as two nights since
One met the Duke 'bout midnight in a lane
Behind St. Mark's Church, with the leg of a man
Upon his shoulder, and he howl'd fearfully;
Said he was a wolf, only the difference
Was, a wolf's skin was hairy on the outside,
His on the inside; bade them take their swords,
Rip up his flesh, and try: straight, I was sent for,
And having minister'd unto him, found his grace
Very well recover'd.

PESCARA: I am glad on't.

DOCTOR: Yet not without some fear
Of a relapse. If he grow to his fit again,
I'll go a nearer way to work with him
Than ever Paracelsus dream'd of; if
They'll give me leave, I'll buffet his madness out of him.

Stand aside; he comes.

Enter FERDINAND, MALATESTE, CARDINAL, and BOSOLA

FERDINAND: Leave me.

MALATESTE: Why doth your lordship love this solitariness?

FERDINAND: Eagles commonly fly alone: they are crows,
Daws, and starlings that flock together. Look,
What's that follows me?

MALATESTE: Nothing, my lord.

FERDINAND: Yes.

MALATESTE: 'Tis your shadow.

FERDINAND: Stay it; let it not haunt me.

MALATESTE: Impossible, if you move, and the sun shine.

FERDINAND: I will throttle it.

MALATESTE: O, my lord, you are angry with nothing.

FERDINAND: You are a fool:
How is't possible I should catch my shadow,
Unless I fall upon't? When I go to hell,
I mean to carry a bribe; for, look you,
Good gifts evermore make way for the worst persons.

PESCARA: Rise, good my lord.

FERDINAND: I am studying the art of patience.

PESCARA: 'Tis a noble virtue.

FERDINAND: To drive six snails before me from this town
To Moscow; neither use goad nor whip to them,
But let them take their own time; (the patient'st man i'th' world
Match me for an experiment) and I'll crawl
After like a sheep-biter.

CARDINAL: Force him up.

FERDINAND: Use me well, you were best.
What I have done, I have done: I'll confess nothing.

DOCTOR: Now let me come to him. Are you mad,
My lord, are you out of your princely wits?

FERDINAND: What's he?

PESCARA: Your doctor.

FERDINAND: Let me have his beard saw'd off,
And his eyebrows fil'd more civil.

DOCTOR: I must do mad tricks with him, for that's the only way on't.- I have brought your grace a salamander's

skin, to keep you
From sun-burning.

FERDINAND: I have cruel sore eyes.

DOCTOR: The white of a cockatrix's egg is present remedy.

FERDINAND: Let it be new-laid one, you were best.
Hide me from him: physicians are like kings,
They brook no contradiction.

DOCTOR: Now he begins to fear me:
Now let me be alone with him.

FERDINAND tries to undress, but they seize him

CARDINAL: How now? Put off your gown?

DOCTOR: Let me have
Some forty urinals filled with rose-water:
He and I'll go pelt one another with them.
Now he begins to fear me. Can you fetch a frisk, sir?
Let him go, let him go upon my peril:
I find by his eye he stands in awe of me;
I'll make him as tame as a dormouse.

FERDINAND: Can you fetch your frisks, sir! I will stamp him
Into a cullis, flay off his skin, to cover one of the anatomies
This rogue hath set i'th' cold yonder in Barber-Chirugeon's-hall.
Hence, hence! you are all of you like beasts for sacrifice:
There's nothing left of you, but tongue and belly,
Flattery and lechery.

FERDINAND runs off

PESCARA: Doctor, he did not fear you thoroughly.

DOCTOR: True; I was somewhat too forward.

BOSOLA: Mercy upon me, what a fatal judgement
Hath fall'n upon this Ferdinand!

PESCARA: Knows your grace
What accident hath brought unto the prince
This strange distraction?

CARDINAL: [*aside*] I must feign somewhat— Thus they say it grew:
You have heard it rumour'd for these many years,
None of our family dies but there is seen
The shape of an old woman, which is given
By tradition to us to have been murder'd
By her nephews, for her riches. Such a figure
One night, as the prince sat up late at's book,
Appear'd to him; when, crying out for help,
The gentleman of's chamber, found his grace
All on a cold sweat, alter'd much in face
And language: since which apparition,
He hath grown worse and worse, and I much fear
He cannot live.

BOSOLA: Sit, I would speak with you.

PESCARA: We'll leave your grace,
Wishing to the sick prince, our noble lord,
All health of mind and body.

CARDINAL: You are most welcome.

Exit all but CARDINAL and BOSOLA

Are you come? so. [*aside*] This fellow must not know
By any means I had intelligence
In our duchess' death; for though I counsell'd it,
The full of all th' engagement seem'd to grow
From Ferdinand— Now, sir, how fares our sister?
I do not think but sorrow makes her look
Like to an oft-dy'd garment: she shall now
Taste comfort from me. Why do you look so wildly?
O, the fortune of your master here, the prince,
Dejects you; but be you of happy comfort:
If you'll do one thing for me, I'll entreat,
Though he had a cold tombstone o'er his bones,
I'd make you what you would be.

BOSOLA: Anything,
Give it me in a breath, and fly to't:
They that think long, small expedition win,
For musing much o'th' end, cannot begin.

Enter JULIA

JULIA: Sir, will you come in to supper?

CARDINAL: I am busy; leave me.

JULIA: [*aside*] What an excellent shape hath that fellow!

Exits

CARDINAL: 'Tis thus. Antonio lurks here in Milan:
Enquire him out, and kill him. While he lives,
Our sister cannot marry, and I have thought
Of an excellent match for her. Do this, and style me
Thy advancement.

BOSOLA: But by what means shall I find him out?

CARDINAL: There is a gentleman call'd Delio,
Here in the camp, that hath been long approv'd
His loyal friend. Set eye upon that fellow;
Follow him to mass; maybe Antonio,
Although he do account religion
But a school-name, for fashion of the world
May accompany him; or else go enquire out
Delio's confessor, and see if you can bribe
Him to reveal it. There are a thousand ways
A man might find to trace him; as to know
What fellows haunt the Jews, for taking up
Great sums of money, for sure he's in want;
Or else to go to th' picture-makers, and learn
Who bought her picture lately: some of these
Happily may take.

BOSOLA: Well, I'll not freeze i'th' business:
I would see that wretched thing, Antonio,
Above all sights i'th' world.

CARDINAL: Do, and be happy.

Exits

BOSOLA: This fellow doth breed basilisks in's eyes,
He's nothing else but murder; yet he seems
Not to have notice of the duchess' death.
'Tis his cunning: I must follow his example;
There cannot be a surer way to trace
Than that of an old fox.

Enter JULIA with a gun

JULIA: So, sir, you are well met.

BOSOLA: How now?

JULIA: Nay, the doors are fast enough:
Now, sir, I will make you confess your treachery.

BOSOLA: Treachery!

JULIA: Yes, confess to me
Which of my women 'twas you hired to put
Love-powder into my drink?

BOSOLA: Love-powder?

JULIA: Yes, when I was at Malfi.
Why should I fall in love with such a face else?
I have already suffer'd for thee so much pain,
The only remedy to do me good,
Is to kill my longing.

BOSOLA: Sure your pistol holds
Nothing but perfumes, or kissing-comforts. Excellent lady!
You have a pretty way on't to discover
Your longing. Come, come, I'll disarm you,
And arm you thus: yet this is wondrous strange.

JULIA: Compare thy form and my eyes together,
You'll find my love no such great miracle. Now you'll say
I am wanton: this nice modesty in ladies
Is but a troublesome familiar
That haunts them.

BOSOLA: Know you me, I am a blunt soldier.

JULIA: The better;
Sure, there wants fire, where there are no lively sparks
Of roughness.

BOSOLA: And I want compliment.

JULIA: Why, ignorance in courtship cannot make you do amiss,
If you have a heart to do well.

BOSOLA: You are very fair.

JULIA: Nay, if you lay beauty to my charge,
I must plead unguilty.

BOSOLA: Your bright eyes
Carry a quiver of darts in them, sharper
Than sun-beams.

JULIA: You will mar me with commendation,
Put yourself to the charge of courting me,
Whereas now I woo you.

BOSOLA: [*aside*] I have it; I will work upon this creature—
Let us grow most amorously familiar:
If the great cardinal should see me thus,
Would he not count me a villain?

JULIA: No, he might count me a wanton,
Not lay a scruple of offence on you;
For if I see, and steal a diamond,
The fault is not i'th' stone, but in me the thief
That purloins it. I am sudden with you:
We that are great women of pleasure, use to cut off
These uncertain wishes and unquiet longings,
And in an instant join the sweet delight
And the pretty excuse together. Had you been i'th' street,
Under my chamber window, even there
I should have courted you.

BOSOLA: O, you are an excellent lady!

JULIA: Bid me do somewhat for you presently,
To express I love you.

BOSOLA: I will, and if you love me,
Fail not to effect it. The cardinal is grown wondrous melancholy:
Demand the cause, let him not put you off
With feign'd excuse; discover the main ground on't.

JULIA: Why would you know this?

BOSOLA: I have depended on him,
And I hear that he is fall'n in some disgrace
With the emperor; if he be, like the mice
That forsake falling houses, I would shift
To other dependence.

JULIA: You shall not need follow the wars:

I'll be your maintenance.

BOSOLA: And I your loyal servant;
But I cannot leave my calling.

JULIA: Not leave
An ungrateful general, for the love of a sweet lady?
You are like some cannot sleep in feather-beds,
But must have blocks for their pillows.

BOSOLA: Will you do this?

JULIA: Cunningly.

BOSOLA: Tomorrow, I'll expect th'intelligence.

JULIA: Tomorrow! Get you into my cabinet;
You shall have it with you. Do not delay me,
No more than I do you: I am like one
That is condemn'd; I have my pardon promis'd,
But I would see it seal'd. Go, get you in:
You shall see me wind my tongue about his heart,
Like a skein of silk.

Exit Bosola

Enter CARDINAL and SERVANTS

CARDINAL: Where are you?

SERVANTS: Here.

CARDINAL: Let none, upon your lives

Have conference with the prince Ferdinand,
Unless I know it.

Exit servants

In this distraction, he may reveal the murder.
Yond's my lingering consumption:
I am weary of her, and by any means
Would be quit of.

JULIA: How now, my lord, what ails you?

CARDINAL: Nothing.

JULIA: O, you are much alter'd!
Come, I must be your secretary, and remove
This lead from off your bosom: what's the matter?

CARDINAL: I may not tell you.

JULIA: Are you so far in love with sorrow,
You cannot part with part of it? or think you
I cannot love your grace when you are sad
As well as merry? or do you suspect
I, that have been a secret to your heart
These many winters, cannot be the same
Unto your tongue?

CARDINAL: Satisfy thy longing:
The only way to make thee keep my counsel
Is not to tell thee.

JULIA: Tell your echo this,
Or flatterers, that like echoes still report
What they hear though most imperfect, and not me;
For, if that you be true unto yourself,
I'll know.

CARDINAL: Will you rack me?

JULIA: No, judgment shall
Draw it from you: it is an equal fault,
To tell one's secrets unto all or none.

CARDINAL: The first argues folly.

JULIA: But the last tyranny.

CARDINAL: Very well; why, imagine I have committed
Some secret deed, which I desire the world
May not hear of.

JULIA: Therefore may not I know it?
You have conceal'd for me as great a sin
As adultery. Sir, never was occasion
For perfect trial of my constancy
Till now: sir, I beseech you-

CARDINAL: You'll repent it.

JULIA: Never.

CARDINAL: It hurries thee to ruin: I'll not tell thee.
Be well advis'd, and think what danger 'tis
To receive a prince's secrets: they that do,
Had need have their breasts hoop'd with adamant
To contain them. I pray thee yet be satisfied;
Examine thine own frailty; 'tis more easy
To tie knots, than unloose them: 'tis a secret
That, like a lingering poison, may chance lie
Spread in thy veins, and kill thee seven year hence.

JULIA: Now you dally with me.

CARDINAL: No more, thou shalt know it.
By my appointment, the great Duchess of Malfi,
And two of her young children, four nights since,
Were strangl'd.

JULIA: O heaven! sir, what have you done?

CARDINAL: How now! how settles this? think you
Your bosom will be a grave dark and obscure enough
For such a secret?

JULIA: You have undone yourself, sir.

CARDINAL: Why?

JULIA: It lies not in me to conceal it.

CARDINAL: No! Come, I will swear you to't upon this book.

JULIA: Most religiously.

CARDINAL: Kiss it.
Now you shall never utter it; thy curiosity
Hath undone thee: thou art poison'd with that book;
Because I knew thou couldst not keep my counsel,
I have bound thee to't by death.

Enter BOSOLA

BOSOLA: For pity sake, hold.

CARDINAL: Ha, Bosola!

JULIA: I forgive you
This equal piece of justice you have done;
For I betray'd your counsel to that fellow:
He overheard it; that was the cause I said
It lay not in me to conceal it.

BOSOLA: O, foolish woman,

Couldst not thou have poison'd him?

JULIA: 'Tis weakness,
Too much to think what should have been done.
I go, I know not whither.

Dies

CARDINAL: Wherefore com'st thou hither?

BOSOLA: That I might find a great man, like yourself,
Not out of his wits, as the Lord Ferdinand,
To remember my service.

CARDINAL: I'll have thee hew'd in pieces.

BOSOLA: Make not yourself such a promise of that life,
Which is not yours to dispose of.

CARDINAL: Who plac'd thee here?

BOSOLA: Her lust, as she intended.

CARDINAL: Very well: now you know me
For your fellow-murderer.

BOSOLA: And wherefore should you lay your fair marble colours
Upon your rotten purposes to me?
Unless you imitate some that do plot great treasons,
And when they have done, go hide themselves i'th' graves
Of those were actors in't?

CARDINAL: No more;
There is a fortune attends thee.

BOSOLA: Shall I go sue to fortune any longer?

'Tis the fool's pilgrimage.

CARDINAL: I have honours in store for thee.

BOSOLA: There are a many ways that conduct to seeming
Honour, and some of them very dirty ones.

CARDINAL: Throw to the devil
Thy melancholy. The fire burns well;
What need we keep a stirring of't, and make
A greater smother? thou wilt kill Antonio?

BOSOLA: Yes.

CARDINAL: Take up that body.

BOSOLA: I think I shall
Shortly grow the common bier for church-yards.

CARDINAL: I will allow thee some dozen of attendants,
To aid thee in the murder.

BOSOLA: O, by no means.
Physicians that apply horseleeches to any rank swelling,
Use to cut off their tails, that the blood may run through them
The faster: let me have no train when I go to shed blood,
Lest it make me have a greater when I ride to the gallows.

CARDINAL: Come to me after midnight, to help to remove that body
To her own lodging: I'll give out she died o'th' plague;
'Twill breed the less enquiry after her death.

BOSOLA: Where's Castruchio, her husband?

CARDINAL: He's rode to Naples, to take possession
Of Antonio's citadel.

BOSOLA: Believe me, you have done a very happy turn.

CARDINAL: Fail not to come: there is the master-key
Of our lodgings; and by that you may conceive
What trust I plant in you.

BOSOLA: You shall find me ready.

Exit CARDINAL

O, poor, Antonio, though nothing be so needful
To thy estate, as pity, yet I find
Nothing so dangerous! I must look to my footing:
In such slippery ice-pavements, men had need
To be frost-nail'd well, they may break their necks else;
The precedent's here afore me. How this man
Bears up in blood! seems fearless! why, 'tis well:
Security some men call the suburbs of hell,
Only a dead wall between. Well, good Antonio,
I'll seek thee out; and all my cares shall be
To put thee into safety from the reach
Of these most cruel biters, that have got
Some of thy blood already. It may be,

I'll join with thee, in a most just revenge:
The weakest arm is strong enough, that strikes
With the sword of justice. Still methinks the duchess
Haunts me: there, there!- 'tis nothing but my melancholy.

O Penitence, let me truly taste thy cup,
That throws men down, only to raise them up!

Exits

Act V, scene iii

A church graveyard

Enter ANTONIO and DELIO

DELIO: Yond's the cardinal's window. This fortification
Grew from the ruins of an ancient abbey;

And to yond' side o'th' river lies a wall,
Piece of a cloister, which in my opinion
Gives the best echo that you ever heard,
So hollow and so dismal, and withal
So plain in the distinction of our words,
That many have suppos'd it is a spirit
That answers.

ANTONIO: I do love these ancient ruins.
We never tread upon them, but we set
Our foot upon some reverend history:
And, questionless, here in this open court,
Which now lies naked to the injuries
Of stormy weather, some men lie interr'd
Lov'd the church so well, and gave so largely to't,
They thought it should have canopied their bones
Till doom's-day; but all things have their end:
Churches and cities, which have diseases like to men,
Must have like death that we have.

ECHO: Like death that we have.

DELIO: Now the echo hath caught you.

ANTONIO: It groan'd, methought, and gave
A very deadly accent.

ECHO: Deadly accent.

DELIO: I told you 'twas a pretty one: you may make it
A huntsman, or a falconer, a musician,
Or a thing of sorrow.

ECHO: A thing of sorrow.

ANTONIO: Ay sure, that suits it best.

ECHO: That suits it best.

ANTONIO: 'Tis very like my wife's voice.

ECHO: Ay, wife's voice.

DELIO: Come, let us walk farther from't.
I would not have you go to th' cardinal's tonight:
Do not.

ECHO: Do not.

DELIO: Wisdom doth not more moderate wasting sorrow,
Than time: take time for't: be mindful of thy safety.

ECHO: Be mindful of thy safety.

ANTONIO: Necessity compels me.
Make scrutiny throughout the passes
Of your own life, you'll find it impossible
To fly your fate.

ECHO: O fly your fate!

DELIO: Hark! the dead stones seem to have pity on you,
And give you good counsel.

ANTONIO: Echo, I will not talk with thee,
For thou art a dead thing.

ECHO: Thou art a dead thing.

ANTONIO: My duchess is asleep now,
And her little ones, I hope sweetly: O heaven,
Shall I never see her more?

ECHO: Never see her more.

ANTONIO: I mark'd not one repetition of the echo
But that; and on the sudden, a clear light
Presented me a face folded in sorrow.

DELIO: Your fancy merely.

ANTONIO: Come, I'll be out of this ague,
For to live thus is not indeed to live;
It is a mockery and abuse of life:
I will not henceforth save myself by halves;
Lose all, or nothing.

DELIO: Your own virtue save you.
I'll fetch your eldest son, and second you:
It may be that the sight of his own blood
Spread in so sweet a figure, may beget
The more compassion.

However, fare you well.
Though in our miseries fortune have a part,
Yet in our noble sufferings she hath none;
Contempt of pain, that we may call our own.

They exit

Act V, scene iv

The CARDINAL'S palace

Enter CARDINAL, PESCARA, MALATESTE, RODERIGO, GRISOLAN

CARDINAL: You shall not watch tonight by the sick prince;
His grace is very well recover'd.

MALATESTE: Good, my lord, suffer us.

CARDINAL: O, by no means:
The noise and change of object in his eye
Doth more distract him: I pray, all to bed;
And though you hear him in his violent fit,
Do not rise, I entreat you.

PESCARA: So, sir; we shall not.

CARDINAL: Nay, I must have you promise
Upon your honours, for I was enjoin'd to't
By himself; and he seem'd to urge it sensibly.

PESCARA: Let our honours bind this trifle.

CARDINAL: Nor any of your followers.

MALATESTE: Neither.

CARDINAL: It may be, to make trial of your promise,
When he's asleep, myself will rise and feign
Some of his mad tricks, and cry out for help,
And feign myself in danger.

MALATESTE: If your throat were cutting,
I'd not come at you, now I have protested against it.

CARDINAL: Why, I thank you.

GRISOLAN: 'Twas a foul storm tonight.

RODERIGO: The Lord Ferdinand's chamber shook like an osier.

MALATESTE: 'Twas nothing but pure kindness in the devil,
To rock his own child.

Exit all but the Cardinal

CARDINAL: The reason why I would not suffer these
About my brother, is because at midnight
I may with better privacy convey
Julia's body to her own lodging. O, my conscience!
I would pray now; but the devil takes away my heart
For having any confidence in prayer.
About this hour I appointed Bosola
To fetch the body: when he hath served my turn,
He dies.

Exit CARDINAL, enter BOSOLA

BOSOLA: Ha! 'twas the cardinal's voice; I heard him name
Bosola, and my death: listen, I hear one's footing.

Enter FERDINAND

FERDINAND: Strangling is a very quiet death.

BOSOLA: [*aside*] Nay then, I see I must stand upon my guard.

FERDINAND: What say to that? whisper softly; do you agree to't?
So, it must be done i'th' dark; the Cardinal
Would not for a thousand pounds the doctor should see it.

Exit

BOSOLA: My death is plotted; here's the consequence of murder.
We value not desert nor Christian breath,
When we know black deeds must be cur'd with death.

Enter SERVANT and ANTONIO

SERVANT: Here stay, sir, and be confident, I pray:
I'll fetch you a dark lantern.

Exit

ANTONIO: Could I take him at his prayers,
There were hope of pardon.

BOSOLA: Fall right my sword:
I'll not give thee so much leisure as to pray.

ANTONIO: O, I am gone! Thou hast ended a long suit
In a minute.

BOSOLA: What art thou?

ANTONIO: A most wretched thing,
That only have the benefit in death,
To appear myself.

Enter SERVANT with a light

SERVANT: Where are you, sir?

ANTONIO: Very near my home. Bosola?

SERVANT: O, misfortune!

BOSOLA: Smother thy pity, thou art dead else. Antonio?
The man I would have sav'd 'bove mine own life!
We are merely the stars' tennis balls, struck and banded
Which way please them. O good Antonio,
I'll whisper one thing in thy dying ear,
Shall make thy heart break quickly. Thy fair duchess
And two sweet children—

ANTONIO: Their very names
Kindle a little life in me.

BOSOLA: —are murder'd.

ANTONIO: Some men have wish'd to die
At the hearing of sad tidings; I am glad
That I shall do't in sadness. I would not now
Wish my wounds balm'd nor heal'd, for I have no use
To put my life to. In all our quest of greatness,

Like wanton boys, whose pastime is their care,
We follow after bubbles blown in th' air.
Pleasure of life, what is't? only the good hours
Of an ague; merely a preparative to rest,
To endure vexation. I do not ask
The process of my death; only commend me
To Delio.

BOSOLA: Break, heart!

ANTONIO: And let my son fly the courts of princes.

Dies

BOSOLA: Thou seem'st to have lov'd Antonio?

SERVANT: I brought him hither,
To have reconcil'd him to the Cardinal.

BOSOLA: I do not ask thee that:
Take him up, if thou tender thy own life,
And bear him where the lady Julia
Was want to lodge. O my fate moves swift!
I have this Cardinal in the forge already,
Now I'll bring him to th' hammer. O direful misprision!
I will not imitate things glorious,
No more than base; I'll be mine own example.-
On, on, and look thou represent, for silence,
The thing thou bear'st.

They exit with the body

Act V, scene v

The CARDINAL'S apartments

Enter CARDINAL, with a book

CARDINAL: I am puzzled in a question about hell:
He says, in hell there's one material fire,
And yet it shall not burn all men alike.
Lay him by. How tedious is a guilty conscience!
When I look into the fish-ponds in my garden,
Methinks I see a thing arm'd with a rake,
That seems to strike at me.

Enter BOSOLA and SERVANT

Now, art thou come? thou look'st ghastly;
There sits in thy face some great determination,
Mix'd with some fear.

BOSOLA: Thus it lightens into action:
I am come to kill thee.

CARDINAL: Ha! help! our guard!

BOSOLA: Thou art deceiv'd;
They are out of thy howling.

CARDINAL: Hold; and I will faithfully divide

Revenues with thee.

BOSOLA: Thy prayers and proffers
Are both unseasonable.

CARDINAL: Raise the watch: we are betray'd!

BOSOLA: I have confin'd your flight:
I'll suffer your retreat to Julia's chamber,
But no further.

CARDINAL: Help! we are betray'd!

Enter MALATESTE, PESCARA, RODERIGO, and GRISOLAN, above

MALATESTE: Listen.

CARDINAL: My dukedom for rescue!

RODERIGO: Fie upon his counterfeiting.

MALATESTE: Why, 'tis not the Cardinal.

RODERIGO: Yes, yes, 'tis he:
But I'll see him hang'd ere I'll go down to him.

CARDINAL: Here's a plot upon me; I am assaulted! I am lost
Unless some rescue!

GRISOLAN: He doth this pretty well;
But it will not serve to laugh me out of mine honour.

CARDINAL: The sword's at my throat!

RODERIGO: You would not bawl so loud then.

MALATESTE: Come, come, let's go to bed: he told us thus much aforehand.

PESCARA: He wish'd you should not come at him; but believe't,
The accent of the voice sounds not in jest:
I'll down to him, howsoever, and with engines
Force ope the doors.

Exit

RODERIGO: Let's follow him aloof,
And note how the Cardinal will laugh at him.
Exit above, Malateste, Roderigo, and Grisolan

BOSOLA: There's for you first,
'Cause you shall not unbarricade the door
To let in rescue.
He kills the servant

CARDINAL: What cause hast thou to pursue my life?

BOSOLA: Look there.

CARDINAL: Antonio!

BOSOLA: Slain by my hand unwittingly:
Pray, and be sudden: when thou kill'd'st thy sister,
Thou took'st from justice her most equal balance,
And left her naught but her sword.

CARDINAL: O mercy!

BOSOLA: Now it seems thy greatness was only outward;
For thou fall'st faster of thyself than calamity
Can drive thee: I'll not waste longer time; there.
Stabs him

CARDINAL: Thou hast hurt me.

BOSOLA: Again.

CARDINAL: Shall I die like a leveret,
Without any resistance? Help, help, help!
I am slain.

Enter FERDINAND

FERDINAND: Th' alarum! give me a fresh horse;
Rally the vaunt-guard, or the day is lost.
Yield, yield: I give you the honours of arms,
Shake my sword over you; will you yield?

CARDINAL: Help me, I am your brother!

FERDINAND: The devil? My brother fight upon the adverse party?

He wounds the Cardinal, and (in the scuffle) gives Bosola his death wound

There flies your ransom.

CARDINAL: O justice!
I suffer now for what hath former been:
Sorrow is held the eldest child of sin.

FERDINAND: Now you're brave fellows.
Caesar's fortune was harder than Pompey's;
Caesar died in the arms of prosperity,
Pompey at the feet of disgrace.
You both died in the field,
The pain's nothing. Pain many time is taken away with
The apprehension of greater, as the toothache with the sight
Of a barber that comes to pull it out: there's philosophy for you.

BOSOLA: Now my revenge is perfect. Sink, thou main cause
Of my undoing. The last part of my life
Hath done me best service.
He stabs Ferdinand

FERDINAND: Give me some wet hay, I am broken-winded.

I do account this world but a dog-kennel:
I will vault credit and affect high pleasures,
Beyond death.

BOSOLA: He seems to come to himself, now he's so near the bottom.

FERDINAND: My sister, O my sister! there's the cause on't.
Whether we fall by ambition, blood, or lust,
Like diamonds, we are cut with our own dust.

Dies

CARDINAL: Thou hast thy payment too.

BOSOLA: Yes, I hold my weary soul in my teeth;
'Tis ready to part from me. I do glory
That thou, which stood'st like a huge pyramid
Begun upon a large and ample base,
Shalt end in a little point, a kind of nothing.

Enter PESCARA and the others

PESCARA: How now, my lord!

MALATESTE: O, sad disaster!

RODERIGO: How comes this?

BOSOLA: Revenge for the Duchess of Malfi, murder'd
By the Arragonian brethren; for Antonio,
Slain by this hand; for lustful Julia,
Poison'd by this man; and lastly for myself,
That was an actor in the main of all
Much 'gainst mine own good nature, yet i'th' end
Neglected.

PESCARA: How now, my lord!

CARDINAL: Look to my brother:
He gave us these large wounds, as we were struggling
Here i'th' rushes. And now, I pray, let me
Be laid by and never thought of.

Dies

PESCARA: How fatally, it seems, he did withstand
His own rescue!

MALATESTE: Thou wretched thing of blood,
How came Antonio by his death?

BOSOLA: In a mist: I know not how:
Such a mistake as I have often seen
In a play. O, I am gone!
We are only like dead walls, or vaulted graves,
That ruin'd, yield no echo. Fare you well.
It may be pain, but no harm to me to die
In so good a quarrel. O, this gloomy world!
In what a shadow, or deep pit of darkness,
Doth womanish and fearful mankind live!
Let worthy minds ne'er stagger in distrust
To suffer death or shame for what is just:
Mine is another voyage.

Dies

PESCARA: The noble Delio, as I came to th' palace,
Told me of Antonio's being here, and show'd me
A pretty gentleman, his son and heir.

Enter DELIO, and Antonio's son

MALATESTE: O sir, you come too late!

DELIO: I heard so, and
Was arm'd for't ere I came. Let us make noble use
Of this great ruin; and join all our force
To establish this young hopeful gentleman
In's mother's right. These wretched eminent things
Leave no more fame behind 'em, than should one

Fall in a frost, and leave his print in snow:
As soon as the sun shines, it ever melts,
Both form and matter. I have ever thought
Nature doth nothing so great for great men,
As when she's pleas'd to make them lords of truth:
Integrity of life is fame's best friend,
Which nobly, beyond death, shall crown the end.

Chapter 11

Study Questions

Q1. Give a brief introduction to Webster's 'The Duchess of Malfi'?

Or

Q. Many Renaissance tragedies seem to have been influenced by Senecan tragedy. (Shakespeare's Hamlet, for example). Does the Duchess of Malfi have Senecan elements?

Or

Q. State and discuss the various perceptions of "The Duchess of Malfi"

Or

Q. Discuss 'The Duchess of Malfi' as Webster's masterpiece.

Webster's The Duchess of Malfi was written in 1613 or 1614 and had at least two successful productions in London before it was published in 1623 under the title "The Tragedy of the Duchesse of Malfi". Generally considered to be Webster's masterpiece, it tells the story of a young widow who marries against the wishes of her powerful brothers, setting off a storm of revenge. The startling violence, the unbelievable plot twists, the mysterious motives of the brothers, and the calm strength of the Duchess have made The Duchess of Malfi a subject for fierce debate for hundreds of years. Critics and reviewers have loved or hated the play, with equal fervor.

The Duchess of Malfi is considered one of Webster's two greatest works and one of the canonical works of Jacobean drama. It is also roundly criticized as being weak, confusing, and illogical. In his thorough overview of more than three centuries of criticism, John Webster and His Critics 1617-1964, Don D. Moore writes that there may be no one other than Webster "whose plays have received a more varied reception and whose critics have been so divided among themselves on whether the writer was due praise or excoriation.

The Duchess's story is based on actual events that took place in Italy in the early sixteenth century. Webster freely borrowed elements of his story from several sources, including William Painter's popular collection of stories, The Palace of Pleasure (1566-1567), and Sir Philip Sidney's romance, Arcadia (1590), and also borrowed dramatic elements from the Revenge Tragedy tradition, but he adapted the source materials to suit his own themes and dramatic purpose.

The Duchess of Malfi presents a complex mixture of different types of popular Renaissance tragedies. There are elements of revenge tragedy (such as Kyd's Spanish Tragedy, or Tourneur's Revenger's Tragedy), romantic tragedy (Romeo and Juliet, Othello, Ford's Tis Pity She's a Whore), and political tragedy (Macbeth, King Lear, Marlowe's Edward II). Critical opinion about the ways Webster presents the Duchess is divided. Some critics blame her for being irresponsible, bold and too passionate. Others praise her for her courage in fighting against tyrannical authority.

The Duchess of Malfi gives us a glimpse into the politics of seventeenth century English marriage, social mobility, and the law. Additionally, we can use reactions to Webster's work as a means of judging the attitudes of seventeenth century English society; Webster's play paints a vivid portrait of Jacobean society's relationship with women, and outlines the norms surrounding marriage, the freedom of women, and the state of patriarchy in England.

Upon closer examination it becomes clear that the plight of the Duchess mirrors at least two real life cases. Our ability to consider the fictitious Duchess' situation in relation to women's plight sheds even more light on the relationship of women to, and as, property, both in and outside the confines of marriage. As a result, this Jacobean tragicomedy not only entertains and transports us, it can also teach us about the English past, the status of noble women, and about the patriarchal system's transitional nature during the seventeenth century.

The Duchess of Malfi is ostensibly a story of resistance of a willful widow who actively defies her brothers' wishes and refuses to be constrained by (male) authority. While her brothers, Ferdinand and the Cardinal, "would not have her marry again" (I.i.265), she immediately sets out to do so, declaring: "If all my royal kindred / Lay in my way unto this marriage, / I'd make them my low foot-steps" (I.i.348-50).(18) When she does marry (soon after), she not only marries in secret, she also marries out of class, choosing Antonio Bologna, her household steward. Before we know it, she has also had several children - provocative signs to her brothers (who have little room to talk) of a sexuality gone wild. Her actions peg her as a woman willing and eager to fight back, to prevent anyone (even her new husband, who is already her subordinate) from taking charge of her body and desires.She does have grounds for asserting such authority. She is, after all, an aristocratic widow with claims on a duchy and with autonomy so legitimate that her brothers must use clandestine means to restrain her. Yet at stake in the play is not merely the question (or problem) of a widow's unique rights, independence, and power and how they can or cannot be contained by male authority. At issue too is the prospect of female self-fashioning and the kind of voice and agency it carries. Though in part The Duchess of Malfi dramatizes what men can do to women, at its core is rather what women can do to men.

That the duchess will act on her will comes as no surprise, given her initial asides. What is puzzling, and revealing, however (especially since she seems to have married as much to exhibit her autonomy as to satisfy herself), is that she does so through submission. On the one hand, she dares "old wives" to report that she "winked, and chose a husband" (I.i.355-6). On the other, she keeps her move into marriage and sexuality under close cover. When the "deadly air" (III.i.56) of a "scandalous report" (III.i.47) actually approaches her, her honour, and her brothers, she proclaims her innocence. In the face of the suspecting Ferdinand, she denies the truth and assures him that she will marry only "for [his] honour" (III.i.44). Pretending to be deeply troubled by rumors "touching [her] honour" (III.i.48) and helpless to intervene, she leaves the remedy in his hands. It is only later, when he overhears her speaking of her closeted sex life (she thinks to Antonio), that she confesses to her marriage. Yet when she does, she strategically hides her husband's identity and his problematic social standing and underplays the implications of all her secrecy, insisting: "I have not gone about, in this, to create / Any new world, or custom" (III.ii.111-2).

To some degree, the duchess's posture of "innocence" (III.i.55) is a matter of survival, forced upon her by a family and society intent on keeping the widow under wraps. At the end of the play, when her secret is out, her time to live is up. Importantly, however, hers is not a simple case of co-optation, a forced relinquishing of her desires. Instead, her ostensible compliance marks a move into will and desire, giving her significant leverage to do as she pleases, to have her cake and eat it too in a society that would have no more cakes and ale.

Her gains are truly extraordinary, at least for a female character on the early modern stage, and the play amplifies their significance by underscoring the pressures that surround her. By the end of act II, the duchess's reputation is under siege and her life threatened. Ferdinand, an early modern Wolman, vilifies her as "a notorious strumpet" and is ready to "purge" her "infected blood" (II.iv.26) and, even to the Cardinal's horror, "[hew] her to pieces" (II.iv.31). At the beginning of act III, her infamy has spread to the "common rabble," which, according to Antonio, "does directly say / She are a strumpet"

(III.i.25-6). Yet in the meantime, during a leap of two children and several years, this "excellent / Feeder of pedigrees" (III.i.5-6) is living and producing heirs at liberty. And her brothers, the representatives of church and state, have not said a word, at least not one that stops her. To some degree, the play smoothes over this gap in time and plot, unprecedented in Jacobean tragedy, by having characters talk about it, about how time and children fly. Nonetheless, it remains so jarring that critics have questioned the text's authority and coherence. But whatever its textual origins, the break work dramatically to underscore the duchess's unprecedented freedom, to highlight the remarkable, though invisible, license that comes with visible compliance. Secretly autonomous, she is overtly submissive to her brothers' constraints; overtly submissive, she seems at once untouched and untouchable. Under the cover of patriarchal authority, she can act on her will.

In the end, of course, the duchess is caught, confined, tormented by madmen, and turned into "a box of worm seed" (IV.ii.124) at the murderous hands of Bosola, Ferdinand's right-hand man. Yet tellingly, when her subjugation becomes reality, a matter of force rather than choice, she no longer complies. When there is nothing left to gain from submission, she asserts her will directly, making clear the uncompromised and uncompromising nature of her voice. As long as there is hope for release, as long as Ferdinand (as Bosola pretends) will entertain reconciliation, the duchess displays "a behaviour so noble / As gives a majesty to adversity" (IV.i.5-6), and asks for her brother's pardon, still (if Bosola is right) "passionately apprehend[ing] / Those pleasures she's kept from" (IV.i.14-5). But once Ferdinand himself gives up his guise of innocence and betrays his undaunted aggression, so also does her. When he brings her the hand of (he pretends) Antonio and denounces her children as "bastards" (IV.i.36), she lambastes him for denying the legitimacy of her marriage and "violat[ing] a sacrament o' th' Church" (IV.i.39) - once again invoking a patriarchal authority to authorize herself, but this time openly against him. It is then that she "account[s] this world a tedious theater" where she "play[s] a part... 'gainst [her] will" (IV.i.83-

4), and then that she refuses to play it. It is also then that she resists Bosola's efforts to dominate and destroy her, and then that she declares herself "Duchess of Malfi still" (IV.ii.142).

In locating this, her signal moment of self-assertion, in the midst of her confinement and immediately before her death, Webster may be underscoring the vacuity of such expression in an era only beginning to come to terms with interiority, as some have argued.(22) But he may also be dramatizing what he has been showing throughout - the possibility of self-assertion within circumscription. Even if the self in question is not yet fully interiorized, articulated, or defined, the duchess's claim is neither vacuous nor defeating. For it is she who ultimately gets the last word. After her death, her voice reverberates from the grave, echoing warnings to Antonio that could (if this were not Jacobean tragedy) save his life. And at the end of the play, we hear that one of her and Antonio's sons will inherit the duchy - importantly, through his "mother's righht" (V.v.113). She is "Duchess of Malfi still."

Significantly, it is from a position as wife and not widow, the ruled rather than the unruly, that the duchess has established her "right"; through marriage and not widowhood that she has acted on her desires. In Elizabethan drama, when marriage figures as a means to power, it is predominantly as a means to male power - a means for men to safeguard (male) society from oversexed and overactive women, to manipulate, appropriate, traffic in, and otherwise dominate women. Yet in The Duchess of Malfi and plays emerging in the surrounding decades, when the debate about women is also in full and vigorous swing, the illusion (probably always an illusion) that women could be contained through marriage is seriously challenged.

The *Duchess of Malfi* has been interpreted in many different ways since it was first performed nearly 400 years ago. Some have seen it as a cautionary tale that shows what can happen when women marry without being granted the "proper" consent, while others argue that it is a feminist story of a strong woman ahead of her time.[1] I argue that neither of these interpretations is entirely correct, rather, *The Duchess of Malfi* is a study of an emancipated widow that reflects the great social and political transitions found in Jacobean England. The Duchess's life mirrors the plight of real seventeenth century women cannot be ignored, thus she serves not only as a role model, but also as a tragic reminder of the world in which she had to function. The Duchess's fight for autonomy and self-determination is, on the one hand, inspiring, yet given her ultimate failure, disheartening on the other.

Q2. Briefly summarize the play, "The Duchess of Malfi"

Or

Q. Write a short note on "The Duchess of Malfi"

John Webster's "Duchess of Malfi"—a tale of incest, jealousy, madness, and murder—could be written for a Tarentino film. The Jacobean Tragedy, The Duchess of Malfi portrays the result of a young widow's refusal to obey her brothers' command never to remarry. After secretly marrying Antonio and having several children together, the Duchess is unfortunately found out by her brothers. The Duchess' natural revolt leaves her at the mercy of her corrupt and imbalanced brothers. The brothers seek revenge and lead to a tragically bloody death and the ruin of all characters in the play. The tragedy is a quick tale of love, obsession, madness and voyeurism.

Ferdinand, one of the Duchess' brothers, is often shown as a weak, imbalanced character susceptible to the corrupting influence of his brother, The Cardinal. Ferdinand is a tragic villain driven mad by his unbalanced and unnatural obsession for his sister. The Duchess is a strong woman who simply doesn't see that what she is doing is so wrong. The introductory scene between The Duchess and Antonio shows a true love between these two characters. The tender family unit we see develop between these two characters, creates a depth and anchoring to this tragedy that is necessary for the arch of the play. The sincere regard found in these lovers is remarkable in this fast-paced production and juxtaposes their happiness and lightness to the dark and despairing characters of Ferdinand and his corrupt brother.

Traditionally played as the overall mastermind of the play, the Cardinal is the brain behind his brother's passion. A greedy, calculating villain, The Cardinal is the instrument behind the tragedy and is only out to keep the Duchess' money in the family. He uses his brother's unnatural love for the Duchess to manipulate him into agreeing to not let the Duchess marry so they can keep control of her estates and fortune.

The play is engaging and a joy to watch. The presentation of the torture and murder of The Duchess, created a disturbingly realistic presentation of death in the tragedy. "The Duchess of Malfi" is an excellent example of how tragically apt to today's violent society, Jacobean drama remains.

Q3. Draft a biographical sketch of John Webster.

Or

Q. What do you know about the life of Webster.

Very little is known about the life of John Webster. He was the son of a London carriage maker, John Webster, who was a member of the Merchant Taylors' Company before being made free in 1571. His father married on November 4, 1577, to Elizabeth Coates. It is assumed that John Webster was born soon after, but since the parish records were destroyed in the great fire of London in 1666, no accurate date exists. It is possible that John Webster attended the respected Merchant Taylor's school but there is no evidence to the same. There is a record of a John Webster entered at Middle Temple, one of the Inns of Court, in 1598, but it is not certain that he was John Webster, the playwright.

For the life of Webster the dramatist, however, as opposed to Webster the private man, we have a few facts. He comes into our notice—fairly young, it is to be presumed—in 1602. He had a hand in several plays that we know of during that year: *Caesar's fall, Two Shapes, Christmas Comes But Once a Year,* and at least one part of *Lady Jane.* His collaborators were

Munday, Drayton, Middleton, Heywood, Chettle, Smith, and Dekker. It was the beginning, as far as we know, of a close connection with Dekker and a long one with Heywood. Webster was writing for both Henslowe's companies, *Caesar's Fall* and *Two Shapes* for the Admiral's men, *Christmas Comes but Once a Year* and *Lady Jane* for Worcester's men. Writing for Henslowe was not the best school for genius. No high artistic standard was exacted. It rather implies poverty, and certainly means scrappy and unserious work. It may have given Webster—it would have given some people—a sense of the theatre. But he emerged with so little facility in writing and so little aptitude for a good plot (in the ordinary sense), that one must conclude that his genius was not best fitted for theatrical expression, into which it was driven. There are other periods and literary occupations it is harder to imagine him in. But I can figure him as a more or less realistic novelist of the present. His literary skill, his amazing genius for incorporating fragments of his experience, his "bitter flashes" and slow brooding atmosphere of gloom, would have been more tremendous untrammeled by dramatic needs. His power of imaginative visualization was often superfluous in a play. Like most of his gifts it is literary. It is just what one keenly misses in most novels. One can see, almost quote from, a rather large grey-brown novel by John Webster, a book full of darkly suffering human beings, slightly less inexplicable than Dostoyevsky's, but as thrilling, figures glimpsed by sudden flashes that tore the gloom they were part of; a book such that one would remember the taste of the whole longer than any incident or character.... But these imaginations are foolish in a Heraclitan world.

The earliest known records of Webster's employment as a playwright are found in the diary of theatre manager Phillip Henslowe at the beginning of the new century. Among the payments which Henslowe noted in his diary in 1602 were those made to Webster, Anthony Munday, Michael Drayton "and the rest" for a play entitled *Caesar's Fall*. Over the next decade or so, Henslowe's records show Webster collaborating with Heywood, writing a prologue to Marston's *Malcontent*, and composing his two masterpieces *The White Devil* and *The Duchess of Malfi.*

Webster has sometimes been criticized for the limited scope of his plays. He knows nothing, for instance, of the tenderness and pleasant fantasy of Shakespeare. It was mankind's anguish and evil alone which captured his imagination. T.S. Eliot described Webster as the poet who was "much possessed by death, and saw the skull beneath the skin."

In his other masterpiece, *The Duchess of Malfi,* Webster deals with a more innocent pair of lovers. The widowed Duchess of Malfi is forbidden to marry again by her brothers—Duke Ferdinand and the Cardinal—because they covet her estate. Unbeknownst to her brothers, however, the Duchess falls in love with her steward Antonio, and they marry secretly. The two lovers live happily for a time and the Duchess gives birth to three children, but when their marriage is discovered, the evil of the world stages a macabre dance around the little family from which there is no escape. A splendid nightmare, *The Duchess of Malfi* bears witness to a sensitive spirit, overwhelmed by the horror and despair of the world.

After *The Duchess of Malfi,* Webster lapsed into mostly second-rate work. Around 1620, he wrote *The Devil's Law Case* and collaborated a year later with Middleton on *Anything for a Quiet Life.* About 1625 he collaborated on *The Fair Maid of the Inn* with Massinger and ford and on *A Cure for a Cuckold* with Heywood. And sometime before his death (probably in the 1630s), he composed the Roman tragedy *Appius and Virginia.*

After Webster's death, the Elizabethan theatre began to decline. The stage was filled with mediocre writers such as Glapthorne, Brome, Markham, Suckling and D'Avenant, reputed to be Shakespeare's illegitimate son. Then in 1642, the Puritans closed the public theatres, and there was darkness.

Q4. Discuss the various themes in Webster's 'The Duchess of Malfi'

Or

Q. 'The Duchess of Malfi' discusses sways through themes of Horror, Corruption and Reality.

Horror, corruption, revenge and integrity linger deep in the backbone of the play, *The Duchess of Malfi*

Machinations, neurosis, incest, and bloody vengeance, all shot through with brilliantly inventive, knotty and darkly poetic language; *Duchess* invites its audience to take a walk on the wild side.

While the eighteenth century, before Garrick at least, and the Victorians after him were able to bowdlerise his near contemporary Shakespeare and come up with something more to their liking, Webster proved far less tractable. Even William Archer, a discerning critic and one of the National Theatre's founding fathers, found the play "intolerable", and it's easy to see why.

Themes central to *The Duchess of Malfi* include identity, sexuality, and power, which are all closely intertwined in the tragedy. The theme of identity is carried through the play in several ways. The twin relationship between Ferdinand and the Duchess makes the characters mirrors for each other; the frequent presence of mirrors as stage props makes the metaphor explicit. The Duchess also battles with the issue of conflicting public and private identities: her status as aristocratic lady contests with her love for the lower-born Antonio, and the connection between birth and identity is an open question throughout the play. Her brothers press upon her the identity of the virtuous widow, one that she is unwilling to accept. When Duchess says, "I am Duchess of Malfi still," it is not clear whether she is affirming or lamenting this identity.The theme of sexuality is tied to identity, particularly in regards to Ferdinand and the Duchess; his apparent desire for her is a perversion of socially acceptable sexuality as well as a kind of narcissism. Sexuality is generally linked to danger and violence, as the most explicitly sexual characters are shown to be the most evil. Even the comparatively healthy sexuality of the Duchess is considered suspect, a sign of excess passion, even if it is not, as Ferdinand and the Cardinal would imagine, a mark of depravity. Moreover, although the Duchess has neither Ferdinand's incestuous desires nor the Cardinal's affairs, it is in one sense her sexuality that propels the violence of the play. The desire for power, however, is also a controlling force in the drama; the Duchess's brothers are driven by a desire to control the family fortune. More generally, however, the play opens the question of the bases of power and authority, and who rightfully holds it. The corrupted authority of Ferdinand and the Cardinal casts doubt on the power they wield, while the nobility of the Duchess as she faces her death suggests the possibility of a different sort of authority.

Appearances and Reality

Repeated throughout *The Duchess of Malfi* is the idea that people cannot be trusted, that things are not as they appear. People, both the essentially good people and the villains, disguise their bodies and their motives. Several instances of pretending and concealing occur to set the tone for the rest of the play: the Cardinal pretends to have no interest in Bosola; he is hired to spy on the Duchess, pretending only to tend her horses; the Duchess pretends to have no interest in marriage; Cariola hides behind the arras without Antonio's knowledge and promises the Duchess that she will "conceal this secret from the world / As warily as those that trade in poison / Keep poison from their children." Antonio, who is known for his honesty, agrees to keep the marriage a secret. The Duchess complains that women of wealth and stature cannot be honest about their feelings, but are "forced to express our violent passions / in riddles, and in dreams, and leave the path / of simple virtue, which was never made / to seem the thing it is not."

Further incidents of deception and disguise occur throughout the play. The Duchess and Antonio invent stories to conceal the birth of their first child and their plans to escape to Ancona. Ferdinand brings the Duchess a dead man's hand that he knows she will take for Antonio's and shows her wax figures that look like her husband and children. Bosola visits the imprisoned Duchess in disguise, appearing as an old man and a bellman. Even Bosola's one kindness to the Duchess is a deception, as he tells the dying Duchess that her husband is alive and reconciled with her brothers. The Cardinal kills Julia (with whom he has been having an affair without her husband's knowledge) by giving her a poison disguised as a holy book, not knowing that Julia has deceived him by hiding Bosola behind the door.

Although none of these deceptions brings about its desired end, the characters turn again and again to secrecy and disguise to solve their problems, as though they know no other way to move in the world. It is not an optimistic picture, as Bosola realises just before he dies: "O, this gloomy world! / in what a shadow or deep pit of darkness, / Doth womanish and fearful mankind live!" If the world is steered not by God but by uncaring stars, and if men and women cannot trust their own perceptions to steer through it, it is a gloomy world, indeed.

The Cardinal, Bosola, and Ferdinand die without anyone coming to save them, because the Cardinal has lied to keep the servants from entering his chambers.

Fate and Belief

Considering that one of the main characters of *The Duchess of Malfi* is a Cardinal, one of the highest-ranking officials in the Roman Catholic Church, there is a surprising lack of reference to God in the play. The characters do not turn to God for help in trouble, and they do not seek forgiveness when they come to believe they have acted wrongly. The only certainty in life is death, and there is no promise here of an afterlife. The world of *The Duchess of Malfi* is controlled not by God, but by fate.

Of all the characters, it is Bosola who most changes during the play, and whose psychology is revealed the most clearly. As he watches the conduct of the three siblings, he comes to a new understanding of the differences between a good servant and a good man, and he grows in respect for the honesty of Antonio and the dignity of the Duchess. If anyone were going to turn to God in the end, it would be Bosola, but he does not. Instead, when he realises that he has accidentally killed Antonio, he utters the line that expresses the world view for the entire play: "We are merely the stars' tennis-balls, struck and banded / which way please them."

Ferdinand is most conscious of his religion, but his Christianity is not a religion of love but one of vengeance, not of forgiveness but of damnation. In act 2, in his anger at learning of the Duchess's child, Ferdinand's first instinct is to call her "a sister damn'd." Naming wild punishments he would like to administer to her, he declares that he would like to have the Duchess and the unknown father of the child "burnt in a coal-pit" with no vents, so that "their curs Ed smoke might not ascend to heaven." In act 4, he brings a series of horrors to the Duchess to drive her to despair, so that she will renounce God and be sent to hell when he has her murdered. Ferdinand is so clearly insane, that his understanding of religion must be seen as a product of rage, not of religious teaching.

Other characters turn elsewhere for their understanding of the world. Antonio learns by astrological calculation that his first child will have a "short life" and a "violent death." The Cardinal, whose lavish lifestyle and mistress would seem to distance him from the teachings of his church, does not suggest that the Duchess pray for guidance if she finds herself tempted to remarry, but advises that "your own discretion / Must now be your director." Cariola warns the Duchess not to use a false religious pilgrimage to fool her brothers, but the Duchess rejects the warning, calling Cariola "a superstitious fool." Although she faces her death on her knees to more easily pass through heaven's gates, there is no real sense of faith in her last speeches.

Q5. Analyze and discuss Webster's play Act wise.

Act I

The Duchess of Malfi is divided into five acts, each comprising several scenes. In the three scenes of act 1, the major characters and conflicts are introduced. The setting is the Italian city of Malfi in the sixteenth century, in the audience chamber or "presence" of the widowed Duchess. Antonio, the Duchess's steward, talks with his friend Delio as they observe the others who pass through the chamber. The first to enter are the Cardinal and Bosola. Although Bosola has recently been released after serving seven years for a murder he committed at the behest of the Cardinal, the Cardinal is cold to him and will not acknowledge his debt.

Ferdinand, the Duke of Calabria, enters with his entourage. Ferdinand learns that Antonio has proven himself the best at a knightly competition, and he congratulates Antonio for his prowess and for his eloquent speech. When the Cardinal reenters with the Duchess, Antonio gives Delio his impression of the three siblings: the Cardinal is jealous and vengeful, Ferdinand is “""""perverse and turbulent,"""""" and the Duchess is sweet and noble. Ferdinand asks the Duchess to accept Bosola as a servant, and she agrees; in fact, the brothers have hired Bosola to spy on the Duchess.

The two brothers warn the Duchess not to remarry, and she promises that she will not. However, as soon as they leave her chamber, she summons Antonio and the two perform a private marriage ceremony, with the Duchess's trusted servant Cariola as witness.

Act II

The second act, which has five scenes, begins several months later, as the Duchess is about to give birth to a child. Her marriage to Antonio is still secret, and she has concealed her pregnancy by wearing loose clothing. Bosola, however, suspects that she is pregnant and tries to trap her by giving her a present of apricots. When she devours them hungrily and then vomits, he has confirmation of the pregnancy but does not reveal what he knows. The incident sends the Duchess into labour, and she is rushed to her chamber.

To avoid suspicion that the Duchess is giving birth, a ruse is invented: it is announced that jewels have been stolen, and everyone must stay in his or her room while a search is conducted. The Duchess delivers a healthy son, and when Cariola tells Antonio the good news, he prepares a set of calculations based on astrology to determine the baby's future. Meanwhile, Bosola sneaks out to the courtyard beneath the Duchess's window and hears her crying out. Antonio finds him there, and they argue about Bosola having left his room. As he leaves Bosola, Antonio accidentally drops the paper on which he has written his astrological notes, and Bosola retrieves it, discovering that a baby has been born to the Duchess—a baby who will have a short life. Bosola knows that Antonio is in on the secret but does not consider that a man of Antonio's social class could be the father.

In Rome, the Cardinal meets in his chamber with Julia, his mistress. Delio arrives and propositions Julia, but she refuses him. In another part of the Cardinal's palace, Ferdinand has received a letter from Bosola, telling him of the baby's birth. The Cardinal and Ferdinand discuss their sister's betrayal, and Ferdinand's rage takes him to the brink of insanity.

Act III

Several years pass before the five scenes in act 3 take place. The Duchess has given birth to two more children, but her marriage is still a secret, and Bosola still has not discovered the identity of the father. Ferdinand, finally stirred to action, arrives at the Duchess's palace to confront her. To play an affectionate joke on her, Antonio and Cariola step out of the room while the Duchess is talking to herself in the mirror, and Ferdinand comes into the room at the same moment. He accuses her of shaming the family with her promiscuity, and although she tells him that she is married, he vows never to look at her again.

Afraid of Ferdinand's anger, the Duchess sends Antonio to safety by pretending that he has stolen money and been banished. Tenderly, the couple say goodbye to each other, planning to reunite in Ancona. In her grief, the Duchess confides in Bosola, telling him everything. Bosola plots to entrap the Duchess and Antonio. He speeds to Rome to tell what he knows and find his reward, and the brothers respond with expected fury. The Cardinal decides to contact the authorities at Ancona and have the Duchess and her family banished.

At the Shrine of Our Lady of Loretto, the Duchess and Antonio review their situation. Bosola brings a letter from Ferdinand calling for Antonio's death, and Antonio and the Duchess say goodbye again. They know that this will be their final parting. Antonio takes their oldest son and flees to Milan. The Duchess is arrested by Bosola, in disguise, and taken by guards to her palace.

Act IV

Act 4: with its two scenes set in the Duchess's chambers, moves quickly. Trying to drive her to despair so that she will be damned as well as killed, Ferdinand arranges for a series of horrors. He visits the Duchess in a darkened room (because he has vowed never to see her again) and places in her hand a dead man's hand that she will assume to be Antonio's. He shows her wax figures that look like the bodies of Antonio and the three children. He arranges for eight madmen to scream outside her window. Through it all, the Duchess maintains her quiet nobility, saying "'"'"'"I am Duchess of Malfi still,"'"'"'" and Bosola begins to feel a grudging respect for her.

Finally, Bosola brings two executioners to the Duchess's chamber, and they strangle her. She faces her death with dignity. Cariola is also strangled, though she resists her death with all her energy. Off stage, the two younger children are strangled. When Ferdinand sees his dead sister, he has a dramatic change of heart, and rather than rewarding Bosola, he blames him for the murders.

Act V

The action of the five scenes of act 5 is also rapid. Four days after the events in the Cardinal has had all of Antonio's property seized. Antonio decides to visit the Cardinal and attempt reconciliation. Ferdinand's madness has increased, and he has been seen digging up bodies in the cemetery and carrying a man's leg over his shoulder. Bosola arrives in Milan, and he and the Cardinal try to determine what the other knows. The Cardinal pretends that he does not know the Duchess is dead, so that he will not seem to have been involved in the murder, but Bosola persuades Julia to find out the truth. The Cardinal confesses to Julia that he has had his sister killed, but then he immediately kills Julia with a poisoned book.

Outside the Cardinal's home, Antonio and Delio speak with a ghostly echo that comes from the Duchess's grave. Bosola vows to protect Antonio from harm, but he accidentally kills Antonio with his sword, mistaking him for the Cardinal, who has promised to kill Bosola. In the final scene, an anguished Bosola kills the Cardinal's servant and stabs the Cardinal. Ferdinand rushes in and stabs Bosola and the Cardinal. Bosola stabs Ferdinand. As they all lie dead, Delio enters with Antonio's son and calls for a unified effort to support the young man as the new Duke.

Q6. Present Webster's View of "The Duchess of Malfi"

"I am confident this work is not unworthy your Honour's perusal for by such poems as this, poets have kissed the hands of great princes, and drawn their gentle eyes to look down upon their sheets of paper, when the poets themselves were bound up in their winding sheets. The like courtesy from your Lordship shall make you live in your grave, and laurel spring out of it; when the ignorant scorners of the Muses (that like worms in libraries seem to live only to destroy learning) shall wither, neglected and forgotten. This work and myself I humbly present to your approved censure, it being the utmost of my wishes, to have your honourable self my weighty and perspicuous comment: which grace so done me, shall ever be acknowledged".

Q7. Webster's play sways in the theme of Unequal power relations. Discuss.

John Webster's play The Duchess of Malfi is an illustration of the unequal power relations between the sexes during the sixteenth century. In the play the brothers Ferdinand and the Cardinal are shown as men who want to control their sister the Duchess by not letting her remarry. Out of this situation emerges the Duchess who, in spite of her promise not to marry again (p. 1298), will do the complete opposite, thus defying male power. Her conversation with Antonio (lines 317-61, pp. 1292-3) is an example of this because in her speech the Duchess intends to make Antonio realise that she is against both the conventions of marriage codes and men's assumptions of women's sexuality.

The duchess, a high-spirited and high-minded widow, reveals her love for Antonio, steward at her court, and secretly marries him, despite the warnings of her brother, Ferdinand, duke of Calabria, and the Cardinal, and immediately after informing them that she has no intention of remarrying. Their resistance appears to be induced by consideration for their high blood, and by, as Ferdinand later asserts, a desire to inherit her property; there is also a strong suggestion of Ferdinand's repressed incestuous desire for her.

The brothers place in her employment as a spy the cynical ex-galley-slave Bosola, who betrays her to them; she and Antonio take flight and separate. She is captured and is subjected by Ferdinand and Bosola to fearful mental tortures, including the sight of the feigned corpse of her husband and the attendance of a group of madmen; finally she is strangled with her two children and Cariola, her waiting woman. Retribution overtakes the murderers: Ferdinand goes mad, imagining himself a wolf; the Cardinal is killed by the now remorseful Bosola, and Bosola is killed by Ferdinand (who, in turn, is also killed by Bosola). Bosola has already killed Antonio, mistaking him for the Cardinal.

Q8. 16th Century play 'The Duchess of Malfi' sends modern-day message. Discuss

"Duchess" takes place in 16th Century Italy during the High Italian Renaissance period. Unbeknownst to, and against the wishes of, her brothers, the young, beautiful Duchess of Malfi marries the steward of her household, Antonio, who is below her class.

A spy named Bosola, planted in her palace by her brothers, reports the births of the Duchess' children. Her brothers become outraged when they discover what the Duchess has done. When her brothers find out the identity of her husband, they move in for revenge. They capture the Duchess and two of her children, confiscate her land and imprison her. Bosola, who becomes her torturer and executioner, has a change of heart as the play progresses and becomes her avenger.

"Bosola has blamed everyone else for the hardships of his life; His choices are motivated by greed and a desire to advance in his career. He has left behind the desire for knowledge and goodness. He thinks, at first, the Duchess is like him, however, when he realises this is not the case, he tries to follow her example."

According to Perkins, the play is an examination of life experiences.

"The Duchess takes risks to shape her life and faces the consequences of her choices. She accepts her consequences with responsibility, not out of guilt. Her brothers and other characters hide their motivations and blame others for their consequences."

"Duchess" was written in the early 17th Century by John Webster, a contemporary of Shakespeare. Webster was a hired-hand playwright at Shakespeare's theater, where the play was first performed in 1614.

The Duchess comes across to the audience as the epitome of stoics and strength of soul and character. At the beginning of the play, she is portrayed as a woman of great integrity and honour, such that Antonio speaks of 'her days are practiced in such noble virtue that sure her nights, nay more her very sleeps are more in heaven than other lady's shrifts'. Indeed, we see her as a noble woman of much childlike innocence and nativity. Even her secret marriage to Antonio is not seen as something of lust and sexual desire, but of a woman's need for companionship and love 'tis not a figure cut in alabaster to kneel at my husband's tomb', something she obviously cannot derive from her villainous brothers. Even at this point, she comes across as a strong character of intense emotion and longing for affection and love that she must resort to a secret marriage. In contrast, her marriage to Antonio seems cleaner than the Cardinal's adulterous relationship with Julia, his mistress. That the Duchess solemnizes their vows shows that she does have moral standards to uphold. Even her 'feigned pilgrimage' to Ancona was something that she and her family did as a real pilgrimage to pay their respect to our Lady of Loretto.

The childlike innocence of the Duchess is seen from the way that she tells Antonio that 'time will easily scatter the tempest' when Antonio brings up the threat of her brothers. Yet, it is because of them that she is made to endure 'the worst torture, pain and fear'. One certainly pities her and feels that she should not be made to suffer so much for following her heart. Indeed, Ferdinand's obsession to 'purge infected blood' seems less a move to right a wrong than out of jealousy 'my imagination carries me to see her in the shameful act of sin'. The Duchess in nobly enduring all his cruel torments becomes a 'reverend monument whose ruins are even pitied'. Yet to a certain extent, while we pity the Duchess, one cannot deny that one feels a great admiration for her strength of character. She accepts suffering as her 'fate' and is 'acquainted with sad misery as the tanned slave is with his oar'.

Even Bosola is able to realise the dignity in which she bears herself up to the suffering that her brothers make her endure 'as majesty gives to adversity; you may discern the shape of loveliness more perfectly in her tears than in her smiles'. One admires her for being so ready to accept her fate, the suffering she endures a mere consequence of her loving Antonio and marrying him. It is also through her suffering that she derives a new found wisdom 'your kiss is colder than I have seen a holy anchorite give to a dead man's skull'. Indeed, she realises the extent of her brother's tyranny and knows that she and Antonio must part. Their last moments together are certainly touching, and one truly pities her for being denied of true love. To lose the love of her life drains her very soul, and she is left empty and without meaning in life 'my laurel is all withered'.

The Duchess accepts her death with humility, 'heaven's gates are not as highly arched as prince's palaces; they that enter there must go on their knees'. Yet to the end, she is dignified 'I am the Duchess of Malfi still'. Indeed, her 'violent death' seems more of a journey to liberation rather than an end in itself. Throughout the play, the Duchess is portrayed as the victim of entrapment, Ferdinand the predator that toys with his prey, the Duchess before killing her.

The Duchess is hence a character to be admired and respected. That she is a historical figure shows that Webster was indeed perceptive in the plight of the Duchess at such a time when her behaviour to marry Antonio outside the social status of her family would have been dealt with death, no question to the reasoning behind it. Webster's play hence is a statement against this convention, and the Duchess comes across as a real person of human emotion that each and every individual can relate to.

Q9. Give a brief introduction to Webster's 'The Duchess of Malfi'?

Or

Q. Many Renaissance tragedies seem to have been influenced by Senecan tragedy. (Shakespeare's Hamlet, for example). Does the Duchess of Malfi have Senecan elements?

Or

Q. State and discuss the various perceptions of "The Duchess of Malfi"

Or

Q. Discuss 'The Duchess of Malfi' as Webster's masterpiece.

Webster's The Duchess of Malfi was written in 1613 or 1614 and had at least two successful productions in London before it was published in 1623 under the title "The Tragedy of the Duchesse of Malfi". Generally considered to be Webster's masterpiece, it tells the story of a young widow who marries against the wishes of her powerful brothers, setting off a storm of revenge. The startling violence, the unbelievable plot twists, the mysterious motives of the brothers, and the calm strength of the Duchess have made The Duchess of Malfi a subject for fierce debate for hundreds of years. Critics and reviewers have loved or hated the play, with equal fervor.

The Duchess of Malfi is considered one of Webster's two greatest works and one of the canonical works of Jacobean drama. It is also roundly criticized as being weak, confusing, and illogical. In his thorough overview of more than three centuries of criticism, John Webster and His Critics 1617-1964, Don D. Moore writes that there may be no one other than Webster "whose plays have received a more varied reception and whose critics have been so divided among themselves on whether the writer was due praise or excoriation.

The Duchess's story is based on actual events that took place in Italy in the early sixteenth century. Webster freely borrowed elements of his story from several sources, including William Painter's popular collection of stories, The Palace of Pleasure (1566-1567), and Sir Philip Sidney's romance, Arcadia (1590), and also borrowed dramatic elements from the Revenge Tragedy tradition, but he adapted the source materials to suit his own themes and dramatic purpose.

The Duchess of Malfi presents a complex mixture of different types of popular Renaissance tragedies. There are elements of revenge tragedy (such as Kyd's Spanish Tragedy, or Tourneur's Revenger's Tragedy), romantic tragedy (Romeo and Juliet, Othello, Ford's Tis Pity She's a Whore), and political tragedy (Macbeth, King Lear, Marlowe's Edward II). Critical opinion about the ways Webster presents the Duchess is divided. Some critics blame her for being irresponsible, bold and too passionate. Others praise her for her courage in fighting against tyrannical authority.

The Duchess of Malfi gives us a glimpse into the politics of seventeenth century English marriage, social mobility, and the law. Additionally, we can use reactions to Webster's work as a means of judging the attitudes of seventeenth century English society; Webster's play paints a vivid portrait of Jacobean society's relationship with women, and outlines the norms surrounding marriage, the freedom of women, and the state of patriarchy in England.

Upon closer examination it becomes clear that the plight of the Duchess mirrors at least two real life cases. Our ability to consider the fictitious Duchess' situation in relation to women's plight sheds even more light on the relationship of women to, and as, property, both in and outside the confines of marriage. As a result, this Jacobean tragicomedy not only entertains and transports us, it can also teach us about the English past, the status of noble women, and about the patriarchal system's transitional nature during the seventeenth century.

The Duchess of Malfi is ostensibly a story of resistance of a willful widow who actively defies her brothers' wishes and refuses to be constrained by (male) authority. While her brothers, Ferdinand and the Cardinal, "would not have her marry again" (I.i.265), she immediately sets out to do so, declaring: "If all my royal kindred / Lay in my way unto this marriage, / I'd make them my low foot-steps" (I.i.348-50). When she does marry (soon after), she not only marries in secret, she also marries out of class, choosing Antonio Bologna, her household steward. Before we know it, she has also had several children - provocative signs to her brothers (who have little room to talk) of a sexuality gone wild. Her actions peg her as a woman willing and eager to fight back, to prevent anyone (even her new husband, who is already her subordinate) from taking charge of her body and desires. She does have grounds for asserting such authority. She is, after all, an aristocratic widow with claims on a duchy and with autonomy so legitimate that her brothers must use clandestine means to restrain her. Yet at stake in the play is not merely the question (or problem) of a widow's unique rights, independence, and power and how they can or cannot be contained by male authority. At issue too is the prospect of female self-fashioning and the kind of voice and agency it carries. Though in part The Duchess of Malfi dramatizes what men can do to women, at its core is rather what women can do to men.

That the duchess will act on her will comes as no surprise, given her initial asides. What is puzzling, and revealing, however (especially since she seems to have married as much to exhibit her autonomy as to satisfy herself), is that she does so through submission. On the one hand, she dares "old wives" to report that she "winked, and chose a husband" (I.i.355-6). On the other, she keeps her move into marriage and sexuality under close cover. When the "deadly air" (III.i.56) of a "scandalous report" (III.i.47) actually approaches her, her honour, and her brothers, she proclaims her innocence. In the face of the suspecting Ferdinand, she denies the truth and assures him that she will marry only "for [his] honour" (III.i.44). Pretending to be deeply troubled by rumors "touching [her] honour" (III.i.48) and helpless to intervene, she leaves the remedy in his hands. It is only later, when he overhears her speaking of her closeted sex life (she thinks to Antonio), that she confesses to her marriage. Yet when she does, she strategically hides her husband's identity and his problematic social standing and underplays the implications of all her secrecy, insisting: "I have not gone about, in this, to create / Any new world, or custom" (III.ii.111-2).

To some degree, the duchess's posture of "innocence" (III.i.55) is a matter of survival, forced upon her by a family and society intent on keeping the widow under wraps. At the end of the play, when her secret is out, her time to live is up. Importantly, however, hers is not a simple case of co-optation, a forced relinquishing of her desires. Instead, her ostensible compliance marks a move into will and desire, giving her significant leverage to do as she pleases, to have her cake and eat it too in a society that would have no more cakes and ale.

Her gains are truly extraordinary, at least for a female character on the early modern stage, and the play amplifies their significance by underscoring the pressures that surround her. By the end of act II, the duchess's reputation is under siege and her life threatened. Ferdinand, an early modern Wolman, vilifies her as "a notorious strumpet" and is ready to "purge" her "infected blood" (II.iv.26) and, even to the Cardinal's horror, "[hew] her to pieces" (II.iv.31). At the beginning of act III, her infamy has spread to the "common rabble," which, according to Antonio, "does directly say / She are a strumpet" (III.i.25-6). Yet in the meantime, during a leap of two children and several years, this "excellent / Feeder of pedigrees" (III.i.5-6) is living and producing heirs at liberty. And her brothers, the representatives of church and state, have not said a word, at least not one that stops her. To some degree, the play smoothes over this gap in time and plot, unprecedented in Jacobean tragedy, by having characters talk about it, about how time and children fly. Nonetheless, it remains so jarring that critics have questioned the text's authority and coherence. But whatever its textual origins, the break work dramatically to underscore the duchess's unprecedented freedom, to highlight the remarkable, though invisible, license that comes with visible compliance. Secretly autonomous, she is overtly submissive to her brothers' constraints; overtly submissive, she seems at once untouched and untouchable. Under the cover of patriarchal authority, she can act on her will.

In the end, of course, the duchess is caught, confined, tormented by madmen, and turned into "a box of worm seed" (IV.ii.124) at the murderous hands of Bosola, Ferdinand's right-hand man. Yet tellingly, when her subjugation becomes reality, a matter of force rather than choice, she no longer complies. When there is nothing left to gain from submission, she asserts her will directly, making clear the uncompromised and uncompromising nature of her voice. As long as there is hope for release, as long as Ferdinand (as Bosola pretends) will entertain reconciliation, the duchess displays "a behaviour so noble / As gives a majesty to adversity" (IV.i.5-6), and asks for her brother's pardon, still (if Bosola is right) "passionately apprehend[ing] / Those pleasures she's kept from" (IV.i.14-5). But once Ferdinand himself gives up his guise of innocence and betrays his undaunted aggression, so also does her. When he brings her the hand of (he pretends) Antonio and denounces her children as "bastards" (IV.i.36), she lambastes him for denying the legitimacy of her marriage and "violat[ing] a sacrament o' th' Church" (IV.i.39) - once again invoking a patriarchal authority to authorize herself, but this time openly against him. It is then that she "account[s] this world a tedious theater" where she "play[s] a part... 'gainst [her] will" (IV.i.83-4), and then that she refuses to play it. It is also then that she resists Bosola's efforts to dominate and destroy her, and then that she declares herself "Duchess of Malfi still" (IV.ii.142).

In locating this, her signal moment of self-assertion, in the midst of her confinement and immediately before her death, Webster may be underscoring the vacuity of such expression in an era only beginning to come to terms with interiority, as some have argued. But he may also be dramatizing what he has been showing throughout - the possibility of self-assertion within circumscription. Even if the self in question is not yet fully interiorized, articulated, or defined, the duchess's claim is neither vacuous nor defeating. For it is she who ultimately gets the last word. After her death, her voice reverberates from the grave, echoing warnings to Antonio that could (if this were not Jacobean tragedy) save his life. And at the end of the play, we hear that one of her and Antonio's sons will inherit the duchy - importantly, through his "mother's right" (V.v.113). She is "Duchess of Malfi still."

Significantly, it is from a position as wife and not widow, the ruled rather than the unruly, that the duchess has established her "right"; through marriage and not widowhood that she has acted on her desires. In Elizabethan drama, when marriage figures as a means to power, it is predominantly as a means to male power - a means for men to safeguard (male) society from oversexed and overactive women, to manipulate, appropriate, traffic in, and otherwise dominate women. Yet in The Duchess of Malfi and plays emerging in the surrounding decades, when the debate about women is also in full and vigorous swing, the illusion (probably always an illusion) that women could be contained through marriage is seriously challenged.

The *Duchess of Malfi* has been interpreted in many different ways since it was first performed nearly 400 years ago. Some have seen it as a cautionary tale that shows what can happen when women marry without being granted the "proper" consent, while others argue that it is a feminist story of a strong woman ahead of her time.[1] I argue that neither of these interpretations is entirely correct, rather, *The Duchess of Malfi* is a study of an emancipated widow that reflects the great social and political transitions found in Jacobean England. The Duchess's life mirrors the plight of real seventeenth century women cannot be ignored, thus she serves not only as a role model, but also as a tragic reminder of the world in which she had to function. The Duchess's fight for autonomy and self-determination is, on the one hand, inspiring, yet given her ultimate failure, disheartening on the other.

Q10. Briefly summarize the play, "The Duchess of Malfi"

Or

Q. Write a short note on "The Duchess of Malfi"

John Webster's "Duchess of Malfi"—a tale of incest, jealousy, madness, and murder—could be written for a Tarentino film. The Jacobean Tragedy, The Duchess of Malfi portrays the result of a young widow's refusal to obey her brothers' command never to remarry. After secretly marrying Antonio and having several children together, the Duchess is unfortunately found out by her brothers. The Duchess' natural revolt leaves her at the mercy of her corrupt and imbalanced brothers. The brothers seek revenge and lead to a tragically bloody death and the ruin of all characters in the play. The tragedy is a quick tale of love, obsession, madness and voyeurism. Ferdinand, one of the Duchess' brothers, is often shown as a weak, imbalanced character susceptible to the corrupting influence of his brother, The Cardinal. Ferdinand is a tragic villain driven mad by his unbalanced and unnatural obsession for his sister. The Duchess is a strong woman who

simply doesn't see that what she is doing is so wrong. The introductory scene between The Duchess and Antonio shows a true love between these two characters. The tender family unit we see develop between these two characters, creates a depth and anchoring to this tragedy that is necessary for the arch of the play. The sincere regard found in these lovers is remarkable in this fast-paced production and juxtaposes their happiness and lightness to the dark and despairing characters of Ferdinand and his corrupt brother.

Traditionally played as the overall mastermind of the play, the Cardinal is the brain behind his brother's passion. A greedy, calculating villain, The Cardinal is the instrument behind the tragedy and is only out to keep the Duchess' money in the family. He uses his brother's unnatural love for the Duchess to manipulate him into agreeing to not let the Duchess marry so they can keep control of her estates and fortune. The play is engaging and a joy to watch. The presentation of the torture and murder of The Duchess, created a disturbingly realistic presentation of death in the tragedy. "The Duchess of Malfi" is an excellent example of how tragically apt to today's violent society, Jacobean drama remains.

Q11. What are the standards and values by which the court of Malfi lives?

The values that govern character's decisions in The Duchess of Malfi are diametrically opposed to the modern day ethos by which we are accustomed to live. The play is set in a time and society where today's basic sociability, fairness and freedom from oppression were completely unheard of and unprecedented. Those in power saw no point to their authority if they did not take full advantage of their influence, nobody would lookout for anyone else and people's livelihoods depended on kings' fickle whims. Corruption was rife, fuelled by the ruthless backstabbing and do-or-die attitude. In fact, the play starts by amalgamating and spotlighting the flaws with the court system by referring to Antonio's recent excursion and comparing Malfi with the vastly different French court.

Antonio is clearly a newly-converted Francophile and describes his experiences in glowing terms, emphasising its superiority with a pithy, italicised aphorism to show that the French head-of-state fully understands how his decisions affect the people - should someone "poison't near the head, Death and diseases through the whole land spread" (I, i, l. 14-5). Coining a superb simile in describing the court as "like a common fountain" (I, i, l. 12), the French communal spirit and sharing lifestyle is drawn to the audience's attention. Unlike the Duke of Calabria, the King does not punish freedom of speech and feels duty-bound to deracinate the inveterate "corruption of the times" (I, i, l. 18).

Antonio is one of the most admirable characters and one of the few in the play's opening who displays an attractive side to their personality. He clearly has positive values, as shown by his adulation of the progressive French régime, and heaps encomia on aspects he respects while rightly deploring contemptible behaviour. He has perceptive vision and cogently describes people he sees in precisely terse thumbnail sketches. Perhaps most admirable, is the way he is able to condemn] characters without a hint of self-promotion, arrogance or snatching at the moral high ground. Indeed, Antonio is a man of much humility and wisdom - his summing up is precise and he sees through to hidden aspects of people's agendas. After Bosola leaves at the end of the first scene, Antonio sapiently notes that "this foul melancholy will poison all his goodness" (I, i, l.77-8), and the reader has a sneaking suspicion his prophecy may just turn out to be realised. Antonio is usually honest and says what he thinks, unlike the other more conniving and duplicitous courtiers.

The only other characters that attract a semblance of esteem are Delio, for his kindly politeness, and non-judgmental lack of presumption; the Duchess; and Bosola, for his mastery of language. Delio listens carefully to his friend's descriptions then comes to his own conclusions of the people he sees. The "right noble Duchess" (I, ii, l. 112) is a breath of fresh air - astute, witty, unintimidated and she speaks with such wisdom one would think she has lived to twice her years. Antonio is so keen in his praise of her that Delio warns him that he has almost become like a "wire-drawer" (I, ii, l. 131). Bosola is an insightful realist with a good understanding of the use of analogies and allusions as well as astute judgement - saying of the Cardinal "this fellow were able to possess the greatest devil, and make him worse" (I, i, l. 47-8), he exhibits a rare acumen.

The Cardinal is one of the story's most despicable characters. He is morally repugnant and highly hypocritical. Holding a high position in the church, he should be expected to be a positive example of piousness and religious reverence. Conversely, the Cardinal is dishonest and corrupt. He is a churchman involved in the vile slave trade, with a seemingly secular materialist trader's mind and no conscience. He speaks of his "galleys" (I, ii, l. 73) laden with emaciated ill-treated prisoners in an entirely offhand and nonchalant manner and is acceptingly aware of his brother's incestuous abuse of his sister, the Duchess. He displays flagrant amorality, and lives a frivolous life complete with betting, "dance, court ladies, and... combats" (I, ii, l. 80). His celibacy and vows instantly forgotten, the Cardinal goes further to defile the Church's beliefs when his deception and bribery is made clear. Bosola has been cheated out of his salary for a certain anticlerical "service" and other aspects of his life are not those usually expected from a clergyman - Antonio shrewdly likens him to seemingly transparent and clear pond water that has a proliferation of unsightly toads hidden just beneath the surface. The Cardinal is a man prone to jealousy, and is wickedly scheming as he takes full advantage of his elevated position. His latent insecurity means he "strews in his way flatterers" (I, ii, l. 86-7), and it has been said that "they do flatter him most" (I, ii, l. 109). The Cardinal has the most cold, slyly cunning, ruthless and hypocritical rôle in the play. He tries to restrict the Duchesses' freedoms, restraining her with overly pious warnings, and there seems to be no end to his hypocrisy and simultaneous high-mindedness when he says that only the "most luxurious, will wed twice" (I, ii, l. 221-2).

Mistreated by the Cardinal is Bosola. He is a very bitter man obsessed with eloquent death imagery who feels hard done by and left bootless: "only the reward of doing well, is the doing of it!" (I, i, l. 33) This quotation also speaks to the audience to show that he is a cold-hearted and sadistic person gaining pleasure from the more questionable deeds and jobs he has carried out. He resents the Cardinal's attitude to him and the debt owed, as well as being vengeful and highly unforgiving. Bosola's ruthlessness and determination leads him to desperately "thrive some way" (I, i, l. 38). We get the impression that Bosola is a man who will do whatever it takes to get what he thinks he deserves and to advance in life. He is hardy and somewhat spiteful in his opinions of Ferdinand and the Duke, who are rich and powerful, but only manage to attract "crows, 'pies and caterpillars" (I, i, l. 52-3). He is cunning, and always aware of the emotions around him. However, whenever he is approached for work, Bosola instinctively assumes he is wanted as a hitman - "Whose throat must I cut?" (I, ii, l. 173) he asks Ferdinand. Perhaps because he is always doing other people's dirty deeds (a fact he is only too aware of), he sees himself as almost subhuman, accepting the employment offer with the words "I am your creature" (I, ii, l. 210). However, Bosola is not only a talented wordsmith with a firm grasp of metaphor, as he often exhibits high intelligence (he was a highly regarded student of philosophy) and makes his exit with the gnomic apothegm, "Sometimes the devil doth preach" (I, ii, l. 215).

Ferdinand is quite a disgusting man. Lascivious, lecherous and equally as fond of ithyphallic innuendo as of his own sister, he makes very suggestive and dirty remarks, prostituting the very language he speaks. From a psychological point of view, Ferdinand clearly harbours strong insecurities. He surrounds himself with adoring and eager-to-please sycophants who attend to his every caprice and are constantly trying to gain favour by impressing him. They crack opaquely moronic jokes to make him laugh, and uproariously guffaw at the slightest hint from Ferdinand of poor paronomasia. Ferdinand needs constant reassurance from his courtiers but is dishonest and cruel. Ferdinand tells them, "laugh when I laugh," (I, ii, l. 46) and, as well as his assault of the Duchess, is described as an "ill man" (I, ii, l. 199) and "the devil" (I, ii, l. 199) by Bosola - himself not the most righteous character.

From just the first couple of scenes, the casual reader can easily discern which personal qualities are most important and how certain characters are successful. Money is clearly a central aspect of life in the Italian courts and Bosola is "lur'd" (I, ii, l. 155) to Ferdinand by his promise that "there's gold" (I, ii, l. 170). Money is also equally important to the aristocracy, as the Cardinal goes to extreme measures to avoid Bosola and the debt he owes. The overwhelming feeling is that, to be successful, one must be ruthless and as corrupt as possible. As a result, power and status are also very important things to have on your side and Ferdinand assumes Bosola wants this too - he temptingly hints, "thou mayst arrive at a higher place by't" (I, ii, l. 186-7). We also find that it is beneficial to be a pragmatic realist and adhere to the harsh, devious Machiavellian model of maintaining political power by underhand means with deceit and without morality. People believed that, in ruling, the end justified whatever means were necessary and knowledge meant power; hence people talked behind each other's backs and gleaned as much useful information out of each other as possible. Phoney civility could get courtiers a long way if they pleased the higher classes sufficiently, and several characters such as Rodgerigo and Castruchio seem to favour following this method. The Cardinal looks as though he has reached his elevated position only by extirpating himself from his conscience and things such as respect and position are clearly very important in court society. A moral character that would stick to ethical beliefs would not last long in this world of corruption and mercilessness. Right and wrong (only in respect to what is owed to you) is a vital issue and it is very important to learn to mix with the right people in order to rise to the highest echelons of the court

Overall, the emphasis in the Italian court of Malfi seems to rest on material worldly goodness such as money, appearance and status rather than aspects some would consider more important - spiritual well-being, conscience and morals.

Q12. Draft a biographical sketch of John Webster.

Or

Q. What do you about the life of Webster.

Very little is known about the life of John Webster. He was the son of a London carriage maker, John Webster, who was a member of the Merchant Taylors' Company before being made free in 1571. His father married on November 4, 1577, to Elizabeth Coates. It is assumed that John Webster was born soon after, but since the parish records were destroyed in the great fire of London in 1666, no accurate date exists. It is possible that John Webster attended the respected Merchant Taylor's school but there is no evidence to the same. There is a record of a John Webster entered at Middle Temple, one of the Inns of Court, in 1598, but it is not certain that he was John Webster, the playwright.

For the life of Webster the dramatist, however, as opposed to Webster the private man, we have a few facts. He comes into our notice—fairly young, it is to be presumed—in 1602. He had a hand in several plays that we know of during that year: *Caesar's fall, Two Shapes, Christmas Comes But Once a Year,* and at least one part of *Lady Jane*. His collaborators were Munday, Drayton, Middleton, Heywood, Chettle, Smith, and Dekker. It was the beginning, as far as we know, of a close connection with Dekker and a long one with Heywood. Webster was writing for both Henslowe's companies, *Caesar's Fall* and *Two Shapes* for the Admiral's men, *Christmas Comes but Once a Year* and *Lady Jane* for Worcester's men. Writing for Henslowe was not the best school for genius. No high artistic standard was exacted. It rather implies poverty, and certainly means scrappy and unserious work. It may have given Webster—it would have given some people—a sense of the theatre. But he emerged with so little facility in writing and so little aptitude for a good plot (in the ordinary sense), that one must conclude that his genius was not best fitted for theatrical expression, into which it was driven. There are other periods and literary occupations it is harder to imagine him in. But I can figure him as a more or less realistic novelist of the present. His literary skill, his amazing genius for incorporating fragments of his experience, his "bitter flashes" and slow brooding atmosphere of gloom, would have been more tremendous untrammeled by dramatic needs. His power of imaginative visualization was often superfluous in a play. Like most of his gifts it is literary. It is just what one keenly misses in most novels. One can see, almost quote from, a rather large grey-brown novel by John Webster, a book full of darkly suffering human beings, slightly less inexplicable than Dostoyevsky's, but as thrilling, figures glimpsed by sudden flashes that tore the gloom they were part of; a book such that one would remember the taste of the whole longer than any incident or character.... But these imaginations are foolish in a Heraclitan world.

The earliest known records of Webster's employment as a playwright are found in the diary of theatre manager Phillip Henslowe at the beginning of the new century. Among the payments which Henslowe noted in his diary in 1602 were those made to Webster, Anthony Munday, Michael Drayton "and the rest" for a play entitled *Caesar's Fall*. Over the next decade or so, Henslowe's records show Webster collaborating with Heywood, writing a prologue to Marston's *Malcontent*, and composing his two masterpieces *The White Devil* and *The Duchess of Malfi*.

Webster has sometimes been criticized for the limited scope of his plays. He knows nothing, for instance, of the tenderness and pleasant fantasy of Shakespeare. It was mankind's anguish and evil alone which captured his imagination. T.S. Eliot described Webster as the poet who was "much possessed by death, and saw the skull beneath the skin."

In his other masterpiece, *The Duchess of Malfi*, Webster deals with a more innocent pair of lovers. The widowed Duchess of Malfi is forbidden to marry again by her brothers—Duke Ferdinand and the Cardinal—because they covet her estate. Unbeknownst to her brothers, however, the Duchess falls in love with her steward Antonio, and they marry secretly. The two lovers live happily for a time and the Duchess gives birth to three children, but when their marriage is discovered, the evil of the world stages a macabre dance around the little family from which there is no escape. A splendid nightmare, *The Duchess of Malfi* bears witness to a sensitive spirit, overwhelmed by the horror and despair of the world.

After *The Duchess of Malfi,* Webster lapsed into mostly second-rate work. Around 1620, he wrote *The Devil's Law Case* and collaborated a year later with Middleton on *Anything for a Quiet Life*. About 1625 he collaborated on *The Fair Maid of the Inn* with Massinger and ford and on *A Cure for a Cuckold* with Heywood. And sometime before his death (probably in the 1630s), he composed the Roman tragedy *Appius and Virginia.*

After Webster's death, the Elizabethan theatre began to decline. The stage was filled with mediocre writers such as Glapthorne, Brome, Markham, Suckling and D'Avenant, reputed to be Shakespeare's illegitimate son. Then in 1642, the Puritans closed the public theatres, and there was darkness.

Q13. Discuss the various themes in Webster's 'The Duchess of Malfi'

Or

Q. 'The Duchess of Malfi' discusses sways through themes of Horror, Corruption and Reality

Horror, corruption, revenge and integrity linger deep in the backbone of the play, *The Duchess of Malfi*

Machinations, neurosis, incest, and bloody vengeance, all shot through with brilliantly inventive, knotty and darkly poetic language; *Duchess* invites its audience to take a walk on the wild side.

While the eighteenth century, before Garrick at least, and the Victorians after him were able to bowdlerise his near contemporary Shakespeare and come up with something more to their liking, Webster proved far less tractable. Even William Archer, a discerning critic and one of the National Theatre's founding fathers, found the play "intolerable", and it's easy to see why.

Themes central to *The Duchess of Malfi* include identity, sexuality, and power, which are all closely intertwined in the tragedy. The theme of identity is carried through the play in several ways. The twin relationship between Ferdinand and the Duchess makes the characters mirrors for each other; the frequent presence of mirrors as stage props makes the metaphor explicit. The Duchess also battles with the issue of conflicting public and private identities: her status as aristocratic lady contests with her love for the lower-born Antonio, and the connection between birth and identity is an open question throughout the play. Her brothers press upon her the identity of the virtuous widow, one that she is unwilling to accept. When Duchess says, "I am Duchess of Malfi still," it is not clear whether she is affirming or lamenting this identity.The theme of sexuality is tied to identity, particularly in regards to Ferdinand and the Duchess; his apparent desire for her is a perversion of socially acceptable sexuality as well as a kind of narcissism. Sexuality is generally linked to danger and violence, as the most explicitly sexual characters are shown to be the most evil. Even the comparatively healthy sexuality of the Duchess is considered suspect, a sign of excess passion, even if it is not, as Ferdinand and the Cardinal would imagine, a mark of depravity. Moreover, although the Duchess has neither Ferdinand's incestuous desires nor the Cardinal's affairs, it is in one sense her sexuality that propels the violence of the play. The desire for power, however, is also a controlling force in the drama; the Duchess's brothers are driven by a desire to control the family fortune. More generally, however, the play opens the question of the bases of power and authority, and who rightfully holds it. The corrupted authority of Ferdinand and the Cardinal casts doubt on the power they wield, while the nobility of the Duchess as she faces her death suggests the possibility of a different sort of authority.

Appearances and Reality

Repeated throughout *The Duchess of Malfi* is the idea that people cannot be trusted, that things are not as they appear. People, both the essentially good people and the villains, disguise their bodies and their motives. Several instances of pretending and concealing occur to set the tone for the rest of the play: the Cardinal pretends to have no interest in Bosola; he is hired to spy on the Duchess, pretending only to tend her horses; the Duchess pretends to have no interest in marriage; Cariola hides behind the arras without Antonio's knowledge and promises the Duchess that she will "conceal this secret from the world / As warily as those that trade in poison / Keep poison from their children." Antonio, who is known for his honesty, agrees to keep the marriage a secret. The Duchess complains that women of wealth and stature cannot be honest about their feelings, but are "forced to express our violent passions / in riddles, and in dreams, and leave the path / of simple virtue, which was never made / to seem the thing it is not."

Further incidents of deception and disguise occur throughout the play. The Duchess and Antonio invent stories to conceal the birth of their first child and their plans to escape to Ancona. Ferdinand brings the Duchess a dead man's hand that he knows she will take for Antonio's and shows her wax figures that look like her husband and children. Bosola visits the imprisoned Duchess in disguise, appearing as an old man and a bellman. Even Bosola's one kindness to the Duchess is a deception, as he tells the dying Duchess that her husband is alive and reconciled with her brothers. The Cardinal kills Julia (with whom he has been having an affair without her husband's knowledge) by giving her a poison disguised as a holy book, not knowing that Julia has deceived him by hiding Bosola behind the door.

Although none of these deceptions brings about its desired end, the characters turn again and again to secrecy and disguise to solve their problems, as though they know no other way to move in the world. It is not an optimistic picture, as Bosola realises just before he dies: "O, this gloomy world! / in what a shadow or deep pit of darkness, / Doth womanish and fearful mankind live!" If the world is steered not by God but by uncaring stars, and if men and women cannot trust their own perceptions to steer through it, it is a gloomy world, indeed.

The Cardinal, Bosola, and Ferdinand die without anyone coming to save them, because the Cardinal has lied to keep the servants from entering his chambers.

Fate and Belief

Considering that one of the main characters of *The Duchess of Malfi* is a Cardinal, one of the highest-ranking officials in the Roman Catholic Church, there is a surprising lack of reference to God in the play. The characters do not turn to God for help in trouble, and they do not seek forgiveness when they come to believe they have acted wrongly. The only certainty in life is death, and there is no promise here of an afterlife. The world of *The Duchess of Malfi* is controlled not by God, but by fate.

Of all the characters, it is Bosola who most changes during the play, and whose psychology is revealed the most clearly. As he watches the conduct of the three siblings, he comes to a new understanding of the differences between a good servant and a good man, and he grows in respect for the honesty of Antonio and the dignity of the Duchess. If anyone were going to turn to God in the end, it would be Bosola, but he does not. Instead, when he realises that he has accidentally killed Antonio, he utters the line that expresses the world view for the entire play: "We are merely the stars' tennis-balls, struck and banded / which way please them."

Ferdinand is most conscious of his religion, but his Christianity is not a religion of love but one of vengeance, not of forgiveness but of damnation. In act 2, in his anger at learning of the Duchess's child, Ferdinand's first instinct is to call her "a sister damn'd." Naming wild punishments he would like to administer to her, he declares that he would like to have the Duchess and the unknown father of the child "burnt in a coal-pit" with no vents, so that "their curs Ed smoke might not ascend to heaven." In act 4, he brings a series of horrors to the Duchess to drive her to despair, so that she will renounce God and be sent to hell when he has her murdered. Ferdinand is so clearly insane, that his understanding of religion must be seen as a product of rage, not of religious teaching.

Other characters turn elsewhere for their understanding of the world. Antonio learns by astrological calculation that his first child will have a "short life" and a "violent death." The Cardinal, whose lavish lifestyle and mistress would seem to distance him from the teachings of his church, does not suggest that the Duchess pray for guidance if she finds herself tempted to remarry, but advises that "your own discretion / Must now be your director." Cariola warns the Duchess not to use a false religious pilgrimage to fool her brothers, but the Duchess rejects the warning, calling Cariola "a superstitious fool." Although she faces her death on her knees to more easily pass through heaven's gates, there is no real sense of faith in her last speeches.

Q14. Study the character of Bosola –Is he truly evil or just mislead?

We are introduced to Bosola by Delio in Act 1 Sc 1 as 'a fellow seven years in the galleys for a notorious murder'. The audience immediately sees him as an evil character capable of murder. Even though Antonio perceives him as a potentially valiant character "He's very valiant', he also realises that he 'like moths in a cloth do hurt for want of wearing'. Hence, Bosola is seen as one who has some inkling of goodness in him but it is overshadowed by his 'close rearing'. Antonio realises that Bosola if not used well would become a bad person. The idea of a nature of goodness overpowered by the nurture by 'black malcontents' is the result that is Bosola. He is the 'court gall', a bitter character who would 'rail at things which he wants' and would do anything to achieve.

The bitterness of Bosola's character is brought out in his conversation with the Cardinal. He laments on it all being a 'miserable age', where 'the only reward for doing well is the doing of it'. He is seen as a character who has been taken advantage of by the corrupted court and who has learnt to deal with his consequence 'blackbirds fatten best in hard weather'. We thus realise that the hardness of his character is brought out by the need for survival. He is a neglected character who has learnt to 'thrive' in his own way. He is obviously angered by the disease of corruption in the italian court 'for places in the court are like beds in the hospital'. It is to survive that Bosola becomes an 'invisible devil in flesh'. Yet while Bosola agrees to play the role of Ferdinand's avengement to the Duchess in her 'marraige' to Antonio, it is Bosola who deems Ferdinand as a 'corrupter and an impudent traitor'. One sees that Bosola does have some ethical sense to see that he is about to commit an evil 'the ill man can invent'. To a certain extent, one realises that Bosola agrees to murder not because he enjoys it, but because he needs to survive.

Yet despite these redeeming characteristics of Bosola, he will always be one associated with the dark. The language that he uses is crude with grotesque and horrific imagery. 'a rotten dead body we delight, to hide it in rich tissue'. He is an unsavoury character and is morally repungant to our senses. Yet his crudeness does hold a certain truth at times and one realises that it is Bosola's own encounter with life that gives him such bitter cynicism. 'man stands amazed to see his deformity in any other creature but himself'. Indeed, one realises that Bosola's character is not brought about by a stark change in character, but an uncovering of the facade of coarseness and evil to reveal his true character, one who only works to be paid and who when taken advantage of seeks to find his own justice because there would be no other way to achieve it. He understands that it is the only way to survive in the court would be to become the worst of them all. 'i look no higher than i can reach'. He cannot aspire to happiness but only to survive.

One realises that true evil is not part of his nature when in accidentally inducing labour for the Duchess, he apologises 'I am sorry' and leaves. Indeed, that even Antonio makes use of Bosola's character to 'give out that Bosola hath poisoned them' shows that while Bosola may play the role of the murderer, he is very much a victim of it all. He hides in the darkness to protect himself. It is only at the end that he allows his true nature to overpower his nurture. Indeed, it is true that his character changes little, for in being made the scapegoat of the Duchess death, he can no longer conceal his hatred for corruption and his desire for justice. We see this in his character from the beginning when he smile at being able to 'make her brother's galls overflow their livers'. He enjoyed seeing the anger and frustration of Ferdinand and the Cardinal to learn of their adulterous sister more than the role of the murderer. Indeed, he speaks of 'this base quality of intelligencer' and one feels that he certainly means it.

Indeed, it is ironic that Bosola is the one who imprisons the Duchess in her own castle for in the exploration of this concern of entrapment and imprisonment of the play, one realises that Bosola is also victim of entrapment. He assumes the darkness to survive in the dark and corrupt court. He 'thrives' because he chooses to abandon his morals and love of justice that he may survive in the court. He kills the Duchess and shows her no mercy because it is his profession to carry out the Cardinal's orders. Yet he tells Ferdinand that 'you may discern the shape of loveliness more perfect in her tears than her smiles'. He is clearly touched by the stoism of the Duchess and he is angered when he does not receive payment for killing her. He was angered, not at being unpaid, but because he had been made to go against his character and ethics to kill the Duchess and then is blamed for it. We see his true character and the facade in conflict when he speaks of wanting to 'save your life' and lamenting on 'this world a tedious theatre'.

Hence, it is NOT a change of character from evil to good that we see in Bosola, but a battle of his conscience with his evil deeds. He was never an evil character, only one who was bitter about his situation and who in seeing the integrity and stoism displayed by the Duchess, realised the own quality within himself.

Q15. What are the principal themes of the Duchess of Malfi? Does the play have a "moral"?

Or

Q. Explore the theme of Victim v/s Villain in Webster's "The Duchess of Malfi"

According to Robert Ornstein, we should expect a Renaissance tragedy to display "a depth of vision that penetrates the surface violence or anarchy of life to illumine the underlying pattern and meaning of man's fate".[1] Ornstein infers that Renaissance drama should a reveal a sense of divine morality and purpose beneath the exterior confusion of life. However, is it necessarily true that Renaissance playwrights desired to exhibit such a virtuous texture, or did they perhaps wish to shock us with the suggestion that horror penetrates deeper than the skin?

This is certainly a view implied by *The Duchess of Malfi:* "Why do you laugh? Methinks you that are/ courtiers should be my touchwood [...]/ laugh when I laugh. Ferdinand demands that his courtiers laugh only when he deems it appropriate; a desire that is itself laughable. He is attempting to assert his position as a Machiavellian prince, but his words undermine him and he is instead cast as a figure of jest. However, this apparent harmlessness is a facade: "What appears in him mirth is merely outside" (I.i.170). Antonio declares that the humour of Ferdinand's character is actually only a shell. Once this is broken, the audience will be able to see his true personality. Contrary to Ornstein's belief, Antonio suggests that horror is not superficial. Instead, what might initially appear amusing, can in fact be terrifying: "You are my sister-/ this was my father's poniard. Do you see? / I'd be lath to see't look rusty" (I.i.330-33). Ferdinand's threat to murder his sister if she should remarry might be perversely amusing, yet it exposes the sinister and perhaps even incestuous nature of the play. Ferdinand and the Cardinal are determined that only they should possess the Duchess, a fact that is borne out most vehemently by the imprisonment and grotesque torture of her: "Here's a hand/ to which you have vowed much love; the ring upon it you gave" (IV.i.43-44). Ferdinand gives the Duchess what she thinks to be the hand of Antonio, tricking her into believing that both her husband and her children have been murdered. The Duchess's 'crime' in marrying her steward surely does not befit such cruelty. "It has often been pointed out that there is a violation of the correct 'order' which is supposed to have affected Jacobean audiences with the moral force of a tragic 'flaw' but [...] the play entirely assumes the audience's complicity and therefore approval of the Duchess's action". If the Duchess's punishment is not intended by Webster to be a moral lesson to the audience, teaching them not to break social boundaries, then what is its purpose? As the Cardinal's reaction to her marriage intimates, it is perhaps still related to her disregard for their noble blood: "Shall our blood/ the royal blood of Castile and Aragon/ be thus attainted?" (II.v.22-24). The Cardinal makes this statement before he knows the identity of his sister's lover. He therefore cannot be aware that she has married a person of lower birth. He is therefore concerned only with the fact that her blood has been poisoned by someone outside of her family. It might be argued that the Duchess's first marriage renders this argument void, but we know nothing of her original husband or the circumstances of his death. Instead, the hint of incest is reconfirmed by Ferdinand: "I could kill her now/ in you, or in me, for I do think/ it is some sin is us heaven doth revenge" (II.v.63-65). James L. Calderwood suggests that Ferdinand's outburst represents an identification of "his latent desire with her realised desire"; that Ferdinand associates his sister's sexual fulfilment with his unconscious yearning for her. Indeed, it might even be suggested that Ferdinand not only longs for a incestuous relationship, but that he and his siblings are the product of one: "You never fixed your eye on three fair medals/ Cast in onè figure" (I.i.188-89). Much is made of the fact that the Duchess and her two brothers are startling similar in appearance. Whilst this alone does not confirm an incestuous family history, we might wish to reinterpret Ferdinand's original threat: "You are my sister-/ this was my father's poniard [...]/ I'd be loth to see't look rusty" (I.i.330-33). Ferdinand's warning infers a sexual relationship between his father and the Duchess: a relationship that he threatens to recreate.

How though, do Ferdinand's bizarre sexual desires relate to his horrific torture of his sister? According to Calderwood, Ferdinand "seeks the purgation of his own tainted blood in the purging of hers". He is repulsed by the realization of his desire and so wishes to cleanse the perceived sins of the Duchess so that he might also cleanse his own. I would suggest the opposite. In imprisoning his sister Ferdinand is attempting to fulfill his lust:

Bosola Why do you do this?

Ferdinand to bring her to despair (IV.ii.116-17)

With the most disturbing line of the play, Ferdinand declares his intention to deprive the Duchess of hope. He desires her complete subjection to his will. He is not purging his sins, but indulging in them: "Damn her! That body of hers" (IV.ii.122). Ferdinand cannot escape his monstrous passion for the Duchess as his desires overcome him entirely:

[...] let them practice together, sing and dance,
and act their gambols to the full oath' moon.
If she can sleep the better for it, let her (IV.ii.129-31)

In tormenting his sister with frolicking madmen, designed to keep her awake at night, Ferdinand is envisaging his own rape of the Duchess. By "seeing the skull beneath the skin", Webster has not found morality, but the ultimate horror and taboo.

Duchess challenges traditional social conventions by expressing her love for a person of lower birth. Ornstein almost compares the Duchess to Shakespeare's Cleopatra, inferring that, in death, she can transcend the immorality of life. Yet whilst the Duchess is virtuous "I forgive them" [her executioners] (IV.ii.206) we must not overlook the fact that we do not learn her true name. The Duchess is denied an identity even when she is seemingly a symbol of absolute virtue. Her moral "victory" then, is somewhat confused.

The ambiguity that pervades morality is expressed by the respective murderers of Edward and the Duchess: "These hands were never stained with innocent blood/ nor shall they now be tainted with a king's" (24.80-81). Lightborne's apparent attempt to reassure Edward is purposely vague. It might be suggested that he is deceiving Edward, for evidently he will murder him. Such an interpretation though, would force us to apply a moral reading to Lightborne's actions, when what he says is not actually false. At this moment in the play, Edward is no longer king. Lightborne's hands will not be stained with the blood of a monarch, but with that of a common man. The morality of Light borne is of no concern. He is merely playing his part in the play and in history. In contrast, Bosola does deceive the Duchess "Come, be of comfort; I will save your life" (IV.i.86). Although Bosola questions Ferdinand's treatment of the Duchess and intends to protect her, he is unable to fulfill his vow. He might not appear in his "own shape", but Bosola is still the Duchess's executioner: "I am come to make thy tomb" (IV.ii.114). His disguise cannot, excuse him from her murder. Despite wishing to find the virtues of the Duchess in himself, Bosola still allows horror to conquer. The failure of morality is finally highlighted by Bosola's accidental killing of Antonio: "The man I would have saved 'above mine own life!" (V.v.53). although attempting to revenge the wrongs of himself, Ferdinand and the Cardinal, Bosola shows that ultimately, virtue can never be victorious.

Therefore, is "the skull beneath the skin" the vision of a moralist or a purveyor of horror? This is perhaps best answered by the conclusions of the plays themselves. Both end with the rightful heir taking their place. However, in *Edward the Second,*

King Edward III has a voice: "Accursed head! / Could I have ruled then as I do now/ Thou hadst not hatched this monstrous treachery (25.95-97)? Edward III promises to be a strong ruler. In a play that dramatizes violence but apparently eschews morality, there is still hope. Marlowe clearly displays the horrors of life yet, in refusing to seek justification for them, he finds nothing worse. In contrast, the son of Antonio and the Duchess can make no speech. He is left an orphan, to be the prey of more powerful men. The Duchess might have achieved a spiritual victory, but horror has not been vanquished. Instead, by penetrating the surface anarchy of life we find, not a divine moral pattern, but a cycle of terror.

Q16. The idea of entrapment and confinement is represented throughout the play. The soul is seen as a prisoner of the body, which will only be liberated in death. Discuss.

By hiring Bosola to spy on the Duchess, the Cardinal and Ferdinand set a trap to ensnare the Duchess as men set traps to capture wild creatures in order to kill them. The Duchess is warned that if she is being caught, would be killed, thus Ferdinand's warning to her that 'your darkest actions, nay, your private's thoughts will come to light'. The Cardinal's comment 'the marriage night is the entrance to some prison' are not prophecies, but threats. Bosola's task is therefore set out, to first entrap the Duchess and then to secure her in her imprisonment.

Even though Bosola's intelligence takes years to produce the results required by the brothers, their threats have an immediate fulfillment in the life of the Duchess: their determined wills and the atmosphere of her own poisoned court limit her activities. Her marriage ceremony is literally confined within the walls of her chamber. In this sense, her marriage night is indeed, 'the entrance to some prison'. Like a prisoner, her movements and emotions are restricted. Even the imagery in her words to Antonio convey the idea of imprisonment 'this lowly roof of yours is too low built' and her speaking of not being 'the figure cut in alabaster, kneels at my husband's tomb'.

The idea of betrayal through violent entrapment is present in Antonio's recognition, after the birth of his 1st child that Bosola is trying to undermine him. The concept of something precious being contained in something frail, parallel to that of the soul being imprisoned in the body, is reflected in Ferdinand's cry 'Foolish man, that ever will trust their honour in a bark, made of so slight, weak bulrush, as is woman, apt every minute to sink it.'

When her brothers know that the Duchess and Antonio have fallen into the trap of a secret marriage Ferdinand goes to take them both in her lodgings. Their married happiness is seen to include Antonio's teasing, which leads to his leaving his wife alone. So the poniard which might have killed Antonio is presented by Ferdinand as a warning - or as a hint to commit suicide to Antonio's wife. Ignoring the hint, the Duchess plans to secure life and liberty, first for her husband and then for herself and her children. In doing so, she rashly accepts Bosola's advice, which in itself is a snare. He suggests a 'feigned pilgrimage', but the Duchess and her family make a properly pious devotion at the shrine at our Lady of Loretto; her brother the Cardinal, on the contrary, resigns his religious vestments to be acoutred as a soldier before banishing the Duchess and her family. Witnessed by pilgrims who comment on his cruel bearing, the Cardinal vents his rage upon his sister by tearing off her wedding ring.

Indeed, one sees the Duchess as one not only imprisoned physically by her brothers, but also one trapped in her role 'we are forced to woo because none dare woo us'. The imagery of the wooing scene suggests, prophetically, not only restraint, but madness and violent death. Nevertheless, a happier instance of the image of confinement occurs in the Duchess's reply to Antonio's question about her brothers 'Do not think of them, all discord without circumference, is only to be pitied, and not feared' This may be interpreted as a reference to the wedding ring that she has given to Antonio, or to the confinement of the wife's arms as she embraces her husband.

The idea of the Duchess as a trapped bird is alter underlined by the way that Ferdinand toys with her before having her killed. Immediately after being captured she asks Bosola 'to what prison' she must go to, but he insists that he brothers 'mean you safety and pity'. The Duchess by now knows better. The trapping net becomes a symbol of necessary evil which will reveal well; just as death is an evil, which at the Last Judgment will reveal the good of the soul. This appears in the conclusion of the Duchess's fable of the Salmon and the Dogfish (Act 3 v133-38)

Images of imprisonment occur most frequently in Act 4. The Duchess treatment within her own palace suggests the she is confined as a punishment and restrained as if she were mad. Cariola assures her that she will like 'to shake this durance off', but the Duchess mind turns again to contemplate the snared bird - which is how Bosola has taught her to think of herself 'the robin red breast and the nightingale, never live long in cages'. Earlier, the Duchess had envied the bird's ability to 'choose their mates and carol their sweet pleasures to the spring'.

The final symbol of the Duchess's confinement is the coffin itself, her 'last presence chamber' and her final thought is of a confinement that leads immediately to liberty. So she exalts her executioners for an instant 'yet stay, heaven gates are not so highly arched as princes palaces; they enter there must go upon their knees'. 'Straight is the gate and narrow is the way' the implied contrast is with the space, the broad way that leads to perdition. Though the Duchess dies in Act 4, the image which has hitherto been so closely associated with her persists. Bosola. Who ensnared her for her brothers is able to confine the Cardinal to the room in which the Duchess's death is to be avenged. So caught, the Cardinal cries 'shall I die like a leveret without any resistance?'

Hence, the theme of imprisonment is indeed an important one in the play. It is not only the Duchess who is imprisoned but most of the characters in the play. Ferdinand as much as he imprisons the Duchess in her chambers, is also imprisoned by his anger which takes over his reasoning 'why do you make of yourself so wild a tempest?' Indeed, the idea of the characters each being confined by themselves is a predominant idea in the play.

Q17. What implies when the lead character Duchess says. "I am Duchess of Malfi still"

Or

Q. What is the effect and significance of the line "I am the Duchess of Malfi still" (Act 4, scene 2, line 128)?

One of the most significant ideas about both of these plays is that in each the heroine dies or is eliminated before the end. This particular line in defence of identity from *The Duchess of Malfi,* "I am Duchess of Malfi still," may therefore be related to both plays, although we see a more poignant example in Webster's text. The remaining characters in each play must also survive without the heroines. Their actions following the deaths of both the Duchess and Hermione seem to give testimony to the significance of these women, and to the continuing importance of their identity. *The Duchess of Malfi* perhaps shows this idea more so than does *The Winter's Tale,* though Shakespeare's play deals with Hermione's death in a unique way. Throughout Webster's play, the Duchess has to deal with domineering and cruel brothers, and her new domestic identity has to be hidden for the most part—her relationship with Antonio and her children initially remains in the private sphere of the play. Hermione, on the other hand, is a married woman and a queen, and as such is duty-bound to have children. Her maternity, however, is used against her as a tangible way to prove that she was unfaithful to her husband. Both women are condemned for their maternity as tangible evidence of their supposed transgression. Yet after their deaths, those who condemned Hermione and the Duchess are remorseful or suffering themselves.

In *The Duchess of Malfi,* after the duchess has been killed, we see significant interaction between Ferdinand, the doctor, and also the Cardinal, as he observes his brother in a state of madness. Pescara initially asks the doctor about Ferdinand's condition, and is answered:

I'll tell you:
In those that are possessed with't there overflows
such melancholy humour, they imagine
themselves to be transformed into wolves.
Steal forth to churchyards in the dead of night,
And dig dead bodies up: as two nights since
One met the Duke, 'bout midnight in a lane
Behind St. Mark's church, with the leg of a man
Upon his shoulder; and he howl'd fearfully:
Said he was a wolf: only the difference
Was, a wolf's skin was hairy on the outside,
His on the inside: bad them take their swords,
Rip up his flesh, and try: straight I was sent for,
And having ministered to him, found his Grace
Very well recovered. (V, ii. 7-21)

The Cardinal seems somewhat surprised to observe this strange behaviour in his brother, though he is aware of the reason for it, as he shows by feigning an answer to Pescara who asks how Ferdinand came to be this way. In *The Winter's Tale,* the elimination of the maternal figure is dealt with differently, most likely because of the differing circumstances of Hermione and the Duchess. Hermione was a queen, the mother of a prince, and clearly entitled to recognition and privilege. Although the Duchess was part of the nobility, her marriage to Antonio was a common one, and she had clearly married beneath her own social class. For these reasons the Duchess's children were not officially recognized. Due to these differences between the two characters, there are varying responses to their deaths—in *The Duchess of Malfi* we have a character going mad, where as in *The Winter's Tale,* Leontes is simply remorseful. He realises that he has been wrong and deserves to be spoken of as such, but he is not punished with madness. As he says to Paulina:

Go on, go on;

Thou canst not speak too much: I have deserved

all tongues to speak their bitterest. (III, ii. 215-217)

He vows every day to visit the chapel where the bodies of the queen and prince will lie, and "tears shed there shall be [his] recreation"(III, ii. 240-241). Despite the different responses to the elimination of the Duchess and Hermione, it is clear that both of these women were significant to the text and to the other characters. Their identities will be remembered and continue to influence the rest of the play after they have disappeared from the text.

Although the removal of both of these women from the texts is significant, the Duchess's death is more heroic than Hermione's. Though we hear Paulina say that the Queen has died as a result of the news of Mamillius' death, Shakespeare provides a dubious magical solution in *The Winter's Tale* by bringing Hermione back to life at the play's conclusion. Perhaps we may assume that Hermione didn't die at all, but rather was kept in hiding somewhere until her identity became less threatening or influential. Hermione was portrayed while alive in the text, as a faithful wife and true mother. Despite Leontes' accusations it is clear that her character was admirable and heroic, and the fact that she "dies" unfairly makes this fact all the more evident. Kept in the domestic arena, Hermione would have been a mother who had an important influence over her child, as is shown by the naming of her child through Antigonus's dream. However, restoring her life at the end of the play, after Perdita has grown up motherless, and Mamillius of course has died, perhaps reflects the concern that society had for maternal power. Hermione's identity is no longer a threat at the end of the play, and her nurturing, motherly skills are no longer needed. The Duchess, however, retains her maternal identity; she is still the Duchess of Malfi after she dies, and in fact one of her children still survives, though he has been separated from her. Although Hermione is a maternal character to be admired, that particular aspect of her identity has been taken away, and she reenters the play's action as an older woman who can have no true influence or nurturing role in the family to whom she has returned.

Q18. Critically study the character of Bosola as presented by Webster.

Or

Q. It is not a change of character from evil to good that we see in Bosola, but a battle of his conscience with his evil deeds. Do you agree?

Or

Q. How does Bosola react to the growing conflict within him? What role does he attempt to play as the bellman? In what sense does the Duchess seem heroic? What is the source of her strength? How does her death contrast with that of Cariola? How does Webster keep Bosola a fairly sympathetic figure even though he has helped murder the Duchess? How might we explain Ferdinand's crazed reaction to the Duchess's death? What explains Bosola's sudden change from murderer to revenge of the Duchess's death?

We are introduced to Bosola by Delio in Act 1 Sc 1 as 'a fellow seven years in the galleys for a notorious murder'. The audience immediately sees him as an evil character capable of murder. Even though Antonio perceives him as a potentially valiant character "He's very valiant', he also realises that he 'like moths in a cloth do hurt for want of wearing'. Hence, Bosola is seen as one who has some inkling of goodness in him but it is overshadowed by his 'close rearing'. Antonio realises that Bosola if not used well would become a bad person. The idea of a nature of goodness overpowered by the nurture by 'black malcontents' is the result that is Bosola. He is the 'court gall', a bitter character who would 'rail at things which he wants' and would do anything to achieve.

The bitterness of Bosola's character is brought out in his conversation with the Cardinal. He laments on it all being a 'miserable age', where 'the only reward for doing well is the doing of it'. He is seen as a character who has been taken advantage of by the corrupted court and who has learnt to deal with his consequence 'blackbirds fatten best in hard weather'. We thus realise that the hardness of his character is brought out by the need for survival. He is a neglected character who has learnt to 'thrive' in his own way. He is obviously angered by the disease of corruption in the Italian court 'for places in the court are like beds in the hospital'. It is to survive that Bosola becomes an 'invisible devil in flesh'. Yet while Bosola agrees to play the role of Ferdinand's avengement to the Duchess in her 'marriage' to Antonio, it is Bosola who deems Ferdinand as a 'corrupter and an impudent traitor'. One sees that Bosola does have some ethical sense to see that he is about to commit an evil 'the ill man can invent'. To a certain extent, one realises that Bosola agrees to murder not because he enjoys it, but because he needs to survive.

Yet despite these redeeming characteristics of Bosola, he will always be one associated with the dark. The language that he uses is crude with grotesque and horrific imagery. 'A rotten dead body we delight, to hide it in rich tissue'. He is an unsavory character and is morally repugnant to our senses. Yet his crudeness does hold a certain truth at times and one realises that it is Bosola's own encounter with life that gives him such bitter cynicism. 'Man stands amazed to see his deformity in any other creature but himself'. Indeed, one realises that Bosola's character is not brought about by a stark change in character, but an uncovering of the facade of coarseness and evil to reveal his true character, one who only works to be paid and who when taken advantage of seeks to find his own justice because there would be no other way to achieve it. He understands that it is the only way to survive in the court would be to become the worst of them all. 'I look no higher than I can reach'. He cannot aspire to happiness but only to survive.

One realises that true evil is not part of his nature when in accidentally inducing labour for the Duchess; he apologizes

'I am sorry' and leaves. Indeed, that even Antonio makes use of Bosola's character to 'give out that Bosola hath poisoned them' shows that while Bosola may play the role of the murderer, he is very much a victim of it all. He hides in the darkness to protect himself. It is only at the end that he allows his true nature to overpower his nurture. Indeed, it is true that his character changes little, for in being made the scapegoat of the Duchess death, he can no longer conceal his hatred for corruption and his desire for justice. We see this in his character from the beginning when he smiles at being able to 'make her brother's galls overflow their livers'. He enjoyed seeing the anger and frustration of Ferdinand and the Cardinal to learn of their adulterous sister more than the role of the murderer. Indeed, he speaks of 'this base quality of intelligencer' and one feels that he certainly means it.

Indeed, it is ironic that Bosola is the one who imprisons the Duchess in her own castle for in the exploration of this concern of entrapment and imprisonment of the play, one realises that Bosola is also victim of entrapment. He assumes the darkness to survive in the dark and corrupt court. He 'thrives' because he chooses to abandon his morals and love of justice that he may survive in the court. He kills the Duchess and shows her no mercy because it is his profession to carry out the Cardinal's orders. Yet he tells Ferdinand that 'you may discern the shape of loveliness more perfect in her tears than her smiles'. He is clearly touched by the stoics of the Duchess and he is angered when he does not receive payment for killing her. He was angered, not at being unpaid, but because he had been made to go against his character and ethics to kill the Duchess and then is blamed for it. We see his true character and the facade in conflict when he speaks of wanting to 'save your life' and lamenting on 'this world a tedious theatre'.

Hence, it is not change of character from evil to good that we see in Bosola, but a battle of his conscience with his evil deeds. He was never an evil character, only one who was bitter about his situation and who in seeing the integrity and stoics displayed by the Duchess, realised the own quality within himself.

Q19. Draft a character sketch of The Duchess.

Or

Q. Does stoic philosophy cast light on the Duchess's story? Does she have the characteristics of a stoic?

Or

Q. In the wooing and wedding scene that takes place in Act 1, scene 2, traditional gender roles are reversed. Is the Duchess's willingness to take the masculine role portrayed as heroic? Does she retain any traditional feminine qualities?

Her struggle for autonomy is lamentable on many levels. First, it is important to note that, while we understand her deepest thoughts and are privy to her most intimate moments, we are never told her given name. She is known throughout the play merely as "the Duchess," a title which she would not have had were it not for her now-deceased first husband. Time and again reviewers have praised the Duchess for her strength, passion, courage, ambition, and cunning, yet they have nearly universally failed to recognize that these traits were not simply desirable facets of her character, but were integral to her very survival. She is a completely isolated character, utterly alone in the world, associated with no female companions of her own rank.She is young, has lost her husband, has been left with a young son and daughter to rise, and has been forbidden by her brothers to remarry. Regarding her as a "strong" woman, considering her circumstances, is the least amount of credit one can give her.

The Duchess's status as a wealthy widow can be regarded as both and asset and a liability. The most positive way to interpret her widowhood would be to focus on the new, special rights accorded to her upon becoming a dowager, namely, freedom from the laws of covertures, the system of laws that applied to married and never-before-married women. Under the system of covertures, women were governed by their closest male relative, usually their father or husband. This male relative enjoyed sole control over the fate of the woman's property, money, and any other chattels. Women under covertures had no legal standing, and were, themselves, considered property. Widowed women, however, were not bound by these constraints, and thus exercised full legal authority over their person, property, and chattels. Widows were allowed to enter into legally binding contracts, could bring a suit before a court, and were not subject to any male's personal authority. Another benefit to widowhood under the laws of seventeenth century England concerned the control of widows' dowries. Upon the death of one's husband, the dowry of the wife was returned to her and she was given sole control over one third of her husband's lands and property for the remainder of her lifetime. Widows were free to remarry or to remain single. Further, if a woman chose to remarry but did not wish to lose control over her dower portion, she could turn it over to a trustee, thereby safeguarding her control of the property while at the same time eliminating the chance that her new husband could seize its control.

Despite these freedoms, few women wished to remain unmarried after the death of their husbands. For many women, widowhood actually resulted in an increased dependency on male family members to secure the political and/or social favours previously sought on their behalf by their husbands. Additionally, they often suffered a loss of kinship connection to their husband's family, thus making it even more difficult to repay the favours granted to her by her new advocates. Furthermore, many women saw remarriage as a wonderful tool with which they could advance themselves both socially and financially. They retained the social status of their deceased husband until remarriage, thus they could use the title "Duchess," "Marchioness," or "Countess" to attract a man of similar social ranking, along with their dower portions, which provided them excellent dowries to offer their suitors. Lastly, in an age when most women defined themselves in terms of their husbands and families, widowhood left many women with a feeling of insecurity and purposelessness. In effect, women would often lose themselves when they lost their husbands. Remarriage could provide definition, a renewed sense of purpose, and a feeling of belonging that was absent from their lives in the widowed state.

The Duchess of Malfi doubtless felt the pressures, both positive and negative, associated with widowhood, and there is evidence that she experienced some difficulty reconciling the two. She is clearly aware of her rights as a widow, yet she still allows herself to be constrained by the traditional patriarchal elements of her society. On one hand she asserts her freedom by marrying Antonio against the wishes of her brothers, yet on the other, most notably in her conversation with Ferdinand in Act I, scene 1, lines 290-304, she allows Ferdinand and the Cardinal to attack her virtue, and then adds the self-defeating comments in which she likens herself to a diamond whose value increases each time it is passed through another man's hand.[6] By sexualizing herself and allowing the innuendoes about the lustiness of widows to go unchecked, she allows herself to be degraded. This sort of incongruous behaviour continues throughout the play as the Duchess time and again reconfirms her brothers' assumptions. When Ferdinand attacks her motives for remarriage, she only replies "If all my royal kindred/ Lay in my way unto this marriage, / I'd make them my low footsteps...Let old wives report/ I winked and chose a husband" (I.1.332-4; 339-40).

Despite these self-defeating comments early in the play, the Duchess continues to act as though she regards herself as a free, autonomous woman. She marries her steward, Antonio, despite the objection of others, and even comments on the odd role reversal found in their courtship, "The misery of us that are born great: / we are forced to woo because none dare woo us" (I.1.431-2). She also represents herself as the sole heir and acting ruler of the Duchy of Malfi, as we see in her death scene when she asks Bosola, "Am I not thy Duchess?" and then answers herself, "I am Duchess of Malfi still" (IV.2.127; 134). Despite these efforts to assert her independence, her work is undone by her controlling brothers. In I.1.246-7, Ferdinand tells Bosola that "she's a young widow, / I would not have her marry again." When she does, he retaliates by telling the Pope who, "fore hearing of her looseness, / Hath seized into th'protection of the church/ the dukedom which she held as a dowager" (III.4.31-34). With this duplicitous act, we see, as apparently the Duchess does not, that her "freedom" never truly existed. She was allowed its illusion as long as it remained convenient for her brothers, but once she began to assert herself it was taken from her. Considering the problems the Duchess encounters after following her own course, we see that her real strength of character lies not in her determination to marry the man of her choosing, or in her general defiance of her brothers; rather, it can be found in her ability to endure the grief she brings upon herself as a result of her independent thoughts and actions.

The complexity of the Duchess's plight, such as the question of remarriage, lends a great deal of realism to Webster's play; fortunately, his taste for realism extends beyond the question of remarriage versus widowhood, and encompasses a great many more issues. The relationship of the Duchess and Antonio gives us an excellent insight into the state of matrimonial custom and law during the seventeenth century. Because the Duchess and Antonio married secretly with only Cariola the waiting-woman as a witness, their marriage falls into the canonical category *per verba de presenti*, or, an orally contracted marriage deemed wholly binding by the Roman Catholic Church. According to canon law, any oral contract of marriage executed in the present tense and in front of a witness was substantially, though not ceremonially, complete. The church recognized such unions; however they were not binding under civil law until they were formally and publicly solemnized in a church ceremony. Until the marriage was solemnized, women were not subject to the laws of covertures, no dower rights were conferred, and, according to civil authorities, any children born of the marriage would be ruled illegitimate. We can assume that the Duchess and Antonio's marriage was at some time formalized, as the question of the children's legitimacy is never broached. Given both the civil advantages and the church's belief that marriage is a sacrament, marriages performed away from the church were considered less desirable than those performed in a more traditional manner at the church doors, one of the most public places in any community. Despite this preference for public marriage, the church did recognize that the traditional posting of the banns and public celebration was sometimes, for whatever reason, not always feasible. This recognition of a binding, yet covert marriage signals a transition in canonical thought. Here we see a shift from the focus on community, as evidenced with the public marriage ceremony, to a focus on the individual, as shown through the tolerance of private ceremony.

The Duchess and Antonio's marriage also signals a shift in marital expectations and customs found throughout seventeenth century English culture. By this time, the public had become familiar with the notion of romantic love in marriage through works such as Chrétien de Troyes' Arthurian romances and Shakespeare's *Romeo and Juliet* and *Sonnets*. Further, they were accustomed to recognizing the power of lust in an open, honest manner, as shown in French *fabliaux* and Chaucer's "Miller's" and "Clerk's" Tales. Exposure to these tales of love and lust slowly led the English population to regard them as valid, or at least potentially valid, reasons for instigating a marital relationship. While the traditional notion of marriage based solely on economic and political factors had certainly not fallen by the wayside, people at this time were beginning to ask themselves if the marriage relationship wasn't deep and complex enough to accommodate feelings of love and affection. The middle and lower classes were the first to embrace these notions, as they had the least to gain or lose from marriage alliances, but by the seventeenth century, love matches like that of the Duchess and Antonio were not unheard of among the aristocracy. The Duchess had already married for the "right" reasons, and, in her widowhood, sought to marry for love (dare we say even, lust) and companionship, while her brothers, for whom the traditional modes of marriage proved more convenient, held fast to the marriage practices of the past. What we see here is the beginning of an ideological clash, one that would not fully resolve itself until the late nineteenth century, between marriages based on duty, and favoured by proponents of patriarchy, and marriages based on love, promoted by champions of the individual.

In addition to reflecting the changing nature of the marriage relationship in Jacobean England, we can find in the characters of the Duchess and Antonio traces of the new social mobility that was working its way into English society at the time. As her title indicates, the Duchess is the ruler of Malfi; she also claims lineage in the royal houses of Castile and Aragon. By virtue of her pedigree, her social status is unquestioned and immutable. Antonio, however, does not enjoy this same background. He is what could be called a "self-made" courtier. He has no impressive pedigree, but has worked his way into his position through hard work and (presumably) good networking skills. It is important to note that the first glimpse we are given of Antonio is at a joust he has just won. He is pleased with his success in this sport of the nobility, while Ferdinand, an observer of noble blood, is bored with the tourney. Antonio appreciates where he is; Ferdinand takes it for granted.Antonio's success is a classic example of the possibility for social advancement in Jacobean England. By approaching the proper people and successfully performing the right tasks, Antonio's identity became "mobile" and carried him into the upper echelons of society.

As a steward of the household, Antonio is valued by all, but as a marriage prospect for the Duchess, is soon cast as a feared interloper. Frank Whigham contends that Antonio's successful social ascendance accounts for Ferdinand's incestuous desires for his sister. Whigham argues that Ferdinand's attraction to the Duchess belies his insecurity about the maintenance of his house, and that he, above all, is seeking to prevent contamination of the bloodline. This desperate move to keep outsiders out is understandable in a time when any well-connected commoner, it seems, can enter the aristocracy if he plays his cards right.

Interestingly, Ferdinand is not the only person who seems intimidated by Antonio's newfound status as a Duchess's husband. Antonio himself seems a bit frightened by his situation. He has certainly improved his social ranking, yet, by virtue of its clandestine nature, he cannot openly enjoy his new status. In III.2.147-9, Antonio hides while Ferdinand threatens the Duchess. Antonio's initial reaction is to defend his wife, yet knows he must remain hidden. When he does emerge to console her, he is terrified by another knock at the door, and cries out, "How now! Who knocks? More earthquakes?" (l. 155). He wants to exercise his new role to its fullest, yet he cannot without jeopardizing both himself and the Duchess.Antonio's unease with his new role is also evidenced by his self-deprecating humour. He teases the Duchess that his "rule is only in the night" (III.2.8). Later, when asked by Cariola why he rises so early in the morning, he jokes that "Labouring men/ Count the clock oftenest Cariola, / Are glad when their task's ended" (III.2.17-9). He purports to be tired of "laboring" with the Duchess all night when in reality he must rise early so as to avoid detection. Because he must keep it a secret, his sexual relationship with the Duchess seems more akin to adultery than it does to Holy Matrimony. These "jokes" that Antonio makes indicate that, deep down, he is really very insecure in his new position. He doubtless had few qualms about his previous social advances, yet those were always undertakes with the knowledge that there would be a limit to his success. With his marriage to the Duchess, all social boundaries have been torn down, and Antonio is left without any usable frame of social reference. His commoner's upbringing prepared him to serve, not to be served, and this change, it seems, may be too much for him to handle.

As we have noted, *The Duchess of Malfi* reflects Jacobean society on many levels, thus it should come as no surprise that it was based in part on another societal commentary or that it also has roots in the real lives of at least two noblewomen. Webster acknowledged that he borrowed the names and general plot for his play from the 1566/7 tale of "The Duchess of Malfi, the unfortunate marriage of a Gentleman, called

Antonio Bologna, with the Duchess of Malfi, and the pitiful death of them both," which can be found in William painter's *Palace of Pleasure*.Painter's version of the story does not favour the Duchess at all, and blames her solely for the ruination of herself and Antonio:

> Thus I say because a woman being as it were the Image of sweetness, curtesie and shamefastnesse, so soone as she steppeth out of the right tracte, and leaueth the smel of hir duetie and modestie, bisides the denigration of hir honour, trusteth hir self into infinite troubles and causeth the ruine of such which should be honoured and praised, if womens allurement solicited them no to follie.

Webster's more even-handed depiction of the Duchess might be a result of the influence of two real women's very similar circumstances.

The life of Lady Arbella Stuart bears a striking resemblance to that of the Duchess's, as does the life story of Catherine of Valois. Lady Arbella (1575-1715) was the first cousin of James I, the only child of Charles Darnley (brother of Henry) and Elizabeth, the daughter of Bess of Hardwick. She was considered a likely claimant to the English Throne during the reign of Elizabeth I, and, upon James' ascension to the Throne, was brought to court to serve as the "second lady" of England.She had never married, and in 1610, at age thirty-four, asked her cousin's permission to wed. This was grated with the stipulation that she not marry any foreign prince. Arbella agreed, and soon announced her intention to wed the Oxford scholar William Seymour (who possessed his own, more distant, claim to the Throne). James forbade the marriage, and made them promise to abandon their plans. They agreed, but later defied him and were married that year at Greenwich. James retaliated by imprisoning them. Arbella was sent to Lambeth under house arrest; William was thrown into the Tower. In 1611, Arbella and William coordinated an escape attempt. Arbella successfully crossed the English Channel, but was apprehended off the coast of Calais while she awaited word of William's whereabouts (he apparently did not escape).

Arbella was returned to England and imprisoned in the Tower, where she died of suicide by starvation in 1615. Presumably, William also died at the Tower.

An even closer parallel to the Duchess's life can be found in the case of Catherine of Valois (1401-37) and Owen Tudor (1400-61). Catherine was the widow of Henry V and mother of Henry VI. When Henry V died in 1422, the year of Henry VI's birth, Catherine was forced to become dependent upon her brothers-in-law, John, Duke of Bedford, and Humphrey, Duke of Gloucester. Like many young widows, Catherine wanted to remarry, but in 1428, Gloucester put a bill through Parliament that forbade the Queen Dowager to marry without the king's consent. Given that Henry VI was both a minor and a half-wit, Gloucester was the one whose consent was actually required. During the previous six years, however, Catherine's eye had been drawn to Owen Tudor, a member of Henry V's household whom she had promoted to clerk of her wardrobe in 1422. Owen was poor and a servant, but did come from royal Welsh stock (he was a cousin of Owain Glyndwr). It is likely that at the time of the bill's passage in 1428 Catherine and Owen were already wed. Catherine and Owen had five children together, four of whom survived to adulthood, three sons and a daughter. The children were kept a secret until 1436, when Catherine fell ill and was sent to Bermondsey Abbey. The children were placed in the care of Catherine de la Pole, Abbess of Barking. Catherine of Valois died the following year, in 1437, and Owen was imprisoned twice at Newgate. He later escaped and fled to Wales.

The similarities between the lives of the Duchess, Arbella Stuart, and Catherine of Valois cannot be ignored. All were noble women in socially isolated environments, each was at the mercy of more powerful male relative(s), and the Duchess and Catherine were widows with young sons to rise. All three wanted to remarry but were forbidden to do so, yet each insisted on marrying anyway. Further, each married not only the man of her choice, but someone beneath her on the social scale. Each woman and her husband were subjected to persecution and captivity after the marriage, and each died under unpleasant circumstances while in confinement.

Examining the reception Arbella and Catherine received from their contemporaries can help us understand how the Duchess of Malfi (both as a character and the play as a whole) was regarded, just as analyzing the attitudes revealed in *The Duchess of Malfi* can give us a greater insight into how society treated the true-life cases of Arbella and Catherine. In short, the notion that society and literature often mirror one another is evident here.

Arbella and William's marriage apparently came as somewhat of a surprise to those around them, and was regarded both positively and negatively. Some, such as her cousin James I, thought that she was guilty of shirking her public responsibilities when she married for love, not social or economic gain. He also thought her guilty of violating the norms established by the patriarchal system (since she ignored his express wishes), and that she had committed a terrible breach of decorum by marrying beneath her. Perhaps the most shocking of all to her detractors, Arbella's choice of a mate revealed her sexual desires and identity that most women of the day kept hidden at all costs. Given these charges, it comes as no surprise that many withheld their support of the couple's union. James accused them before the Privy Council of "caprice" and claimed they were guilty of "diver's great and hainous offences" with one another. In reality, James was most hurt by Arbella's refusal to abide by his wishes, as he felt that her rebellion had hurt his honour. Moreover, James was aware that any child born to Arbella and William could offer a claim to his Throne, or could easily become a rallying point for his enemies on the Continent. In 1611 and anonymous Latin treatise, which was perhaps authored unofficially by the palace, circulated around both England and the Continent defending James' dealings with Arbella and William. It argued that Arbella had not in fact married William for love, but rather married him so that she could forge a political alliance with the Seymour family. Such and alliance was unacceptable to

James, thus once he was provoked he had no option but to act as he did. By even mentioning the love aspect of Arbella's and William's relationship, the anonymous author revealed the extent to which he believed many readers would be moved to sympathy in the face of mutual marital affection. If the public would not have deemed love a reasonable motive for marriage, they would have had no reason to support Arbella's and William's cause, thus no "anonymous treatise" would have needed to be circulated. Other opponents of Arbella's and William's marriage condemned them not on legal grounds, but on moral and social ones. One writer argued that their crime was not inappropriate marriage, but was lying, since they had given James their word that they would not wed.

Despite these critics, Arbella and William enjoyed widespread support from nearly all those around them. The court neither condemned nor defended them, but adopted an air of tolerance and acceptance of their relationship. It is unclear whether this was because they had no qualms about the marriage, or whether their personal relationship with the involved parties made them more willing to turn a blind eye "in the name of love." The Lords of the Privy Council and the Queen both accepted Arbella's and William's marriage, and publicly urged James to reconsider his position, as did James' personal physicians. Arbella's servants remained loyal to her, and even followed her into confinement. While there, they worked with William's gaolers to arrange correspondence between the couple, as well as the occasional clandestine meeting. Most telling, the Bishop of Durham often expressed a belief that one day God would soften James' heart toward the couple and that a happy ending would result. Obviously he was not worried about the validity or appropriateness of their marriage or their supposed violation of decorum. Sara Jayne Steen notes that, "clearly some Jacobeans regarded the separation more as a violation of the marriage than the marriage as a violation of anything."

Reactions to the marriage of Catherine of Valois and Owen Tudor are not as well documented as those regarding Arbella

Stuart and William Seymour. Modern sources usually discuss their relationship in conjunction with the reign of Henry V or that of their grandson, Henry (Tudor) VII.

By examining these reactions to real-life events we can see that the public's reaction to *The Duchess of Malfi* was by no means homogeneous. Many critics who study the Jacobean period assume that audiences would have soundly condemned the Duchess for marrying below her station, yet after reading of the widespread support for Arbella Stuart and William Seymour, this assumption falls apart. Why would people have supported, accepted, and advocated the actions of a real couple while at the same time denouncing the same actions of a fictional couple? Rather, it is more likely that audiences of the play, like the acquaintances of Arbella and William, would have had mixed reactions to the Duchess.

One of *the Duchess of Malfi's* chief critics was James I. That the play was written and first performed during Arbella's imprisonment would not have been lost on James. As a result, he did all within his power to distance himself from the play itself and the actions of the murderous Ferdinand. After Arbella's death in 1615, James went to great pains to distance himself from *The Duchess of Malfi*. While the play was first performed in Blackfriars in 1614, it was still fresh in the public's memory when word of Arbella's death emerged the following year. James feared the public would suspect foul play, thus only one day after her death he had a team of six doctors perform an autopsy on her body. An official report was then issued outlining the cause of death, liver failure,[34] and thereby eliminating any speculation of foul play. Further, James ordered Arbella's body removed from the Tower under the cover of darkness, and forbade any royal funeral to be held. The basic funeral readings were performed in a private ceremony as her body was interred in a vault at Westminster Abbey.

A final irony regarding the striking parallels between Arbella's the Duchess's lives can be found in IV.1.75-6, when the Duchess declares, "The church enjoins fasting:/ I'll starve myself to death." Arbella refused all medical treatment beginning in 1614, thus she had already begun to starve herself to death by the time these lines were first uttered on the stage. Because of details such as this, one cannot help but marvel at the eerie coincidences between the lives of these two women.

Considering the great of negative publicity the Crown brought to *The Duchess of Malfi*, one must wonder what, if any, positive feedback John Webster received about his play. Happily, the play was a success and enjoyed a great deal of public support (as evidenced by the fact that it is still performed today, nearly four hundred years after its initial performance).

Anti-monarchal forces and proponents of romantic love and individualism were the greatest supporters of the play. They immediately embraced it, and soon the Duchess and her real-life counterpart, Arbella Stuart, was regarded as a role model for others, a Protestant martyr and saint, and a woman of greatness. Anti-monarchal groups cited James' treatment of both his cousin and the play as evidence of his tyrannical ways, and called for his downfall. This widespread public support for the play and the woman unnerved James, as it brought with it, according to Steen, "a hint of unrest." Supporters of the individualistic ideal also championed

Q20. Reaffirm the Male Ambition in John Webster's The Duchess of Malfi

Throughout Webster's tragedy the Duchess is defined not through her ideals, as noble as they may be, but through Webster's characters' twisted definitions of the Jacobean patriarchy. Her demise at the conclusion of act four is indeed caused by her marriage to Antonio. However, the marriage to Antonio can only be seen as indirectly causing her downfall. The marriage is subverted by the Duchess' defiance of her brother's warped sense of patriarchal conventions concerning widowhood. As I hope to show, the Duchess did not defy social conventions concerning the remarrying by widows. Rather, Ferdinand and the Cardinal's depiction of a sadistic patriarchy twist the noble marriage into something horrific and this, not her marriage to Antonio, is the true cause of the Duchess' downfall.

The first lengthy depiction of Ferdinand and the Cardinal clues the reader to the fact that Malfi's patriarchs are disturbed. Although the description comes from Bosola, the reader soon learns that the malcontent's view of the Duchess' brothers is accurate. Bosola describes the pair as "plum trees that grow crooked over / standing pools; they are rich and overlade with fruit, but none but / crows, pies, and caterpillars feed on them" (I.i.46-8). The "crooked" reference applies to their corruption of the court. This corruption is not withheld when concerning their sister and her affairs. Crows, pies (a bird of evil omen), and caterpillars also suggest their corruptive behaviour at court, here symbolized by a stagnant pool where nothing (e.g. equality for women, etc.) can grow or be nurtured.

Antonio's opening description of France's idealist monarchy contrasts what the reader soon discovers to be the corruption of Ferdinand and the Cardinal, Malfi's patriarchs. Antonio states: "Considering duly that a prince's court / Is like a common fountain, whence should flow / Pure silver drops in general, but if 't chance / Some cursed example poison 't near the head, / Death and diseases through the whole land spread" (I.i.11-5). The "cursed example" mentioned is the poison at the head of Malfi's court, namely Ferdinand and the Cardinal's corruption. Antonio also foreshadows the Duchess' death when he instructs Delio that "Though some o' the' court hold it presumption / To instruct princes what they ought to do, / It is a noble duty to inform them / What they ought to foresee. - Here comes Bosola" (I.i.19-22). The "noble duty" to inform the Duchess what she "ought to foresee," her murder, is a duty not undertaken by any of the characters in Webster's drama. The entrance of Bosola here signifies him as the Duchess' executioner. Antonio also comments on the presumption of Ferdinand and the Cardinal to instruct the prince (the Duchess) on how she should run the court of Malfi. As Antonio allusion shows, Ferdinand and the Cardinal's corruption will spread death and disease throughout the land, its wrath not excluding their sister the Duchess. Ironically, the diseases caused by the brothers' corruption inverts on themselves when Ferdinand suffers from lycanthropy at the close of Webster's play.

In Christy Desmet's discussion "In Another Country: Feminist Perspectives on Renaissance Drama," Ferdinand and the Cardinal's motives are made clear. The dialogues of both brothers throughout the first act suggest that Desmet is correct in thinking that they "build their argument on a litany of common female faults: because women are all driven by lust, widows who remarry are not far removed from whores. Naturally shameless, women also neglect their reputation; and weak in both mind and will, they succumb easily to amorous advances and smooth tales of courtship" (Desmet 79). Yet the Duchess' actions seem to refute this concept of widowhood. Indeed, Antonio does not court the Duchess. In fact, the situation is reversed. The Duchess removes her wedding band and places it on Antonio's finger. In a sense she courts him and explains (or perhaps defends) her actions: "We are forced to woo, because none dare woo us; / And as a tyrant doubles with his words / And fearfully equivocates, so we / Are forced to express our violent passions / In riddles and in dreams, and leave the path / Of simple virtue, which was never made / To seem the thing it is not" (I.iii.145-51). Here the Duchess defends her actions through defending Antonio's worthiness of nobility. At the same time, her brothers' twisted ambitions suppress and distort simple virtues into riddles and dreams. Desmet's argument concurs, stating that "not only does Malfi's Duchess work assiduously for virtue during the day, she has such innocent nights that even her dreams are as chaste as other women's 'shrifts' (I.ii.115-33)" (Desmet 79).

A historical comparison between Arabella Stuart and Webster's Duchess lends evidence to the Duchess' remaining within societal norms concerning marriage by widows. Sara Jayne Steen's essay "The Crime of Marriage: Arabella Stuart and The Duchess of Malfi" asserts that "responses to Stuart suggest a more complex historical interpretation is in order" (Steen 62). Steen's argument parallels King James/Ferdinand and Arabella Stuart/ Duchess of Malfi. In a historical context, Stuart's marriage to William Seymour parallels the Duchess' situation. Seymour/Antonio was of a lower station and the marriage was not condoned by King James/Ferdinand. Steen provides evidence that "before Stuart's escape [related to the Duchess' fleeing from Malfi], both young Prince Henry and James's chief adviser, Robert Cecil, urged James to be lenient" and "James's English advisers saw little danger in the marriage". Steen reports that the Florentine secretary, too, recorded the widespread court anticipation of a happy outcome... The people who thought so were engaging in wishful thinking, but to them love was an extenuating circumstance, even at court and even when the woman was of royal blood". Steen's most convincing argument also relates to love as an extenuating circumstance: "Clearly some Jacobeans regarded the separation more as a violation of the marriage than the marriage as a violation of anything". Perhaps Webster intended for his theatrical audience to hold the same views concerning the Duchess' actions. Either way, existing evidence proves that citizens and theater attendees alike would not have automatically condemned the Duchess' marriage to Antonio.

Desmet's argument continues this theory, exploring the idea of the Jacobean female prince's "body politic:" "By emphasizing his sister's femininity, Ferdinand seeks to deprive her not only of her life and political title, but of her very identity. The Duchess defends herself against Ferdinand's stereotypes with stoic exemplars of her own, choosing to die like Brutus's faithful wife Portia". In order to clarify this argument, a further step must be taken. Female sexuality does not inherently threaten the integrity of the body politic until viewed from the corrupt male characters' point of view. No evidence exists within the play which suggests the Duchess uses her sexuality to further her political position. Rather, the Duchess uses her sexuality in order to distinguish a clear separation between her body natural and her body politic; a need for a private life separate from the political realm, a separation her corrupt brothers are unable to recognize. Desmet's argument further substantiates this claim, refuting Lord Tennennhouse's idea that "womanhood and sovereignty are logically incompatible" to "shed light on the fate of Webster's Duchess". Again, these arguments are only justified when viewing the Duchess from her corrupt brothers' point of view. As I intend to show, the Duchess remained within societal sexual limitations concerning widowhood. She only exceeds the boundaries when seen from the twisted views of her corrupt brothers.

Many critics chastised Stuart for her actions. Steen clarifies and refutes their argument: "The crime as Clement Edmonds saw it when he wrote his brother about the marriage was the immorality of lying: the couple had promised that they would never marry without consent, then did so, and that was wrong. A pamphlet writer branded Stuart a descendant of Eve, an unruly woman who had 'touched pleasures in order to transgress,' an accusation more revealing of misogynistic than royalist fears". These misogynistic fears parallel Ferdinand and the Cardinal's actions toward their sister. In a sense, the Duchess was forced into lying because of her brothers' irrational fears of losing their places at court. These patriarchal fears instigate the chain reaction leading to the Duchess' downfall by blaming these fears on her marriage to Antonio. Quoting Harley, Steen also provides contextual evidence from the church to support her theory. A Bishop named "Durham assured himself and others 'God in time will move his Majesties hearte to haue Compassion vpon her,' apparently unconvinced that Stuart was damned on theological grounds since he expected God to argue her case". This endorsement from the church suggests that neither Stuart nor the Duchess' actions were outside societal boundaries.

Dympna Callaghan's discussion on "Feminism and Tragedy" falsely agrees with other critics' claims that the Duchess defies the boundaries of family/politic. She states that "Marriage is a 'state' ordained by God, and the implication is that the married state constructs the State (that is the organized, centralized government of a country) and not the other way around. Marriage, moreover, as the foundation of the family, is also the foundation of the family/State analogy. Rebellion over the marriage issue constitutes a very serious threat to the order of the State". A critical point which Callaghan fails to recognize is that the Duchess theoretically already controls the state by her title which should allow her to marry as long as she remains within the societal rules for remarriage. From this perspective, a more rational conclusion would be that Ferdinand's incestuous and political ambitions replace the state's official views on the Duchess' marriage to Antonio.

Elizabeth Oakes, in her essay "The Duchess of Malfi as a Tragedy of Identity," provides further evidence in the play that the Duchess goes to great lengths to remain within societal boundaries for widows. Her argument begins by stating that "the importance of Webster's depiction of the Duchess' widowhood lies not only in his exonerating her but also in his using the dynamics of her marital status to construct and then deconstruct a female hero within the genre of tragedy". Continuing, Oakes argues for the rights of the Duchess' marriage to Antonio: "Although remarriage was not uncommon for widows of all ages [and, in fact, critics have shown that remarriage was common for young widows], a year's wait was customary. As William Heale phrases it, a woman who 'remarrieth within her yeere of mourning, is by the law free from infamy, but by the lawe also adjudged unworthie of mattrimonial dignity.' Although no definite time is reported in the text, the ritual mourning period seems to have passed, because the Duchess has been giving parties. In fact, it is to talk about 'these triumphs [festivities] and this large expense' (I.i.365) that she calls in Antonio to inspect his accounts of her estate. Surely a lady of her rank would not have breached custom so, and surely Ferdinand would have commented on it if she had" (Oakes 55). Ferdinand's lack of comment on this aspect of the Duchess' ambition leads to his own motives. Clearly the Duchess makes every effort to remain within societal boundaries. The problem arises when Ferdinand's assumptions about his sister's ambitions and his own desires, both sexual and political, enter into his decisions.

Oakes' argument proceeds a step further, justifying the Duchess' choice in marriage to the reader. Webster "presents the Duchess as choosing well, diminishing the difference in rank between her and Antonio" Antonio's opening speech signifies his noble ability, relating the purity of the French court to Delio. This speech places Antonio as a noble figure, worthy of marrying the Duchess. In Oakes' words, Antonio's speech "introduces a standard into the play from which we can clearly judge the two brothers... Indeed, they reject him as a spy on the Duchess, deeming him, according to the Cardinal, 'too honest for such business' (I.i.230)". In Webster's tragedy, "before [Antonio] marries the Duchess, he shows some gentlemanly skill when he wins the ring at jousting. Moreover, [he is] morally superior to the brothers". Webster clearly shows that Antonio is worthy of nobility which leads to the corrupt motives of the Cardinal and Ferdinand.

Ferdinand's motives also must be explored in order to justify the Duchess' marriage to Antonio. Partly using a discussion from Nicholas Brooke, Frank Whigham's rational argument sheds light on the Duchess' corrupt brother: "Brooke emphasizes how Ferdinand's courtly appearance constitutes an 'absolute spectacle' ('laugh when I laugh,' 'The Lord Ferdinand / Is going to bed' [III.i.37-8], 'the Lord Ferdinand laughs' [III.iii.54]) (Brooke, 52, 54, 61)... This pattern of distancing objectifies those below Ferdinand, as mere reflective witnesses to his absolute surpassing. His embattled sense of excellence insists on ontological separation from those below, but his frenetic iteration of this motif suggests its ongoing failure" (Whigham 267). This failure of Ferdinand's is perhaps one reason which causes Ferdinand's inability to view Antonio as worthy of acquired nobility. Other of Ferdinand's irrational desires and reasons also suggest his "ongoing failure."

One cannot discuss Ferdinand's motives toward his sister without considering Ferdinand's false assumptions concerning the Duchess' political ambitions. Desmet quotes Leonard Tennenhouse's description of the Duchess' body politic: "In the Jacobean period, however, there appears a second notion of the body politic, which represents 'the female body -... specifically that of the aristocratic female - as the symbol and point of access to legitimate authority, thus as the potential substitute for blood and a basis for counterfeit power.' Under these circumstances, female sexuality threatens the integrity of the body politic". By analyzing Ferdinand's actions throughout the play, the reader can justify this theory as one of Ferdinand's motives for the supression and eventual murder of the Duchess. Therefore, the Duchess does not transgress Jacobean societal boundaries on widowhood, but transgresses only her brother's opinions on how she should conduct her private life.

In "The Duchess of Malfi: tyranny and spectacle" Karin Coddon justifies the Duchess' actions through the malcontent Bosola. Coddon claims that in Webster's tragedy "melancholy is chiefly emblematic and instrumental, bound to visible strategies of corrupt political practices. But this overt appropriation of madness by the authority to which it is ostensibly antagonistic does not structurally efface the space of transgression. Rather, it opens up a different, but significant, site for contestation as well as for subjectivity: the private and domestic sphere that the resolutely sane Duchess and Antonio strive to occupy". This argument reinforces the corruptibility of Ferdinand's desires when contrasted with the "private sphere" the Duchess seeks to obtain. Ferdinand's corruption is seen further when Coddon states that "the spectacle cannot show the ideal but only narrates it, for representation is itself implicated in the corrupt world of dissembling but opaque appearance". This "appearance" represents the public motives of Ferdinand versus his true, private motives, revealed in part when the "madness in the play becomes a material instrument of an equally disordered power". Ferdinand's corrupt desire to control both the public and private life of the Duchess ultimately ends in death and madness. This corruption is the true cause of the Duchess' downfall, a corruption perhaps instigated but not directly caused by her marriage to Antonio.

The masque of madmen Ferdinand sends to the Duchess' chambers in act IV also lends evidence to the Duchess' nobility and Ferdinand's twisted ambition. By presenting the madmen to a sister who still clings to noble virtue, Ferdinand "forces the Duchess to see and experience all those vices which should make her, as a female governor, unfit to rule her dukedom and her fortune... Ferdinand's allegory of woman's proverbial madness, vanity, and impiety is therefore an exercise in identity manipulation; demonstrating through association that the Duchess shares the vices common to all women, he seeks to prove that she is not, properly speaking, a female prince" (Desmet 84). I would take this argument a step further by postulating that the combination of Ferdinand's incestuous desire for his sister and his own political ambition causes his warped sense of female vices and that these vices are initially defined by the patriarchy to subjugate women into subservient roles. While the Duchess' intended separation of body politic and body natural causes much debate, the Duchess' actions and motives are not driven by political ambition, but rather driven by a need to seek her own identity in a world where the patriarchal Ferdinand does not allow her a public or private identity.

Through Ferdinand murdering his sister, Webster attempts to reaffirm a stable patriarchy. Oakes contends that "the Duchess comports herself in a way that is congruent with her society's mores, but not with her brother's wishes, and in the end he wins". The Duchess' claim before she dies that she is "Duchess of Malfi still" (IV.iv.128) can be seen not as an affirmation of her power in the face of patriarchy, but, as Oakes eloquently states, "with that title she negates her relationship with Antonio: she becomes the woman carved in stone that Ferdinand wanted her to be". In other words, the Duchess reverts to Ferdinand's wish for her to be a chaste widow and shuns her marriage to Antonio, ultimately giving in to her brother's depiction of the patriarchy.

Ultimately, Webster's patriarchy fails to reaffirm its stable identity in act five due to the corrupt nature of its leaders. After the Duchess' death and before Antonio is "mistakenly" murdered by Bosola, the corrupt Cardinal and Ferdinand attempt to bring Antonio back to Malfi for execution. The Cardinal gives Antonio's land to his mistress Julia, herself a sign of the Cardinal's corruptibility, and Antonio replies that they "fortify themselves with my ruin!" (V.i.37). The scene here shows that the Cardinal attempts to "fortify" the patriarchy, but ultimately fails to do so due to both his and Ferdinand's corrupt nature. While the Cardinal attempts to reestablish the patriarchy, Ferdinand echoes his own madness with a retreat into lycanthropy, a fitting end for a corrupt political leader.

Q21. Critically study the play" The Duchess of Malfi".

Or

Q Drama arises from conflict of one sort or another. What is the principal conflict underlying the action of the play?

It's not so much that Webster looked beneath the skin, as lifted up a rock and dispassionately observed what wriggled and slithered underneath. The Duchess of Malfi is forced to foreswear remarriage by her brother Ferdinand, the Duke of Calabria. But as is clear from the text and this production, his feelings towards the Duchess (Janet McTeer) are decidedly more than fraternal.

Initial response to Webster's play was strong. For decades the play was one of those commanded by royalty, and it has been performed throughout the centuries as one of the great tragedies of the English Renaissance. The role of the Duchess continues to be a favourite of leading áctresses, including Dame Peggy Ashcroft and Juliet Stevensón. As critic John Russell Brown has suggested, *The Duchess of Malfi* offers a rich variety of interpretive possibilities for the stage, allowing it to retain its relevance for modern audiences. Literary scholars have focused their attention on both the form and the themes of the play. Webster's talent as a technician has been a matter of some debate. In his study of Webster's dramatic art, Charles R. Forker has described Webster as one of the first playwrights successfully to create distinct psychological portraits of his characters, a claim with which later critics have concurred. But because the Duchess dies in the fourth act, the fifth act is sometimes seen as disconnected from the coherent whole of the first four acts.

But equally the Duchess is no shrinking violet; Webster's creation is very much a modern woman; passionate, whose love lists where it will and who will follow her heart's desires.

Early critics considered this a sign of Webster's lesser skill as a playwright, but more recently scholars have suggested that Webster employed a complex structure that is not flawed but rather sophisticated and innovative. Christina Luckyj's study of form in Webster's work proposes a different model for understanding the structure of his plays, suggesting a pattern of repetition and circular movement rather than a linear progression through consecutive acts.

Jacqueline Pearson has considered the play in generic terms, maintaining that the difference between the fifth act and the others is the presence of tragicomic elements, setting the final scenes apart from the pure tragedy of the earlier part of the play. As M. C. Bradbrook has pointed out, *The Duchess of Malfi* also incorporates the dramatic form of the masque, a genre that would have been readily recognized and understood by a Renaissance audience.

A trend toward feminist studies of Renaissance drama in the late 1980s and 1990s brought the Duchess to the attention of several scholars. As a strong, sexual woman who nonetheless dies proclaiming Christian piety and forgiveness, the Duchess has resisted definitive interpretation.

The model of subversion and containment applied by some critics to much Renaissance drama seems to suit the Duchess, who is severely punished for her private violations of patriarchal order. Yet as Emily Bartles has argued, the Duchess's seeming complicity in her "containment" poses a challenge to that model. The containment of her sexuality has particularly interested critics. Dympna Callaghan and Laura Behling are among those feminist scholars who have included the Duchess in studies of the discourse of sexuality. As Behling has suggested, in the character of the Duchess relations between gender, sexuality, and power are brought to the fore, presenting a challenge to traditional notions of authority that is left unresolved.

Chapter 12

Critical Essays

lla Stuart, Catherine of Valois, and The Duchess of Malfi: An Examination of Women, Marriage, and Widowhood in Jacobean England

by Nanci Lamb Roider

Throughout history, man has sought to understand and chronicle himself, his experiences, and his culture. One of the primary ways this has been achieved is through the written word. Writing about one's experiences and surroundings provides not only an outlet for self-expression and understanding, but also provides a means by which future generations can glimpse the past. John Webster's 1614 play The Duchess of Malfi gives us a glimpse into the politics of seventeenth century English marriage, social mobility, and the law. Additionally, we can use reactions to Webster's work as a means of judging the attitudes of seventeenth century English society; Webster's play paints a vivid portrait of Jacobean society's relationship with women, and outlines the norms surrounding marriage, the freedom of women, and the state of patriarchy in England.

Upon closer examination it becomes clear that the plight of the Duchess mirrors at least two real life cases. Our ability to consider the fictitious Duchess' situation in relation to two actual women's plight sheds even more light on the relationship of women to, and as, property, both in and outside the confines of marriage. As a result, this Jacobean tragicomedy not only entertains and transports us, it can also teach us about the English past, the status of noble women, and about the patriarchal system's transitional nature during the seventeenth century.

The Duchess of Malfi has been interpreted in many different ways since it was first performed nearly 400 years ago. Some have seen it as a cautionary tale that shows what can happen when women marry without being granted the "proper" consent, while others argue that it is a feminist story of a strong woman ahead of her time. I argue that neither of these interpretations is entirely correct, rather, The Duchess of Malfi is a study of an emancipated widow that reflects the great social and political transitions found in Jacobean England. The Duchess's fight for autonomy and self-determination is, on the one hand, inspiring, yet given her ultimate failure, disheartening on the other. That the Duchess's life mirrors the plight of real seventeenth century women cannot be ignored, thus she serves not only as a role model, but also as a tragic reminder of the world in which she had to function.

Her struggle for autonomy is lamentable on many levels. First, it is important to note that, while we understand her deepest thoughts and are privy to her most intimate moments, we are never told her given name. She is known throughout the play merely as "the Duchess," a title which she would not have had were it not for her now-deceased first husband. Time and again reviewers have praised the Duchess for her strength, passion, courage, ambition, and cunning, yet they have nearly universally failed to recognize that these traits were not simply desirable facets of her character, but were integral to her very survival. She is a completely isolated character, utterly alone in the world, associated with no female companions of her own rank. She is young, has lost her husband, has been left with a young son and daughter to raise, and has been forbidden by her brothers to remarry. Regarding her as a "strong" woman, considering her circumstances, is the least amount of credit one can give her.

The Duchess's status as a wealthy widow can be regarded as both and asset and a liability. The most positive way to interpret her widowhood would be to focus on the new, special rights accorded to her upon becoming a dowager, namely, freedom from the laws of coverture, the system of laws that applied to married and never-before-married women. Under the system of coverture, women were governed by their closest male relative, usually their father or husband. This male relative enjoyed sole control over the fate of the woman's property, money, and any other chattels. Women under coverture had no legal standing, and were, themselves, considered property. Widowed women, however, were not bound by these constraints, and thus exercised full legal authority over their person, property, and chattels. Widows were allowed to enter into legally binding contracts, could bring a suit before a court, and were not subject to any male's personal authority. Another benefit to widowhood under the laws of seventeenth century England concerned the control of widows' dowries. Upon the death of one's husband, the dowry of the wife was returned to her and she was given sole control over one third of her husband's lands and property for the remainder of her lifetime. Widows were free to remarry or to remain single. Further, if a woman chose to remarry but did not wish to lose control over her dower portion, she could turn it over to a trustee, thereby safeguarding her control of the property while at the same time eliminating the chance that her new husband could seize its control.

Despite these freedoms, few women wished to remain unmarried after the death of their husbands. For many women, widowhood actually resulted in an increased dependency on male family members to secure the political and/or social favours previously sought on their behalf by their husbands. Additionally, they often suffered a loss of kinship connection to their husband's family, thus making it even more difficult to repay the favours granted to her by her new advocates. Furthermore, many women saw remarriage as a wonderful tool with which they could advance themselves both socially and financially. They retained the social status of their deceased husband until remarriage, thus they could use the title "Duchess," "Marchioness," or "Countess" to attract a man of similar social ranking, along with their dower portions, which provided them excellent dowries to offer their suitors. Lastly, in an age when most women defined themselves in terms of their husbands and families, widowhood left many women with a feeling of insecurity and purposelessness. In effect, women would often lose themselves when they lost their husbands. Remarriage could provide definition, a renewed sense of purpose, and a feeling of belonging that was absent from their lives in the widowed state.

The Duchess of Malfi doubtless felt the pressures, both positive and negative, associated with widowhood, and there is evidence that she experienced some difficulty reconciling the two. She is clearly aware of her rights as a widow, yet she still allows herself to be constrained by the traditional patriarchal elements of her society. On one hand she asserts her freedom by marrying Antonio against the wishes of her brothers, yet on the other, most notably in her conversation with Ferdinand in Act I, scene 1, lines 290-304, she allows Ferdinand and the Cardinal to attack her virtue, and then adds the self-defeating comments in which she likens herself to a diamond whose value increases each time it is passed through another man's hand. By sexualizing herself and allowing the innuendoes about the lustiness of widows to go unchecked, she allows herself to be degraded. This sort of incongruous behaviour continues throughout the play as the Duchess time and again reconfirms her brothers' assumptions. When Ferdinand attacks her motives for remarriage, she only replies "If all my royal kindred/ Lay in my way unto this marriage,/ I'd make them my low footsteps...Let old wives report/ I winked and chose a husband" (I.1.332-4; 339-40).

Despite these self-defeating comments early in the play, the Duchess continues to act as though she regards herself as a free, autonomous woman. She marries her steward, Antonio, despite the objection of others, and even comments on the odd role reversal found in their courtship, "The misery of us that are born great:/ We are forced to woo because none dare woo us" (I.1.431-2). She also represents herself as the sole heir and acting ruler of the Duchy of Amalfi, as we see in her death scene when she asks Bosola, "Am I not thy Duchess?" and then answers herself, "I am Duchess of Malfi still" (IV.2.127; 134). Despite these efforts to assert her independence, her work is undone by her controlling brothers. In I.1.246-7, Ferdinand tells Bosola that "she's a young widow,/ I would not have her marry again." When she does, he retaliates by telling the Pope who, "forehearing of her looseness,/ Hath seized into th'protection of the church/ The dukedom which she held as a dowager" (III.4.31-34). With this duplicitous act, we see, as apparently the Duchess does not, that her "freedom" never truly existed. She was allowed its illusion as long as it remained convenient for her brothers, but once she began to assert herself it was taken from her. Considering the problems the Duchess encounters after following her own course, we see that her real strength of character lies not in her determination to marry the man of her choosing, or in her general defiance of her brothers; rather, it can be found in her ability to endure the grief she brings upon herself as a result of her independent thoughts and actions.

The complexity of the Duchess's plight, such as the question of remarriage, lends a great deal of realism to Webster's play; fortunately, his taste for realism extends beyond the question of remarriage versus widowhood, and encompasses a great many more issues. The relationship of the Duchess and Antonio gives us an excellent insight into the state of matrimonial custom and law during the seventeenth century. Because the Duchess and Antonio married secretly with only Cariola the waiting-woman as a witness, their marriage falls into the canonical category per verba de presenti, or, an orally contracted marriage deemed wholly binding by the Roman Catholic Church. According to canon law, any oral contract of marriage executed in the present tense and in front of a witness was substantially, though not ceremonially, complete. The church recognized such unions, however they were not binding under civil law until they were formally and publicly solemnized in a church ceremony. Until the marriage was solemnized, women were not subject to the laws of coverture, no dower rights were conferred, and, according to civil authorities, any children born of the marriage would be ruled illegitimate. We can assume that the Duchess and Antonio's marriage was at some time formalized, as the question of the children's legitimacy is never broached. Given both the civil advantages and the church's belief that marriage is a sacrament, marriages performed away from the church were considered less desirable than those performed in a more traditional manner at the church doors, one of the most public places in any community. Despite this preference for public marriage, the church did recognize that the traditional posting of the banns and public celebration was sometimes, for whatever reason, not always feasible. This recognition of a binding, yet covert marriage signals a transition in canonical thought. Here we see a shift from the focus on community, as evidenced with the public marriage ceremony, to a focus on the individual, as shown through the tolerance of private ceremony.

The Duchess and Antonio's marriage also signals a shift in marital expectations and customs found throughout seventeenth century English culture. By this time, the public had become familiar with the notion of romantic love in marriage through works such as Chrétien de Troyes' Arthurian romances and Shakespeare's Romeo and Juliet and Sonnets. Further, they were accustomed to recognizing the power of lust in an open, honest manner, as shown in French fabliaux and Chaucer's "Miller's" and "Clerk's" Tales. Exposure to these tales of love and lust slowly led the English population to regard them as valid, or at least potentially valid, reasons for instigating a marital relationship. While the traditional notion of marriage based solely on economic and political factors had certainly not fallen by the wayside, people at this time were beginning to ask themselves if the marriage relationship wasn't deep and complex enough to accommodate feelings of love and affection. The middle and lower classes were the first to embrace these notions, as they had the least to gain or lose from marriage alliances, but by the seventeenth century, love matches like that of the Duchess and Antonio were not unheard of among the aristocracy. The Duchess had already married for the "right" reasons, and, in her widowhood, sought to marry for love (dare we say even, lust) and companionship, while her brothers, for whom the traditional modes of marriage proved more convenient, held fast to the marriage practices of the past. What we see here is the beginning of an ideological clash, one that would not fully resolve itself until the late nineteenth century, between marriages based on duty, and favoured by proponents of patriarchy, and marriages based on love, promoted by champions of the individual.

In addition to reflecting the changing nature of the marriage relationship in Jacobean England, we can find in the characters of the Duchess and Antonio traces of the new social mobility that was working its way into English society at the time. As her title indicates, the Duchess is the ruler of Amalfi; she also claims lineage in the royal houses of Castile and Aragon. By virtue of her pedigree, her social status is unquestioned and immutable. Antonio, however, does not enjoy this same background. He is what could be called a "self-made" courtier. He has no impressive pedigree, but has worked his way into his position through hard work and (presumably) good networking skills. It is important to note that the first glimpse we are given of Antonio is at a joust he has just won. He is pleased with his success in this sport of the nobility, while Ferdinand, an observer of noble blood, is bored with the tourney. Antonio appreciates where he is; Ferdinand takes it for granted. Antonio's success is a classic example of the possibility for social advancement in Jacobean England. By approaching the proper people and successfully performing the right tasks, Antonio's identity became "mobile" and carried him into the upper echelons of society.

As a steward of the household, Antonio is valued by all, but as a marriage prospect for the Duchess, is soon cast as a feared interloper. Frank Whigham contends that Antonio's successful social ascendance accounts for Ferdinand's incestuous desires for his sister. Whigham argues that

Ferdinand's attraction to the Duchess belies his insecurity about the maintenance of his house, and that he, above all, is seeking to prevent contamination of the bloodline. This desperate move to keep outsiders out is understandable in a time when any well-connected commoner, it seems, can enter the aristocracy if he plays his cards right.

Interestingly, Ferdinand is not the only person who seems intimidated by Antonio's newfound status as a Duchess's husband. Antonio himself seems a bit frightened by his situation. He has certainly improved his social ranking, yet, by virtue of its clandestine nature, he cannot openly enjoy his new status. In III.2.147-9, Antonio hides while Ferdinand threatens the Duchess. Antonio's initial reaction is to defend his wife, yet knows he must remain hidden. When he does emerge to console her, he is terrified by another knock at the door, and cries out, "How now! Who knocks? More earthquakes?" (l. 155). He wants to exercise his new role to its fullest, yet he cannot without jeopardizing both himself and the Duchess. Antonio's unease with his new role is also evidenced by his self-deprecating humour. He teases the Duchess that his "rule is only in the night" (III.2.8). Later, when asked by Cariola why he rises so early in the morning, he jokes that "Labouring men/ Count the clock oftenest Cariola,/ Are glad when their task's ended" (III.2.17-9). He purports to be tired of "labouring" with the Duchess all night when in reality he must rise early so as to avoid detection. Because he must keep it a secret, his sexual relationship with the Duchess seems more akin to adultery than it does to Holy Matrimony. These "jokes" that Antonio makes indicate that, deep down, he is really very insecure in his new position. He doubtless had few qualms about his previous social advances, yet those were always undertakes with the knowledge that there would be a limit to his success. With his marriage to the Duchess, all social boundaries have been torn down, and Antonio is left without any usable frame of social reference. His commoner's upbringing prepared him to serve, not to be served, and this change, it seems, may be too much for him to handle.

As we have noted, The Duchess of Malfi reflects Jacobean society on many levels, thus it should come as no surprise that it was based in part on another societal commentary or that it also has roots in the real lives of at least two noblewomen. Webster acknowledged that he borrowed the names and general plot for his play from the 1566/7 tale of "The Duchess of Malfi, the infortunate marriage of a Gentleman, called Antonio Bologna, with the Duchess of Malfi, and the pitiful death of them both," which can be found in William painter's Palace of Pleasure.19 Painter's version of the story does not favour the Duchess at all, and blames her solely for the ruination of herself and Antonio:

Thus I say bicause a woman being as it were the Image of sweetnesse, curtesie and shamefastnesse, so soone as she steppeth out of the right tracte, and leaueth the smel of hir duetie and modestie, bisides the denigration of hir honour, trusteth hir self into infinite troubles and causeth the ruine of such which should be honoured and praised, if womens allurement solicited them no to follie.

Webster's more even-handed depiction of the Duchess might be a result of the influence of two real women's very similar circumstances.

The life of Lady Arbella Stuart bears a striking resemblance to that of the Duchess's, as does the life story of Catherine of Valois. Lady Arbella (1575-1715) was the first cousin of James I, the only child of Charles Darnley (brother of Henry) and Elizabeth, the daughter of Bess of Hardwick. She was considered a likely claimant to the English Throne during the reign of Elizabeth I, and, upon James' ascension to the Throne, was brought to court to serve as the "second lady" of England. She had never married, and in 1610, at age thirty-four, asked her cousin's permission to wed. This was grated with the stipulation that she not marry any foreign prince. Arbella agreed, and soon announced her intention to wed the Oxford scholar William Seymour (who possessed his own, more distant, claim to the Throne). James forbade the marriage, and made them promise to abandon their plans. They agreed, but later defied him and were married that year at Greenwich. James retaliated by imprisoning them. Arbella was sent to Lambeth under house arrest; William was thrown into the Tower. In 1611, Arbella and William coordinated an escape attempt. Arbella successfully crossed the English Channel, but was apprehended off the coast of Calais while she awaited word of William's whereabouts (he apparently did not escape). Arbella was returned to England and imprisoned in the Tower, where she died of suicide by starvation in 1615. Presumably, William also died at the Tower.

An even closer parallel to the Duchess's life can be found in the case of Catherine of Valois (1401-37) and Owen Tudor (1400-61). Catherine was the widow of Henry V and mother of Henry VI. When Henry V died in 1422, the year of Henry VI's birth, Catherine was forced to become dependent upon her brothers-in-law, John, Duke of Bedford, and Humphrey, Duke of Gloucester. Like many young widows, Catherine wanted to remarry, but in 1428, Gloucester put a bill through Parliament that forbade the Queen Dowager to marry without the king's consent. Given that Henry VI was both a minor and a half-wit, Gloucester was the one whose consent was actually required. During the previous six years, however, Catherine's eye had been drawn to Owen Tudor, a member of Henry V's household whom she had promoted to clerk of her wardrobe in 1422. Owen was poor and a servant, but did come from royal Welsh stock (he was a cousin of Owain Glyndwr). It is likely that at the time of the bill's passage in 1428 Catherine and Owen were already wed. Catherine and Owen had five children together, four of whom survived to adulthood, three sons and a daughter. The children were kept a secret until 1436, when Catherine fell ill and was sent to Bermondsey Abbey. The children were placed in the care of Catherine de la Pole, Abbess of Barking. Catherine of Valois died the following year, in 1437, and Owen was imprisoned twice at Newgate. He later escaped and fled to Wales.

The similarities between the lives of the Duchess, Arbella Stuart, and Catherine of Valois cannot be ignored. All were noble women in socially isolated environments, each was at the mercy of more powerful male relative(s), and the Duchess and Catherine were widows with young sons to rise. All three wanted to remarry but were forbidden to do so, yet each insisted on marrying anyway. Further, each married not only the man of her choice, but someone beneath her on the social scale. Each woman and her husband were subjected to persecution and captivity after the marriage, and each died under unpleasant circumstances while in confinement.

Examining the reception Arbella and Catherine received from their contemporaries can help us understand how the Duchess of Malfi (both as a character and the play as a whole) was regarded, just as analyzing the attitudes revealed in The Duchess of Malfi can give us a greater insight into how society treated the true-life cases of Arbella and Catherine. In short, the notion that society and literature often mirror one another is evident here.

Arbella and William's marriage apparently came as somewhat of a surprise to those around them, and was regarded both positively and negatively. Some, such as her cousin James I, thought that she was guilty of shirking her public responsibilities when she married for love, not social or economic gain. He also thought her guilty of violating the norms established by the patriarchal system (since she ignored his express wishes), and that she had committed a terrible breach of decorum by marrying beneath her. Perhaps the most shocking of all to her detractors, Arbella's choice of a mate reveaed her sexual desires and identity that most women of the day kept hidden at all costs. Given these charges, it comes as no surprise that many withheld their support of the couple's union. James accused them before the Privy Council of "caprice" and claimed they were guilty of "divers great and hainous offences" with one another. In reality, James was most hurt by Arbella's refusal to abide by his wishes, as he felt that her rebellion had hurt his honour. Moreover, James was aware that any child born to Arbella and William could offer a claim to his Throne, or could easily become a rallying point for his enemies on the Continent. In 1611 and anonymous Latin treatise, which was perhaps authored unofficially by the palace, circulated around both England and the Continent defending James' dealings with Arbella and William. It argued that Arbella had not in fact married William for love, but rather married him so that she could forge a political alliance with the Seymour family. Such and alliance was unacceptable to James, thus once he was provoked he had no option but to act as he did. By even mentioning the love aspect of Arbella's and William's relationship, the anonymous author revealed the extent to which he believed many readers would be moved to sympathy in the face of mutual marital affection. If the public would not have deemed love a reasonable motive for marriage, they would have had no reason to support Arbella's and William's cause, thus no "anonymous treatise" would have needed to be circulated. Other opponents of Arbella's and William;'s marriage condemned them not on legal grounds, but on moral and social ones. One writer argued that their crime was not inappropriate marriage, but was lying, since they had given James their word that they would not wed.

Despite these critics, Arbella and William enjoyed widespread support from nearly all those around them. The court neither condemned nor defended them, but adopted an air of tolerance and acceptance of their relationship. It is unclear whether this was because they had no qualms about the marriage, or whether their personal relationship with the involved parties made them more willing to turn a blind eye "in the name of love." The Lords of the Privy Council and the Queen both accepted Arbella's and William's marriage, and publicly urged James to reconsider his position, as did James' personal physicians. Arbella's servants remained loyal to her, and even followed her into confinement. While there, they worked with William's gaolers to arrange correspondence between the couple, as well as the occasional clandestine meeting. Most telling, the Bishop of Durham often expressed a belief that one day God would soften James' heart toward the couple and that a happy ending would result. Obviously he was not worried about the validity or appropriateness of their marriage or their supposed violation of decorum. Sara

Jayne Steen notes that, "clearly some Jacobeans regarded the separation more as a violation of the marriage than the marriage as a violation of anything."

Reactions to the marriage of Catherine of Valois and Owen Tudor are not as well documented as those regarding Arbella Stuart and William Seymour. Modern sources usually discuss their relationship in conjunction with the reign of Henry V or that of their grandson, Henry (Tudor) VII.

By examining these reactions to real-life events we can see that the public's reaction to The Duchess of Malfi was by no means homogeneous. Many critics who study the Jacobean period assume that audiences would have soundly condemned the Duchess for marrying below her station, yet after reading of the widespread support for Arbella Stuart and William Seymour, this assumption falls apart. Why would people have supported, accepted, and advocated the actions of a real couple while at the same time denouncing the same actions of a fictional couple? Rather, it is more likely that audiences of the play, like the acquaintances of Arbella and William, would have had mixed reactions to the Duchess.

One of The Duchess of Malfi's chief critics was James I. That the play was written and first performed during Arbella's imprisonment would not have been lost on James. As a result, he did all within his power to distance himself from the play itself and the actions of the murderous Ferdinand. After Arbella's death in 1615, James went to great pains to distance himself from The Duchess of Malfi. While the play was first performed in Blackfriars in 1614, it was still fresh in the public's memory when word of Arbella's death emerged the following year. James feared the public would suspect foul play, thus only one day after her death he had a team of six doctors perform an autopsy on her body. An official report was then issued outlining the cause of death, liver failure, and thereby eliminating any speculation of foul play.35 Further, James ordered Arbella's body removed from the Tower under the cover of darkness, and forbade any royal funeral to be held. The basic funeral readings were performed in a private ceremony as her body was interred in a vault at Westminster Abbey.

A final irony regarding the striking parallels between Arbella's the Duchess's lives can be found in IV.1.75-6, when the Duchess declares, "The church enjoins fasting:/ I'll starve myself to death." Arbella refused all medical treatment beginning in 1614, thus she had already begun to starve herself to death by the time these lines were first uttered on the stage. Because of details such as this, one cannot help but marvel at the eerie coincidences between the lives of these two women.

Considering the great of negative publicity the Crown brought to The Duchess of Malfi, one must wonder what, if any, positive feedback John Webster received about his play. Happily, the play was a success and enjoyed a great deal of public support (as evidenced by the fact that it is still performed today, nearly four hundred years after its initial performance).

Anti-monarchal forces and proponents of romantic love and individualism were the greatest supporters of the play. They immediately embraced it, and soon the Duchess and her real-life counterpart, Arbella Stuart, was regarded as a role model for others, a Protestant martyr and saint, and a woman of greatness. Anti-monarchal groups cited James' treatment of both his cousin and the play as evidence of his tyrannical ways, and called for his downfall. This widespread public support for the play and the woman unnerved James, as it brought with it, according to Steen, "a hint of unrest." Supporters of the individualistic ideal also championed both the play and the real couple, as they saw the two as role models for the triumph of companionate marriage and romantic love over the colder, less personal marriage and family relationships of the past.

Victorian-era critics almost unanimously cast their lots in with the supporters of the Duchess and Arbella. They held James personally responsible for not finding Arbella a suitable mate before she reached the age of thirty-four, and also tended to regard Arbella and the Duchess as victims of a cold, uncaring and unfeeling, barbaric society; they often used these cases to congratulate themselves for the advancement of English society. They could look back at this play and Arbella's plight to remind them of just how how far human behaviour had advanced in the past three hundred years.

In short, The Duchess of Malfi was judged by some as a cautionary tale, by others as an inspirational one, and by most as one to be pitied, since "all may be attributed to the great love she had for the person she had chosen to be her husband."

In conclusion, The Duchess of Malfi shows us how literature can mirror everyday life and how everyday life is revealed through the written word. By analyzing the play as a whole, especially the actions and statements of the Duchess and Antonio, we can gain a great deal of insight into the ways Jacobean men and women dealt with issues such as gender roles and expectations, familial pressures, social mobility, sexual desire, and legal responsibility. The seventeenth century was a time of great change in the English mind set, as some elements of society struggled to fulfill the destiny of the Renaissance by uplifting the individual, while others fought to maintain the traditional, community and family oriented mores of the past.

Though John Webster explored these issues nearly 400 years ago, the struggles are not entirely alien to our own late twentieth century experience. Today women must reconcile the pressures of family and work, much as the Duchess had to maintain her relationships with her brothers, her husband, and her subjects in Amalfi. Furthermore, Antonio's struggle for self-definition is a universal one. Upon his marriage to the Duchess, he found himself in a social setting for which he was totally unprepared. This is not unlike the way many of us feel today, given the relative smallness of our world, the isolation brought on by increasing technology, and the seemingly limitless frontier of social interaction. As never before, people of the twentieth century are called upon to relate to others from infinitely varied backgrounds and life experiences, and are expected to navigate the murky waters of human relations flawlessly. Given these circumstances, perhaps Antonio's feelings of insecurity, while not the cornerstone of Webster's play, are in fact the most enduring and universal of all the issues explored in The Duchess of Malfi.

Discussion of Morality and Horror in The Duchess of Malfi and Edward II

According to Robert Ornstein, we should expect a Renaissance tragedy to display "a depth of vision that penetrates the surface violence or anarchy of life to illumine the underlying pattern and meaning of man's fate". Ornstein infers that Renaissance drama should a reveal a sense of divine morality and purpose beneath the exterior confusion of life. However, is it necessarily true that Renaissance playwrights desired to exhibit such a virtuous texture, or did they perhaps wish to shock us with the suggestion that horror penetrates deeper than the skin?

This is certainly a view implied by *The Duchess of Malfi*: "Why do you laugh? Methinks you that are/ courtiers should be my touchwood [...]/ laugh when I laugh. Ferdinand demands that his courtiers laugh only when he deems it appropriate; a desire that is itself laughable. He is attempting to assert his position as a Machiavellian prince, but his words undermine him and he is instead cast as a figure of jest. However, this apparent harmlessness is a facade: "What appears in him mirth is merely outside" (I.i.170). Antonio declares that the humour of Ferdinand's character is actually only a shell. Once this is broken, the audience will be able to see his true personality. Contrary to Ornstein's belief, Antonio suggests that horror is not superficial. Instead, what might initially appear amusing, can in fact be terrifying: "You are my sister-/ This was my father's poniard. Do you see?/ I'd be loth to see 't look rusty" (I.i.330-33). Ferdinand's threat to murder his sister if she should remarry might be perversely amusing, yet it exposes the sinister and perhaps even incestuous nature of the play. Ferdinand and the Cardinal are determined that only they should possess the Duchess, a fact that is borne out most vehemently by the imprisonment and grotesque torture of her: "Here's a hand/ To which you have vowed much love; the ring upon it you gave" (IV.i.43-44). Ferdinand gives the Duchess what she thinks to be the hand of Antonio, tricking her into believing that both her husband and her children have been murdered. The Duchess's 'crime' in marrying her steward surely does not befit such cruelty. "It has often been pointed out that there is a violation of the correct 'order' which is supposed to have affected Jacobean audiences with the moral force of a tragic 'flaw' but [...] the play entirely assumes the audience's complicity and therefore approval of the Duchess's action". If the Duchess's punishment is not intended by Webster to be a moral lesson to the audience, teaching them not to break social boundaries, then what is its purpose? As the Cardinal's reaction to her marriage intimates, it is perhaps still related to her disregard for their noble blood: "Shall our blood/ The royal blood of Castile and Aragon/ Be thus attainted?" (II.v.22-24). The Cardinal makes this statement before he knows the identity of his sister's lover. He therefore cannot be aware that she has married a person of lower birth. He is therefore concerned only with the fact that her blood has been poisoned by someone outside of her family. It might be argued that the Duchess's first marriage renders this argument void, but we know nothing of her original husband or the circumstances of his death.

Instead, the hint of incest is reconfirmed by Ferdinand: "I could kill her now/ In you, or in myself, for I do think/ it is some sin is us heaven doth revenge" (II.v.63-65). James L. Calderwood suggests that Ferdinand's outburst represents an identification of "his latent desire with her realised desire"; that Ferdinand associates his sister's sexual fulfilment with his unconscious yearning for her. Indeed, it might even be suggested that Ferdinand not only longs for a incestuous relationship, but that he and his siblings are the product of one: "You never fixed your eye on three fair medals/ Cast in one figure" (I.i.188-89). Much is made of the fact that the Duchess and her two brothers are startling similar in appearance. Whilst this alone does not confirm an incestuous family history, we might wish to reinterpret Ferdinand's original threat: "You are my sister-/ This was my father's poniard [...]/ I'd be loth to see 't look rusty" (I.i.330-33). Ferdinand's warning infers a sexual relationship between his father and the Duchess: a relationship that he threatens to recreate.

How though, do Ferdinand's bizarre sexual desires relate to his horrific torture of his sister? According to Calderwood, Ferdinand "seeks the purgation of his own tainted blood in the purging of hers". He is repulsed by the realisation of his desire and so wishes to cleanse the perceived sins of the Duchess so that he might also cleanse his own. I would suggest the opposite. In imprisoning his sister Ferdinand is attempting to fulfil his lust:

Bosola Why do you do this?

Ferdinand To bring her to despair (IV.ii.116-17)

With the most disturbing line of the play, Ferdinand declares his intention to deprive the Duchess of hope. He desires her complete subjection to his will. He is not purging his sins, but indulging in them: "Damn her! That body of hers" (IV.ii.122). Ferdinand cannot escape his monstrous passion for the Duchess as his desires overcome him entirely:

[...] let them practise together, sing and dance,

And act their gambols to the full o'th' moon.

If she can sleep the better for it, let her (IV.ii.129-31)

In tormenting his sister with frolicking madmen, designed to keep her awake at night, Ferdinand is envisaging his own rape of the Duchess. By "seeing the skull beneath the skin", Webster has not found morality, but the ultimate horror and taboo. *The Duchess of Malfi* closely resembles Christopher Marlowe's *Edward the Second*: "let us leave the brainsick King/ And henceforth parley with our naked swords" (1.124-25). Mortimer Junior, like Ferdinand, desires to be a Machiavellian prince. It is clear from the beginning of the play that he is not prepared to tolerate the "base minion" (1.132) that is Gaveston, and so commits himself to usurping Edward. Mortimer and his noble followers wish to punish Edward for daring to threaten the social hierarchy:

Edward You that are noble born should pity him

Warwick You that are princely born should shake him off (4.80-81)

As with the Duchess, Edward challenges traditional social conventions by expressing his love for a person of lower birth. Moreover, this person is of course French and male: "I'll bandy with the barons and the earls/ And die or live with Gaveston" (1.136-370). Clearly Edward is not an innocent victim of Mortimer's scheming. He has betrayed his status as a king by declaring his love for a foreign male peasant, yet more importantly he threatens the stability of his nation:

Make several kingdoms of this monarchy,

And share it equally amongst you all,

So that I may have some nook or corner left

To frolic with my dearest Gaveston (4.70-73)

Edward does not care for the future of his realm, but only for Gaveston. His faults though are those of a poor king, not of a man who deserves to be murdered: "They seize Edward and hold him down, laying the table on him. Lightborne murders him with the spit. He screams and dies" (24). The brutal rape of Edward - a confirmation yet also extinction of his sexuality is, like that of the Duchess, a punishment that does not fit his crime.

The parallels between *Edward the Second* and *The Duchess of Malfi* imply that Webster's play, or at least its conclusion, is a re-enactment of Marlowe's: "Know that I am a king" (24.88). Edward's attempt to reassert his position is clearly the futile gesture of a broken man. Yet, it is through his fall that he achieves greatness:

O Gaveston, it is for thee that I am wronged;

For me both thou and both the Spencer's died,

And for your sakes a thousand wrongs I'll take Edward is able to achieve a degree of self awareness, recognising that he has caused the death of his friends. For this, he is prepared to accept his fate. It is tempting therefore to place Edward in the role of a tragic hero, his death creating as it does "the sense of human weakness, claiming pity from utter helplessness and conscious misery".[5] Edward's pain can easily be seen as a moral lesson, a view that would reinforce Ornstein's belief that Renaissance tragedy should find a pattern of fate beneath its violence. However, according to Irving Ribner, "Marlowe [...] does not see in history the working out of any divine providence". *Edward the Second* is not attempting to apply a moral judgement to history. It is instead a reworking of the past in which fate is decided purely by action. This abandonment of virtue highlights the crucial difference between Marlowe's play and that of Webster, whose Duchess is surely a deliberate 'mis-creation' of Edward: "I am Duchess of Malfi still" (IV.ii.141). The Duchess' speech mirrors that of Edward. However, whilst Edward is clearly defeated, the Duchess' reaffirmation of her position is perceived as a sign of strength and resolve. "Her self possession in the face of death is a spiritual victory rather than a glorious defeat". Ornstein almost compares the Duchess to Shakespeare's Cleopatra, inferring that, in death, she can transcend the immorality of life. Yet whilst the Duchess is virtuous "I forgive them" [her executioners] (IV.ii.206) we must not overlook the fact that we do not learn her true name. The Duchess is denied an identity even when she is seemingly a symbol of absolute virtue. Her moral "victory" then, is somewhat confused.

The ambiguity that pervades morality is expressed by the respective murderers of Edward and the Duchess: "These hands were never stained with innocent blood/ Nor shall they now be tainted with a king's" (24.80-81). Lightborne's apparent attempt to reassure Edward is purposely vague. It might be suggested that he is deceiving Edward, for evidently he will murder him. Such an interpretation though, would force us to apply a moral reading to Lightborne's actions, when what he says is not actually false. At this moment in the play,

Edward is no longer king. Lightborne's hands will not be stained with the blood of a monarch, but with that of a common man. The morality of Lightborne is of no concern. He is merely playing his part in the play and in history. In contrast, Bosola does deceive the Duchess "Come, be of comfort; I will save your life" (IV.i.86). Although Bosola questions Ferdinand's treatment of the Duchess and intends to protect her, he is unable to fulfil his vow. He might not appear in his "own shape", but Bosola is still the Duchess's executioner: "I am come to make thy tomb" (IV.ii.114). His disguise cannot, must not, excuse him from her murder. Despite wishing to find the virtues of the Duchess in himself, Bosola still allows horror to conquer. The failure of morality is finally highlighted by Bosola's accidental killing of Antonio: "The man I would have saved 'bove mine own life!" (V.v.53). Although attempting to revenge the wrongs of himself, Ferdinand and the Cardinal, Bosola shows that ultimately, virtue can never be victorious.

Therefore, is "the skull beneath the skin" the vision of a moralist or a purveyor of horror? This is perhaps best answered by the conclusions of the plays themselves. Both end with the rightful heir taking their place. However, in *Edward the Second,* King Edward III has a voice: "Accursed head!/ Could I have ruled then as I do now/ Thou hadst not hatched this monstrous treachery (25.95-97). Edward III promises to be a strong ruler. In a play that dramatises violence but apparently eschews morality, there is still hope. Marlowe clearly displays the horrors of life yet, in refusing to seek justification for them, he finds nothing worse. In contrast, the son of Antonio and the Duchess can make no speech. He is left an orphan, to be the prey of more powerful men. The Duchess might have achieved a spiritual victory, but horror has not been vanquished. Instead, by penetrating the surface anarchy of life we find, not a divine moral pattern, but a cycle of terror.

Chapter 13

Questions for Reading and Review

Your sense of the play's theme or central focus?

1. The dramatic imagery at the beginning of the play contrasts Ferdinand's court, compared to a stagnant pool, with the ideal of a court as a fountain watering the whole land. How does the information we learn about Ferdinand and the Cardinal in the early scenes, together with their behaviour, sustain this sense of corruption and evil?
2. Bosola's dialogue reveals a biting metaphysical wit appropriate to an unemployed scholar. What kind of employment is Ferdinand really offering him when he presents him with the position of the Duchess's Master of Horse? What dilemma does Ferdinand's offer pose for Bosola? What does his distinctive "voice" add to the play as it progresses?
3. How does Webster characterize the relationship between the Duchess and Antonio in their early appearances? Widows were often, in 16th-century conduct books, advised not to remarry for religious reasons. Webster's source, William Painter's *The Palace of Pleasure,* presents Antonio as an example of foolish ambition and the Duchess as an example of lust. What do Webster's attitude toward them and their relationship seem to be? How does the Duchess's attempt to balance her public and private

identities and her vulnerability as a woman who is pressured by male relatives compare with Queen Elizabeth's dilemmas as a female ruler as described in the reading assigned above?

4. How justifiable does Ferdinand's anger in 2.5 seem to be? From what motives does it seem to spring? How, in general, are we invited to view the restrictions placed on the Duchess by Ferdinand and the Cardinal?
5. Acts 2 and 3 is a kind of detective story in which Bosola and Ferdinand try to find out the Duchess's and Antonio's secret. How does the bedroom scene at 3.2 underscore the pathos and precariousness of the Duchess's situation? How does Bosola feel about the role he is playing? How does he rationalize his
6. In Act 4, the conflict is conceived more as a psychological or spiritual struggle between Ferdinand and the Duchess. What is Ferdinand attempting to do to the Duchess by giving her the dead hand and by showing her the fake bodies of Antonio and her children? By presenting her with the masque of madmen?
7. Some critics have objected that by killing off the Duchess in Act 4, Webster has created an anti-climactic dramatic structure. However, if we see the inner struggle of Bosola as a consistent focus of the action, that is not necessarily the case. What are Bosola's goals in Act 5, and who is his main antagonist?
8. Why is it appropriate, given the earlier references in the play to wolves that Ferdinand thinks of himself as a wolf in his madness? How do the scenes with Julia (and with Castrucchio, Pescara, and the other courtiers) help to emphasize the corruption of the Italian courts where the action is supposedly set?

9. Like Shakespeare's *King Lear, The Duchess of Malfi* invites us to speculate about the metaphysical order of things. To what extent does its conclusion show us that "we are merely the stars' tennis balls"? To what extent does it reinforce a sense of poetic justice? Can we apply the term "tragic" to the deaths of Bosola, Antonio, and Ferdinand? In what sense? What is the point of Bosola's final speech? Of Delio's? How would you describe Webster's "moral vision"—his sense of optimism or pessimism about human nature, human happiness, cosmic order?
10. We do not discover that the Duchess intends to marry Antonio until she proposes to him late in Act 1; but we have already seen the quality of his character. What sort of man is he? What dramatic techniques does Webster use to reveal his character to the audience? What is the effect of our getting to "know" him before we find out that the Duchess loves him?
11. Antonio is a commoner and a servant (albeit a high ranking one), rather than a gentleman or a noble. How does he compare to the men of higher social class in the play?
12. In the wooing and wedding scene that takes place in Act 1, scene 2, traditional gender roles are reversed. Is the Duchess's willingness to take the masculine role portrayed as heroic? Does she retain any traditional feminine qualities?
13. Near the end of Act 2, scene 1, the Duchess exits, feeling very ill and about to go into labour. She is absent from the rest of the Act. What are the dramatic effects of Webster's placing the childbirth scene offstage? What are the dramatic effects of the Duchess's long absence from the stage at this point in the play?
14. A "foil" is a character that helps to define and set off another character's personality by contrasting sharply with him or her. Which character serves as the Duchess's "foil"?

15. When Act 3 begins, years have passed and Antonio and the Duchess have had two more children. In light of Act 3, scene 2, how is the marriage relationship going?
16. In Act 3, scene 1, the Duchess's brother, Ferdinand, pretends to be supportive and friendly toward her, but in the next scene, he privately confronts her, rebuking her for her soiled reputation, and presents her with a knife in the hope that she will kill herself rather than live on in dishonour. Instead, the Duchess concocts an elaborate hoax, pretending to accuse Antonio of embezzlement, so that they can both flee Amalfi (she pretending to go on pilgrimage) and rejoin in the safety of another city, Ancona. How does this scene affect our sense of their heroism?
17. Because Bosola is able to trick the Duchess into telling him who her husband is, the escape plan is foiled, and the Duchess's brothers arrange to have her and her family banished from Ancona. Rather than endanger the family by staying together, the Duchess advises that she and Antonio separate. How do the parting scene and the arrest that follows affect our sense of her character? Pay particularly close attention to the imagery in her speeches and to the things she says to and about her children.
18. In *The Duchess of Malfi*, Bosola's melancholy disposition is frequently noted; he is dominated by black bile or melancholy. What do his presence and his commentary on the action contribute to the reader's or audience's sense of the society portrayed in the play? Do you detect a predominance of any other humour (choler, blood, or phlegm) in any other characters?
19. The Duchess's brothers torture her in bizarre ways. In one scene, Ferdinand presents her with a dead man's hand, telling her it is Antonio's, and then shows her a convincing waxworks display of her

family in order to convince her they are dead. Is Webster resorting to pure sensationalism (as in a horror film where the point is to make the audience scream)? Or do you see some larger thematic significance to this scene?

20. Madness is much in evidence in this play: Cariola says she pities the Duchess and thinks her mad, the Duchess is tortured by being kept in the company of madmen, and Ferdinand eventually goes mad. How does the action of the play define madness? And why is it necessary to emphasize it as a theme in telling the story of the Duchess?
21. Is it a dramatic flaw to have the title character of a tragic drama die in the fourth act with an entire fifth act still to come? Does the fact that the Duchess dies in the fourth act change your sense of the play's theme or central focus?

Chapter 14

Quotations

- We are merely the stars' tennis balls, struck and bandied

  Which way please them.

  Bosola, to Antonio after accidentally stabbing him. Act 5, Sc.4

- A Spanish fig for your impudence

  Bosola, to Antonio after being accused of poisoning the Duchess. Act 2, Sc.2

- Do you not weep?

  Other sins only speak; murder shrieks out.

  The element of water moistens the earth,

  But blood flies upwards and bedews the heavens.

  Bosola, to Ferdinand upon gazing on the dead body of the Duchess. Act 4, Sc. 2

- Cover her face. Mine eyes dazzle. She died young.

  Ferdinand, after looking at the dead body of his sister the Duchess. Act 4, Sc.2

- She and I were twins;

  And should I die this instant, I had liv'd

  Her time to a minute.

  Ferdinand, after looking at the dead body of his sister the Duchess. Act 4, Sc.2

- It seems she was born first:

  You have bloodily approv'd the ancient truth,

  That kindred commonly do worse agree

  Than remote strangers.

  Bosola, in response to Ferdinand. Act 4, Sc. 2

- Whether we fall by ambition, blood or lust,

  Like diamonds we are cut with our own dust.

  Ferdinand's dying words. Act 5, Sc.5

- "Diamonds are of most value

  They say, that have pass'd through most jewellers hands"

  The Duchess, talking about remarrying

- "Whores, by that rule, are precious."

  Ferdinand, in response to the above quote.

Bibliography

Abbott, E.A., *A Shakespearian Grammar*, second edition (1870).

Abbot Parry, Edward, *Overbury Mystery: A Chronicle of Fact and Drama of the Law* , Ayer Company, 1972.

Antonio Pérez: El hombre, el drama, la época, Espasa-Calpe, 2 vols., Madrid, 1977.

Baldini, Gabriele, *John Webster e il Linguaggio della Tragedia*, Rome, 1953.

Berry, Ralph, *The Art of John Webster*, The Clarendon Press, Oxford, 1972.

Biedermann, Hans, *Dictionary of Symbolism*, Wordsworth Reference, Hertfordshire, 1992.

Boklund, Gunnar, *'The Duchess of Malfi': Sources, Themes, Characters*, Harvard University Press, Cambridge, MA, 1962.

Bradbrook, M.C., *Themes and Conventions of Elizabethan Tragedy*, Cambridge University Press, Cambridge y Londres, 1935, 2nd edn, 1980.

Brooke, Rupert, *John Webster and the Elizabethan Drama*, Sidgwick & Jackson, London, 1916.

Burton, Robert, *The Anatomy of Melancholy*, ed. A.R. Shiletto, 3 vols. (1893).

Calderwood, J.L., '*The Duchess of Malfi*: Styles of Ceremony', *EIC* 12, 1962.

Camera, M., *Memorie storico-diplomatiche dell'antica città e ducato di Amalfi*, , Salerno, 1876-1881.

Cave, Richard Allen, '*The White Devil*' and '*The Duchess of Malfi*', Text and Performance, Macmillan Education, Basingstoke and London, 1988.

Collins English Dictionary, Harper Collins Publishers, third Edition Updated, Glasgow, 1994.

Cuddon, J.A., *The Penguin Dictionary of Literary Terms and Literary Theory*, Third edition, Pinguin Books, London, 1991.

Dent, R.W., *John Webster's Borrowing*, University of California Press, Berkeley y Los Angeles, 1960.

Dollimore, Jonathan, *Radical Tragedy*, Harvester Wheatsheaf, 1989.

Dyce, Alexander, *The Works of John Webster* , editado por Alexander Dyce, Londres, 1857.

Empson, William, *Essays on Renaissance Literature*, ed. John Haffenden, vol. II., Cambridge University Press, Cambridge, 1994.

Farley-Hills, David, *Jacobean Drama: A Critical Study of the Professional Drama, 1600-25*, Macmillan Press, Londres, 1988.

Findlay, Alison, *A Feminist Perspective on Renaissance Drama* , Blackwell, Oxford, 1999.

Foakes, R.A., *Hamlet versus Lear: Cultural Politics and Shakespeare's Art* , Cambridge, 1993.

Ford, John, *Tis Pity She's a Whore*, ed. By Brian Morris, New Mermaids, A & C Black, Londres, 1998.

Frasser, Antonia, *The Weaker Vessel: Woman's Lot in Seventeenth Century England*, Vintage Books, 1985.

Gerald, John, *Herball*. The Essence Thereof Distilled by Marcus Woodward from the Edition of Th. Johnson, 1636.1927.

Graves, R.B., '*The Duchess of Malfi* at the Globe and Blackfriars', *RenD* N. S. 9 (1978), 193-209.

Hazlitt, W.C., *The Dramatic Works of John Webster*, editado por W.C. Hazlitt, Londres, 1857.

Heineman, Margot, *Puritanism and Theatre: Thomas Middleton and Opposition Drama under the Early Stuarts*, Cambridge University Press, Cambridge, 1980.

Heywood, Thomas, *A Woman Killed with Kindness*, ed. Brian Scobie, The New Mermaids, A. & C. Black, Londres, 1998.

Hoeniger, F.D., *Medicine and Shakespeare in the English Renaissance*, Newark, Delaware, 1992.

Iaggard, William, *The History of Four-Footed Beasts and Serpents and Insects*, Londres, 1607.

Jackson, Macd. P., *Jacobean Drama Studies: Studies in Attribution Middleton and Shakespeare*, Institut für Anglistik und Amerikanistik Universität Salzburg, Austria, 1979.

Jardine, Lisa, *Still Harping on Daughters: Women and Drama in the Age of Shakespeare* , The Harvester Wheatsheaf, Londres, 1989.

John Webster: A Critical Anthology, edited by G.K. and S.K. Hunter, Penguin Critical Anthologies, Harmondsworth, 1969.

John Webster, edited by Brian Morris, Mermaid Critical Commentaries, Ernest Benn, London, 1970.

Jonson, Ben, *Volpone* , ed. Philip Brockbank, The New Mermaids, London/ A & C. Black, Londres,1997.

Lagarde, Fernand, *John Webster*, 2 vols, Toulouse, 1968.

Lake, David J., *The Canon of Thomas Middleton's Plays*, Cambridge University Press, Londres, 1975.

Lamb, Charles, *Specimens of English Dramatic Poets, who lived about the Time of Shakespeare: with notes*, London, 1808.

Leech, Clifford, *John Webster: A Critical Study*, London, 1951.

Leech, Clifford, *John Webster: 'The Duchess of Malfi'*, Studies in English Literature, 8, Edward Arnold, London, 1963.

